Political Parties and Democracy

Political Parties and Democracy

Explorations in History and Theory

ARTHUR LIPOW

LONDON • CHICAGO, IL.

First Published 1996 by Pluto Press
345 Archway Road
London N6 5AA
and 1436 West Randolph,
Chicago, Illinois 60607, USA

British Library Cataloguing in Publication Data
A catalogue record for this book is available from the British Library

ISBN 0 7453 1099 0 hbk

Library of Congress Cataloging in Publication Data
Lipow, Arthur.
Political parties and democracy: explorations in history and theory/[Arthur Lipow].
256p. 22cm.
Includes bibliographical references and index.
ISBN 0–7453–1099–0
1. Democracy. 2. Democracy—Great Britain. 3. Democracy—United States. 4. Political parties—Great Britain. 5. Political parties—United States. 6. Referendum. I. Title.
JC423.L5668 1996
321.8—dc20 95–52788
CIP

Designed and produced for Pluto Press by
Chase Production Services, Chipping Norton, OX7 5QR
Typeset from disk by Stanford DTP Services, Milton Keynes
Printed in the EC by T J Press, Padstow

Contents

Introduction

Although the essays in this book focus primarily on American politics and history, the subject with which they deal – the idea and practice of plebiscitarian politics – will have an interest and relevance for British as well as American readers.

The Labour Party has served here, tacitly, as a model, however imperfect, of the kind of broad, membership-based party which America sorely needs and which the historical liberal reformers – the 'Progressives' – did their best, alas successfully, to prevent through their 'direct democracy' devices. However, the Labour Party is moving slowly, but by no means inevitably, toward a less democratic, top-down form of organization using devices, such as membership referendums, which appear democratic but which are, for reasons which are examined in this volume, instruments of executive manipulation.

Their function is to confer democratic legitimacy on the actions of the leadership; the results, all other things being equal, which, fortunately, they are not, could lead to the destruction of the party Conference and the representative, democratic, structure of the party which ties it to the trade union movement and to ordinary rank-and-file members. Taking control out of the hands of 'activists', who are assumed not to be accountable or representative of the membership, and subjecting decisions to a leadership poll of the membership is an attack on democracy, as Sidney and Beatrice Webb explained so many years ago in *Industrial Democracy*. But, of course, everyone nowadays knows that the Webbs were only 'middle-class socialists' – an epithet which seems particularly ironic when mouthed in hearty populist style by other middle-class socialists.

Briefly, the direction of change in the Labour Party is toward the 'Americanization' of the party and, if some prominent thinkers have their way, of the present party and electoral system. These essays ought to be read carefully as a warning of what lies in store for the supporters of the British labour movement should these trends continue unimpeded. The debased American political system produced by the Progressive reforms is now in terminal decay; perhaps it will be replaced by a genuine two-party system, with a democratically organized membership party on the left confronting the conservative remnants of the two old parties. To advance in Britain along the lines laid out by the critics of 'old-fashioned' parties would not only be to regress to the state in which the American political system finds itself, but to lose the opportunity to build a new politics upon the still healthy democratic political tradition which exists in Britain – one which uses, but is not used by, the new systems of electronic communication.

The British labour movement has created a unique and valuable democratic political culture and it ought not to be destroyed either for the illusion of short-term electoral advantage, or because of the agenda of well-placed elites in party leadership, or in sympathetic think-tanks to create a bogus form of democracy to replace the existing system. The democratic culture of the labour movement is sturdy but one ought not to underestimate how its steady erosion can in the end result in its destruction. None of this is to deny that its improvement, in the form of 'regeneration', is not urgently needed: no one who has observed the Labour Party up close for nearly two decades as I have could possibly deny it. Barbecues and having fun ought to be part of party life, but so should serious discussion and decision making based in a democratically constituted organization. Democracy in modern society requires accountable, representative bodies, bodies which involve the members actively, rather than repelling them for narrow sectarian or petty bureaucratic reasons, and which use the devices of 'direct democracy' – or 'one member, one vote' with which it has been misleadingly equated – sparingly at best, with a continuous awareness of how important an accountable, democratic, representative structure is to a functioning democratic organization.

The information technology revolution through which we are now living holds great promise as well as great danger for democracy and the future of political parties. It may be used either to enhance genuine membership participation through opening up sources of information and making communication easier, or it can become, as in the proposals for a 'lean democracy' cooked up in the British think-tank, Demos, a new form of plebiscitarian manipulation – a cyber-democracy which will undermine already fragile democratic institutions, all in the name (of course) of a higher and more advanced form of democracy.

These are lessons which my American readers ought to know well. But, unfortunately, the undemocratic nature of such direct democracy ideas and their reverse, the idea of genuine participation through democratically organized membership parties and other organizations, are only vaguely understood by most of the American left. However, in the present earthquake which is shaking the American political system to its core, there are clear signs that a new politics based on such a form of organization, one uniquely American, drawing on the deep tradition of democracy in America, is emerging in the form of the New Party and Labor Party Advocates. It is my hope that this volume, which lays bare the Progressive roots of the present-day American political system and the political culture which accompanied it, will contribute in some small way to the rebirth of the idea of democracy grounded in democratic political parties: an idea which was well known before the Progressive reforms managed to snuff it out by their successes.

The theme which runs through these essays is a concern with democracy, authoritarianism and political organization. It will be obvious to the reader that the book which has influenced me the most is Robert Michels' *Political Parties* which I first read at the age of fifteen when I ran across it on the dusty bookshelf of a family friend. I had never heard of it and no one I knew, certainly none of my high school teachers, were aware of it. It had not yet been reprinted, I think, and I desperately wanted to have a copy for myself but was too shy to ask for it, although I doubt it had ever been read by its owners.

A few years later on, to my surprise and delight, I came across it again in Professor Ralph Turner's wonderful course at UCLA on social movements and learned for the first time that it was a classic of political sociology, not political 'science' out of whose boring, formalistic grasp I had removed myself after a year of studying comparative government through a close reading of constitutions – including, absurdly enough, Stalin's 1936 constitution. When it came to the British Constitution, I was as baffled as my instructors: constitutions are either written or they are – well, what was one to make of an unwritten constitution except by learning about the actual organization of politics and the nature of British society? And so I transferred to sociology and went on to study political sociology as a post-graduate student at Berkeley where I was, by a stroke of luck, introduced to the field by Seymour Martin Lipset whose own work had been stimulated by *Political Parties* long before I chanced upon it.

Lipset's interest in politics and political parties and his commitment to democracy stimulated my intellectual development. From *Agrarian Socialism* to *Union Democracy* and, of course, *Political Man*, I learned many answers but, far more important, I learned which questions to ask, questions that have formed the core of my intellectual interests as well as my practical participation in the democratic socialist movement and as an opponent of authoritarian ideas and movements. Lipset guided me not only to a critical reading of Michels, but to Ostrogorski, whose magnificent study of *Democracy and the Organization of Political Parties* is hardly known today, as well as to the also now largely unread classic studies of trade unionism and industrial democracy by Sidney and Beatrice Webb. These works, as will be seen in the essays that follow, particularly the discussion of populism and plebiscitarianism, provide a method of analysis and an insight into democracy within organizations and in politics which has never been surpassed.

My study of the Fabian-like Edward Bellamy 'Nationalist movement', *Authoritarian Socialism in America*, begun under Lipset's supervision, worked at many levels – intellectual, theoretical, and historical – to analyze the nature of authoritarian anti-capitalist politics and to relate it to support for Stalinism among socialist intellectuals such as Sidney and Beatrice Webb during the 1930s and after. A number of the essays in this volume represent an ongoing attempt to work out both the historical and theoretical questions raised by this study. Karl Mannheim's anti-socialist search for an elite to deal with the crises of capitalist society (Chapter 8) as well as Clark Kerr's utopia for managers (Chapter 9), illuminated the deep intellectual roots of the politics of anti-democratic, authoritarian collectivism while clarifying the fundamental difference between it and a genuinely democratic socialism.

In addition, as a result of my research into the history of socialism and liberal reform, which required me to turn the conventional approach of radical critics of American capitalism upside down, one of the discoveries I made about Edward Bellamy's 'Nationalist' movement was the way in which Bellamy's technocratic politics, a forerunner of progressivism, as Sam Haber demonstrates in his book *Efficiency and Uplift*, took up and adopted the 'populist' demand for direct democracy. (This was a discovery that most American political historians are still either oblivious to or sullenly reject as an attack on the progressive synthesis which still weighs heavily on the field, although far less so than when I first wrote.) The Bellamyites saw, rightly, no inconsistency in the rule of experts and strong administrative power and the use of plebiscitarian devices such as the initiative and referendum. This pairing was to be, of course, at the heart of the new liberalism, especially its 'administrative' wing, most closely identified with the ideas of Herbert Croly and the *New Republic* liberals. Indeed, as a footnote to intellectual history, it is worth noting that the first American discovery of Michels' *Political Parties* took place in 1915 in the pages of the *New Republic*, confirming, no doubt, the elitist bias of the new liberals, some of whom drifted, along with Michels in the 1920s, indeed as Croly himself did, into support for Mussolini's fascist state.

The second American discovery (although it was really more of a recovery) of Michels took place in the early 1940s in a different context: young radicals, democratic socialists, a number of whom, like Lipset and Phillip Selznick, were soon to become influential figures in the founding of modern political sociology, grappled with the degeneration of the Russian revolution and the rise of a 'socialism' which was a new form of class society – one that was both deeply anti-democratic and also anti-socialist.

Michels provided a starting point for analysis which no honest democratic socialist confronted with the reality of Stalinism could afford to ignore. Indeed, the fact that its thesis – 'socialists may conquer, but socialism never' – had been taken seriously and not rejected out of hand by pre-Stalinist Marxists like Bukharin shored up what was then very much a minority view on the left. Bukharin's passing acknowledgement in *Historical Materialism* of the possible truth of Michels' thesis confirmed, for the adherents of the theory of Stalinism as a 'bureaucratic collectivist' society, that the idea of a social order which was neither capitalist nor socialist was not as unthinkable from a Marxist standpoint as most of the left, including Trotsky and even most social democrats, thought it to be. Marx, the dominant view held, had written about the transition to feudalism from ancient society, and from feudalism to capitalism. The 'next stage' could only be socialism – even if it was a deformed socialism. For social democrats as well as members and friends of the Communist parties, it was the fact of state ownership and the abolition of private property which clinched the argument. This mechanistic approach now seems absurd, although it is certainly true that a majority of those describing themselves as part of the 'left' still have never really accepted or understood the class nature of Soviet-type regimes. A return to Marx's democratic view of socialism, which is dissected in Chapter 9, would be a breath of fresh air today, especially in light of the dishonest equation of Marx's ideas with totalitarian collectivism.

Today, six years after most of these regimes imploded, a kind of intellectual amnesia combined with an endemic hostility to 'theory', has left the field to the opponents of socialism who see in the demise of communism the failure of socialism. The deep demoralization of the left has led many to abandon socialism in pursuit of a more benevolent kind of capitalism.

My study of Bellamyism, then, turned out to be a study of a forerunner of the new liberalism as well as authoritarian, anti-democratic currents within the socialist movement which found in Stalinism a congenial vision. The insights I had gained from Michels allowed me to see, in its proper context, the plebiscitarian anti-democratic nature of Progressive-style 'direct democracy'.

In the late 1970s and early 1980s, when Progressive-style reform was reborn in the form of the middle-class American reform organization Common Cause, I was able to apply, successfully, I think, this perspective to a critique of the Common Cause agenda, relating its top-down, plebiscitarian form of organization (Common Cause discovered the WATS (wide area telephone service) line as a means of mobilizing its members while at the same time creating a simulacrum of democracy) to its vision of a reformed political system, one in which organized, voluntary, democratic political parties played no role. State subsidies, in the form of the public financing of campaigns and the creation of new, unprecedented, administrative bodies whose purpose is to regulate political life, would complete the transformation of American parties, such as they are, into 'public utilities' as Leon Epstein has approvingly called them. In this respect, Common Cause was, and is, very American: democratic parties and democratic forms of organization play very little role in American politics. The Common Cause vision, then, for all of its 'democratic' rhetoric was profoundly undemocratic: the idea of the administrative regulation of politics which I applied both to the California Fair Political Practices Commission and to the Federal Elections Commission as well as to the host of other, similar, bodies established in many other American states is one which is peculiarly American, although, as I show in the essay on state funding of parties (Chapter 3), the power to inject state money into politics brings a direct form of state control over the practice of politics.

These issues are not at all remote from British politics. The threat of state funding of the parties still hangs over the British political system – it has already crept in through the 'Short funds', which give the leader of the opposition a degree of independence from his party in Parliament and in the country that would not otherwise be possible. With a system of direct state funding of the parties would come, as some of its Liberal proponents made clear to the Houghton Committee, state regulation of the parties, including parliamentary control over their internal life. And, only recently, the prime source of the politics of anti-partyism, Demos, has proposed the creation of 'OFELECT' – an office of truth in elections to oversee political campaigns. The American regulatory control over political life, through the Federal Election Commission and the California Fair Political

Practices Commission, is at least a gleam in the eyes of certain influential thinkers in Britain.

I have included my articles on the reform agenda of Common Cause in this volume (Chapters 4–7): even after 20 years, such is the hold of the progressive mentality on American political scientists and historians, there has yet to be, to my knowledge, a thoroughgoing critical re-evaluation of the undemocratic nature of post-Watergate electoral reform. These articles provide, I think, an essential starting point for such an effort.

A broader examination of the relationship between state funding of politics, civil society and political parties and the issues it raises for democracy is to be found in Chapter 3, which has been revised from a paper first presented to a conference in Tokyo on the role of money in politics.

Along with these essays, there is the essay 'Populism and Direct Democracy' (Chapter 2) which, like most of my work, examines the interplay between ideas and theories and political experience. Chapter 1, 'Direct Democracy and Progressive Political Reform' also first presented as a paper at the American Historical Association, goes to the heart of the Progressive movement's plebiscitarian political reforms which are its legacy – 'curse' would be more accurate – to the American system today.

Throughout this book, Michels' ideas and insights continue to play a key theoretical role, but critically modified, as Lipset did in his classic study of *Union Democracy*. Michels is best known for his 'iron law of oligarchy': 'He who says organization, says oligarchy.' But Michels, subtly contradictory thinker that he is, also says the opposite: democracy requires organization. No one can doubt that even in the most democratic of movements and organizations there exists a strong possibility of oligarchy: it is a tendency but there are also countertendencies. If there is an iron law, I say in the first essay on direct democracy and plebiscitarianism, it is the iron law of *non-organization*. With democratic, participatory organization, there exists the possibility, but not the certainty of rule by an elite; without it, however, the inevitability of oligarchy and the impossibility of democracy.

The issue is not addressed in the theory of 'elite democracy' – in this I differ from Lipset – for reasons I make clear in the essay on populism (Chapter 2). For those who value democracy because effective participation is necessary to the dignity of individual human beings, leaders must be held accountable from below through internally democratic political organizations. This requires a mixture of effective forms of representation and direct participation, none of which is the same as the sham 'direct democracy' which I characterize as 'plebiscitarian'. None of this is to say, of course, that leaders, or 'elites', will cease to exist. Nothing is more manipulative and elitist than the populistic pretence in the world of 'participatory' democracy that leaders are not different from rank-and-file members.

The belief in the inevitability of oligarchy is a self-fulfilling prophecy, both in terms of larger outcomes as well as personal choices, as Michels' own political trajectory demonstrated. Given the monstrous history of the twentieth century, in which the idea of socialism and the democratic ideas of Marx have been turned into their opposite, and the likelihood – not inevitable, note – that the twenty-first century global order under the aegis of really existing capitalism will unleash forces even more monstrous than we have seen in this century, a great deal of sober realism and clear thinking is required. The current rage on the right, in the US, for direct democracy, and its parallel in Britain among the cyber-heads of Demos, whose political lineage, not surprisingly, goes back to *Marxism Today*, rather than to the democratic labour movement, is ample warning of how dangerous are the times we live in. Direct democracy, I hasten to say, if the point is not obvious enough already, is the opposite of participatory, bottom-up democracy: it is a fraudulent use of the forms of democracy – sham democracy – without its prerequisites, which includes organization from below. 'Electronic democracy', based on 'virtual reality' in which truth is infinitely malleable by an elite of mediacrats in place of democratic organizations, is not democracy at all, but a pure illustration of the plebiscitarian, anti-democratic politics against which this book is directed.

This same theme of the interplay between organization and democracy is to be found in the other essays in this volume. 'Civil Society, Democracy and the Cold War' (Chapter 13) was originally presented as a paper at the American Sociological Society meetings. It was surely, in retrospect, wildly optimistic about the emergence of a new democratic socialist current in Eastern Europe. But the foreclosure of this possibility was, after all, as the essay argues, the point of the way in which the Cold War was waged. The totalitarian Communist system imploded, but so devastated was civil society and so repulsive did the citizens of these countries find the word 'socialism' which had been used by the Communists to legitimate its anti-democratic, exploitative rule, that not only socialism but also a democratic political culture hardly flourishes there. The re-appearance of the reformed Communist parties in positions of power is only one indication of this. 'Capitalism' there may be, although its hybrid, still highly statified and bureaucratic form, raises fundamental questions about the nature of modern corporate capitalism and its affinity for 'bureaucratic authoritarian' regimes. Only in Poland, where the Polish working class created a mass labour movement in the form of Solidarity did there exist the possibility of creating an alternative to the economic and social policies to which the final collapse of the Communist regime led.

One can only speculate about what might have been if at the beginning of the 1980s there had not been a renewal of the Cold War but instead the formulation of an alternative, democratic, foreign policy on the part of the United States. Solidarity might have become the basis of a democratic workers' party and the democratic spirit which animated it might have infused Polish society. By the end of the 1980s, the Jaruzelski government collapsed, but many remnants of the old state apparatus remained, including the secret police, while the *nomenklatura* quickly scrambled, as it did in the rest of Eastern Europe and the former

Soviet Union, to appropriate public property and assure itself a leading position in the new system. To discuss these issues with the thoroughness they deserve, however, goes beyond the scope of this introduction.

But, to illustrate the continuing relevance of Michels to these questions, a personal anecdote is appropriate here. I was an observer when the newly elected Solidarity deputies walked into the halls of power. A poorly dressed mixture of intellectuals and workers (the former more numerous than the latter), they had first assembled in the shabby surroundings of the Warsaw University auditorium. And then, suddenly, they found themselves invited to the Palace of Deputies, a beautiful, spacious hall lit by crystal chandeliers and waited upon by the same liveried servants who had served their oppressors. Perhaps it was my imagination, although I think not, but it seemed to me that there unfolded before my eyes in the next few days a process of differentiation which Robert Michels would have appreciated. The workers sat in bunches, clearly dissatisfied with the compromises their leadership was making, while the intellectuals, even the many brave ones who had served long prison sentences, began to experience Power. Jacek Kuron, former Communist turned socialist critic of the regime strutted around on the new parliamentary stage. One could almost see the intellectuals trying on ministerial frock-coats as they strode around the hall. I couldn't resist asking my Polish friends, most of them intellectuals, whether they were familiar with *Political Parties* and resolved on the spot to send them copies in the hope that they might translate it and thereby arm themselves against what was so clearly happening. I never learned whether they were able to do so or even whether they read it, but the power of Michels' insights were confirmed for me once again.

'Transnationalism From Below' (Chapter 14) was presented first at the Central European University; the second version, closer to the present essay, at a conference on NAFTA at the University of Toronto. It argues that the prospect for democracy and social progress in the new, post-Cold War era is intertwined with the fate of the democratic labour movement, nationally as well as internationally. A strong, independent labour movement is a fundamental part of civil society. In the countries of Central and Eastern Europe today, the possibility of creating a democratic political culture in which working people acquire the skills of democracy is, once again, bound up with the development of a strong labour movement.

The essay on 'the new slavery' (Chapter 9), which applies Marx's democratic theory of alienation to an examination of Clark Kerr's industrial relations expert's utopia, as well as the essay on Karl Mannheim, whose work is undeservedly neglected today, continues the theme of the conflict between democracy and authoritarianism and the role of intellectuals in elaborating ideas for top-down utopias as an answer to the ills of capitalism and an alternative to democratic socialism.

I have also taken the opportunity – one might say the luxury – to publish reviews of individual books which, in most cases, have been expanded beyond the limits which zealous editors were willing to allow. The review of Michael

Coren's biography of H.G. Wells (Chapter 10), which sparked a furious response from Michael Foot, whose own forthcoming biography of Wells we look forward to with great interest, once again takes up the theme of authoritarian and anti-democratic ideas on the 'left' as does the review of Robert Hughes' *Culture of Complaint* (Chapter 12). Democracy if it means anything requires freedom of expression which in turn requires practical organization – freedom to organize and to participate effectively in politics as well as economic life. Hence the need for unions and hence too the incompatibility, however unfashionable it may be nowadays to say so, between capitalism and democracy.

Chapter 15 examines the decline of the post-World War II 'middle class' in America – a decline which has helped to fuel the volatility of American politics at the end of the twentieth century and has raised, once again, the hope of a realignment and reorganization of the American political system which can transcend those of its features which the Populist and Progressive reformers created nearly one hundred years ago.

A Final Postword

I tell my students in American politics at Birkbeck College, University of London, that I have learned about American politics by living in Britain and, as an American, studying and participating in the British labour movement, even as I have at the same time kept an active intellectual and practical interest in American politics. Two friends and colleagues, Lewis Minkin and Patrick Seyd, have helped me to understand British politics and the role of the labour movement (in the British sense, of party and trade unions) in creating a democratic political culture in Britain, the absence of which is thereby all the more apparent in America – unless one accepts, as I clearly do not, the form of sham democracy created by the Progressive movement as 'democratic'. I should also like to express my gratitude to Elizabeth Cotton for her assistance in preparing the final manuscript.

It remains only to mention one other friend, Professor Paul Goodman, of the University of California, Davis, Department of History, whose death has deprived his friends and the academic community of a brilliant scholar and a good man. I often talked to Paul about the subject of this book on my frequent visits to Berkeley and I was pleased to learn that he drew upon draft versions of the papers which are published here for his classes on American history. His study of the abolitionist movement, completed just before his death, will, when published, be the best possible memorial for a good friend who was both my intellectual mentor and a model of what a committed scholar ought to be. In the meantime, I dedicate this book to Paul's memory in the hope that it will help in a small way to bring about the realization of our shared vision of a democratic world free of racial and religious prejudice and social and economic injustice.

PART I

Democracy and the Politics of Reform

PART I

Democracy *vs.* the Politics of Reform

CHAPTER 1

Direct Democracy and Progressive Political Reform

Although much of the mythology surrounding the history and meaning of the social and economic reforms of the Progressive movement has been rather effectively demolished by recent historians, the myths about the political reform side of the movement have proven to be peculiarly resistant to critical historical analysis. This is especially true when it comes to the 'direct democracy' movement and its most important achievements in the restructuring of the American political system: the direct primary and the twin devices of direct legislation, the initiative and referendum.[1]

It is hardly surprising that this should be so. Even the most conventional historian can perceive the domination of the American economy by corporate capital and can understand the government's role in fostering the concentration of economic power, in great part using the very regulatory machinery instituted in the Progressive era. But the character and function of the political reforms have remained relatively invisible, like a piece of furniture which blends into the background until we stumble over it in the middle of the night. All of which is to say the obvious: that the political arrangements of the last six or seven decades have been remarkably free from serious ideological or organized political challenge, although of course, a great deal has changed. But to a truly amazing degree, the direction and fundamental outline of the changes which have taken place were set in the Progressive era.[2]

In short, the reforms themselves as well as the underlying ideological assumptions have come to be regarded as part of the natural political order in the United States. It has become as difficult to think about them in a critical way as it has been to think critical thoughts about the supposed necessity of the two-party system in America or to be able to doubt the celebrated genius of the American political system in excluding politics – or 'ideology' as the sociologists put it.

In its classic form, the myth of the democratic nature of Progressive political reform is found in George Mowry's landmark study of California Progressivism. 'The Progressive political reforms', Professor Mowry writes, 'were basic advances.'

> They were, and are, the people's tools for the control of their government. If the great corporations do control the state of California today [Mowry was

> writing at the end of the 1940s, in the era of Artie Samish, the lobbyist 'boss' of California politics], which is extremely debatable, it is by the people's sanction. As long as democratic government exists, the people, if they are concerned enough, can claim their own by effective use of the primary, the initiative, the referendum, the recall, and the free honest ballot.[3]

Although the democratic reputation of the Progressives has been tarnished considerably since Mowry wrote, the views he expressed continue to be resurrected. David Thelen, for example, writes that 'direct democracy was profoundly radical because it was thoroughly democratic'.[4]

To be sure, many historians now regard views such as these with great scepticism. From the vantage point of experience, Mowry's assurances about the workability of these tools sound rather hollow and, in any case, too many studies have demonstrated that the devices of direct democracy did not attain the goal which their advocates allegedly claimed for them. Yet this scepticism has little to do with an understanding of the actual history of the direct democracy movement and its role in the politics of the various classes and groups which supported it. Still less does it stem from a serious attempt to understand the conditions necessary for democratic political participation in the modern world. Rather, such scepticism is mostly an expression of disenchantment – cynicism would be more accurate in most cases – akin to Mowry's own which he unwittingly reveals in blaming the people for not using the tools of democracy provided for them by the Progressive reformers. The underlying thought here is that if flaws in these supposedly democratic political tools have been revealed with the passage of time, then it must be that these are the flaws of democracy itself. Those who pursue this line of thought would agree with the sentiment expressed many years ago by the proto-Progressive, Henry Demarest Lloyd, that 'the average citizen has broken down' in the face of the complexity of modern politics. The reformers, it follows, were guilty of naivete for believing that ordinary people were actually capable of using these democratic devices to govern themselves. Or, to put it bluntly, they were prisoners of their own foolish dogmas for ever having believed that a democratic system, requiring such sustained, direct participation, was possible in a modern industrial society.

Such disenchantment, however, apart from what it says about the collapse of liberal democratic ideas today, leaves the key elements of the myth intact: it assumes that these were indeed democratic devices which were designed to facilitate participation in politics. If they did not work, because the people could not use them, then the goal of a participatory democracy is a utopian one which must be rejected in the name of realism. Social scientists tell us today that democracy can only mean a choice between competing elites and in this conclusion there seems to be tacit agreement from historians, who have not understood the real nature of the direct democracy movement and the structural changes it imposed on American politics.

I must take note, at this point, of the growing number of historians who have recognized that the Progressives' self-proclaimed faith in 'the people' and in the virtues of democracy was greatly dependent on their belief that the people would follow them; those elements who failed to display the proper deference to Progressive leadership were promptly expelled from the sacred category of 'the people'. While this approach is a distinct advance, its proponents have had difficulty in reconciling the elitist and often explicitly anti-democratic sentiments of the reformers with their advocacy of the devices of direct democracy.[5]

What both of these viewpoints fail to see accurately is that these devices, far from being instruments of democratic participation, made citizens into tools used by an elite. It apparently has occurred to few, if any, of the historians or political scientists who have written about the origins of the direct democracy movement that the contemporary enemies of direct democracy, mostly old-fashioned conservatives who had as little use for democracy as their Progressive opponents, were shrewd analysts when they pointed out, as did Henry Jones Ford, for example, in 1909, that 'the pretence of giving power to the people is a mockery. The reality is that it [the direct primary] scrambles power among faction chiefs and their bands, while the people are despoiled and oppressed.' Ford went on to point out, in words that might well be applied to present-day Progressive-bred political nostrums, that 'the fact that it is done in the name of the people, and with the pretence that it is done for the people, ought not to obscure the patent facts of the situation'.[6]

Ford's was a minority voice and the successful institution of the direct primary throughout the states within a few short years left his objections behind for a decade or more. However, despite the well-known pragmatism of the liberal ethos, success does not make truth. Ford was correct in his time about the motives of the reformers and the consequences of their devices, and nothing in the history of the direct primary and direct legislation and their impact upon American politics disproves his basic insight. He was not, as I shall show, alone in this and indeed the sophisticated leaders among the advocates of direct democracy were just as aware as Ford of what the proper role of 'the people' was in their kind of direct democracy.

To put the matter most succinctly: the Progressive reformers did not aim at, nor did they accomplish to any degree, the 'democratization' of the American political system. Such a belief can only rest either on ignorance of the actual ideas or, far more likely, on a tacit acceptance of the political ideology and rhetoric of Progressivism itself. It is absurd to believe that a system which undid the possibility of mass, democratically organized membership participation parties; which aimed at the dismantling of the party system even as it then existed; and which was consciously and deliberately concerned with preventing the emergence of a class party of labour, could ever have eventuated in the 'rule of the people' or represented in the smallest degree a belief, to use Russell B. Nye's words, 'in the ability of the people to rule if given the proper tools'.[7] In 1924, joined in his earlier criticisms by a growing number of political scientists, Henry Jones

Ford could correctly observe that 'whatever assigns to the people power they are unable to wield in effect takes it away from them'. In practice, Ford pointed out, the direct primary had meant

> that the choice will actually be made by the portion of the community so circumstanced as to have the time, means and opportunity of attending to the business and finding their account of it. Therefore the practical effect of the direct primary has been to establish a class rule of a singularly degraded and irresponsible character.[8]

It would be difficult to improve upon Ford's words as a final judgement on the American political system today.

What the Progressives did establish was a plebiscitarian system: a pseudo-democratic 'polling-democracy' to borrow George Gallup's later term for his own extension of this idea. Its essential feature was that it gave the appearance of increased participation while taking away its necessary substance. This system, to which the key is the direct primary, aided and abetted by the spirit and practice of direct legislation, undermined representative institutions, made political parties – even the capitalist political parties – less responsible and less responsive as organizations, and at the same time played a critical role in strengthening the trend toward the autonomization and centralization of power in the hands of the executive branch of state government.

None of this is exactly new. Not, that is, if one is willing to go back to the Progressive era itself and examine the criticisms of those who lost the argument. The old saw about the victors writing the history applies here in spades: the American political culture is so permeated by Progressivism, especially the electoral system it created, that the cogent and prophetic views of its critics have simply gone down the memory-hole. For the most part they have been derided as blinkered conservatives or, in the rhetoric of the Progressives, as tools of the 'boss' and the 'machine' or that standard Progressive devil, the 'special interests' – a hoary and misleading term which continues to haunt American political discourse, testifying once again to the way in which the political culture of Progressivism became the 'American persuasion' in the twentieth century.

Diving into the memory-hole, we find that contemporary conservative and socialist critics alike pointed out the consequences of the Progressive reforms and did so with a cogency and clarity of vision which illuminates the structural sources of the debased existing American political system in which money and celebrity replace issues or 'ideology' and responsible, democratically organized parties are non-existent.

In Wisconsin, for example, both Emanuel L. Philipp, leader of the anti-La Follette 'stalwarts' and Victor Berger of Milwaukee, who was the spokesman of the Socialist Party, perceptively analyzed the consequences of La Follette's direct primary reform. Wrote Berger in 1909:

> A democracy ... or a republic ... is impossible without political parties ... As long as we have democracy, and particularly representative democracy, parties will be absolutely necessary for its expression. There will be either anarchy and crude factionalism or organized political parties.[9]

Philipp's book, *Political Reform in Wisconsin*,[10] published in 1910, was a devastating attack on the pretensions of the Progressive politician, Robert La Follette. In words which are surely a fitting epitaph for the American political system in the twentieth century, Philipp wrote of La Follette's creation, the direct primary,

> The overthrow of parties through the ascendancy of the individual destroys party principles, and individuals take their places with organized personal followings bearing the motto, 'Anything to Win' as their most sacred principle. The discussion of real principles is lost in the public exchange of bitter personalities. Even factional strife, deplorable as such a condition must be, is soon displaced by something worse – personal contests for power.[11]

In the same vein, the *Socialist Call* in 1914 warned socialists about

> the danger to real democracy that there is in the pseudo-democracy that is sweeping the country ... In their eagerness to get the reputation for being democrats, those pseudo-democrats who are running things just now want to break up political parties. If they really wanted to have real democracy they would pattern parties after our party, a group of earnest men and women who have a definite aim ... Then let every man and woman who really believes in that aim get into the party and work.[12]

This came from the opponents of progressivism. But even the advocates of direct democracy often were very aware of the way in which these devices would work. Jonathan Bourne, Jr, a reformed machine politician who seized the opportunity offered him by William S. U'Ren, the founder of the Oregon direct democracy movement, to ride the 'people's power' issue to the US Senate, set forth with marvellous candour the actual relationship between 'the people' and the new type of leader who had sparked the movement. Bourne wrote in 1912 that there are

> ... always ... a few intellectual leaders who are in advance of the masses of the people: but the practical workings of delegated government are such that the masses of people are always in advance of those individuals who secure political but not intellectual leadership ... [The old-style politics] under a system of delegated government, brings into power men who are guided more by selfish interest than by general welfare. Popular government reverses this condition and gives power to intellectual leaders rather than to men whose success is due to skill as 'practical politicians'. ... [Direct legislation] is the practical machinery of intellectual leadership. Without that machinery the intellectual leader is in most cases powerless.[13]

The combination of demagogy and contempt for 'the people' which prompted politicians like La Follette to admit in private that he gave speeches mainly 'to stir the animals up'[14] and which led Lincoln Steffens to characterize him as a 'boss who dictated democracy', was shared by U'Ren who, soon after the passage of direct legislation in Oregon, set forth just what it meant for the people to legislate directly. 'The average man', he told a reporter, 'is either too indolent, too busy, or too distrustful of his own judgement to study or decide for himself upon the details of a law or a great public question. People always ask of a proposition ... "Who is back of it?"' It was for this reason, U'Ren boasted, that 'in all our work we have found the great value of well-known names attached to our measures as officers or members of the committees'.[15]

Where in this is the rational and the educated citizen, or 'faith in the people' which latter-day historians have attributed to the Progressive mind by way of explaining their naivete? Naive? Hardly. Shrewd and manipulative, certainly. The socialist charge that these were 'pseudo-democrats' and that the party system based on the direct primary was a pseudo-democratic, plebiscitarian one, is an entirely accurate characterization of the Progressive's achievement.

That the atomized population, or 'the people', created by the dismemberment of political parties, was to be the tool and the new-style politician the tool-user, rather than the other way around, as the myth of direct democracy has it, was incisively analyzed by Herbert Croly in a well-known and equally well-ignored passage: 'None but an idolator could believe for one moment', Croly wrote,

> that the initiative and referendum ... are instruments of majority rule. They depend on popular action, but the proportion of the people who act and, in particular cases rule is never a majority. They are instruments of minority rule and usually the rule of a very small minority.[16]

Croly, more than anyone else, then or since, was able to articulate the relationship between the administrative state he advocated and the movement for direct democracy. The supposedly separate wings of Progressivism, the populistic and organizationist wings, come together in Croly. Little wonder that he found in William S. U'Ren's plan for executive government in Oregon the very model of his ideal of reform: concentrated authority in the hands of the executive, a diminished role for the legislature, and the tool of direct democracy by which an aggressive, powerful leader could appeal directly to 'the people' over the heads of their elected representatives and the organized political parties.[17]

U'Ren's 'Oregon plan', which was submitted to the voters of Oregon in 1912 and, to U'Ren's chagrin, rejected, illustrates another aspect of the myth – or rather shows the way in which historians who have examined the direct democracy movement have misunderstood the relationship between the supporters of the movement and its leaders who were able to give conscious thought to what the reforms would accomplish. I would not want to give the impression at any point that the movement was a conspiracy; such a broadly-supported set of reforms could hardly have been hatched in a boardroom. Indeed, the short-sighted conservative defenders of the big corporations were genuinely opposed to the direct primary and direct legislation and perhaps even believed their own propaganda about the 'revolutionary' democratic character of direct democracy.[18] However, much, possibly most, of the uncritical writing about the Progressive movement is, one suspects, in reaction to who its enemies were. An editorial in the *Los Angeles Times* denouncing the initiative and referendum as the work of anarchistic, socialistic agitators who would use it to destroy property must have convinced many who hated the *Times*'s reactionary politics to vote for the measures. As in so many other cases, liberal historians also seem to have judged these devices by what their conservative enemies said about them.

The point is that there was, indeed, broad, popular support marshalled for the reforms of the Progressives; there was a populistic wing of the Progressive movement which genuinely reflected lower middle-class and working-class radical sentiment and believed that such devices would give 'the people' power over their own government. In short, in their minds such reforms were democratic and not merely devices by which a new kind of elite of notables could manipulate an unorganized mass to do their will.[19] But this 'populistic' or lower middle-class wing, as in the case of the economic reforms, was dominated by the side of progressivism whose aims were very different and who had only contempt – not to say fear – for the populistic ideas of those whose support they nevertheless required if their plans were to be approved. Precisely how this popular sentiment was harnessed by the elitist and anti-democratic Progressives cannot be dealt with here.

U'Ren's 'Oregon plan' illustrates the point that for the administrative or organizationist wing of progressivism, the 'direct democracy' demand was not counterposed to the rationalization and centralization of executive authority, but was instead its necessary prerequisite insofar as it broke down legislative authority and gave to the governors the power to initiate legislation by going directly to 'the people'. In the case of U'Ren's proposed plan the executive was given power to propose legislation to the representative bodies which he could then dissolve if necessary, calling for new elections. All of this without a party system, so that its superficial resemblance to the British parliamentary system is misleading.[20] Once again, contemporary observers understood this well. Horace E. Flack pointed out in 1911 that the Oklahoma and California systems of direct legislation which permitted the governor to call special elections would directly lessen the power of the legislature and would also allow the governor to assume

> much of the authority as the chief executive of the state and head of a political party. The plan of giving the governor a duty to perform in relation to the initiative appears a rational step toward placing upon him a responsibility commensurate with the additional power.[21]

The 'reorganization movement' in state governments between 1912 and 1920 was directly linked to the way in which such direct democracy devices increased the executive's informal and formal powers and strengthened the autonomy of the executive branch in relation to the legislature.[22] In California, for example, John R. Haynes, the tireless advocate of the initiative and referendum, saw no conflict in serving on a special Governor's committee on 'efficiency and economy in California'. It proposed such a reorganization as a continuation of the 'popular rule' which had, in the words of the commission, so successfully removed 'social unrest' in California.[23]

When it came to assessing the impact of their direct democracy devices on the political system, usually in response to the protests of frightened reactionaries who took seriously the Progressives' demagogic rhetoric about people's rule, the conservative (as opposed to 'populist') nature of such devices was stressed. This was not, as some have suggested, merely a verbal concession, but a statement which drew upon actual experience. It was well known to the advocates of direct democracy, for example, that in England conservatives and others opposed to the threat to the established order posed by the rising Labour Party were urging the adoption of the referendum to check the drift toward socialism; they frequently cited this fact as proof of their conservative intentions. The Swiss experience of conservative rule was well known too, of course, and provided the most important model of how class rule could be fragmented. And whatever fears of radicalism may have been sparked off by the passage of direct legislation in Oregon in 1902, these were soon dissipated by experience, so that even former opponents were mollified and began to see the possibility of using the system for their own ends.[24] But most important of all was the way in which the direct primary system was understood to have made it possible to achieve the Progressive goal of checking the excesses of big capital and providing necessary social reforms in order to head off the 'formation of class parties'.[25]

Just how conservative and how successful, therefore, the Progressive political reforms were – that is, how little they served to democratize American politics – may be grasped merely by stepping back for a moment to look at the party system which resulted. To do so it is important to abandon the usual parochial approach of American historiography and survey the scene from a comparative vantage point. It then becomes possible to ask the all-important question which alone can permit us to evaluate these reform devices: namely, what alternatives to these reforms might have been attempted by way of opening up the political system to genuine democratic control from below – but were not and, indeed, were successfully aborted by the adoption of the Progressives' plebiscitarian devices?

The answer, in brief, is that the system of direct primaries which replaced the convention and the caucus resulted in a party system in the United States which is unique among the capitalist democracies.[26] Only in America is it true that direct membership participation in the parties does not exist except in the sense that individuals register their party preference with an official agency of the state or are habitual voters for one or another party.[27] The parties themselves and the choice of candidates is strictly regulated by law in the states in which the individual parties exist. The political party in the United States is not, therefore, a private voluntary association whose rules and conduct are set by the wishes of its members – democratically or undemocratically – but by legislative enactment, in effect making parties the creature of professional politicians. As a party, control over its own candidates is virtually non-existent; the crude factionalism of which Berger spoke has become the norm in American politics. Not only are the adherents of the dominant parties thereby kept out of the governance of the party, but the ability of minority parties (when they are allowed) to choose their own candidates is frequently subjected to the control of the politicians of the majority two-party system.[28] The American situation is in contrast to the party systems of Western Europe, Australia and New Zealand where the parties are organized as private voluntary associations; although the particular national electoral system obviously impinges upon their internal organization, the program, the rules and by-laws, and the very method of selecting candidates are substantially the private business of the party, its membership, and its leaders.[29]

All of this is so widely taken for granted as the natural state of affairs in America, that even the possibility of an alternative democratic party system has simply vanished from American political discourse, popular as well as academic. Whole books are written about 'participation' in American politics without ever once mentioning the absence of democratic-membership political organizations. It is a demonstration of the 'dog that didn't bark' phenomenon. Even the advocates of 'responsible parties' have, as the years have gone by, tended to forget the idea of democratic-membership political parties, leaving only the idea of disciplined organizations of professional politicians as their ideal of 'party renewal'.

A second and equally well-known fact about the American party system must also be mentioned, because it has been taken for granted for so long that it too is now usually ignored. This is the remarkable fact of the absence of any mass socialist or labour party in the United States, in contrast to every other capitalist democracy where there exist membership parties of the working class which proclaim their adherence to 'socialist' ideas.

For the most part the absence of such a socialist or labour party is dealt with in ideological terms or in relationship to peculiarities of American society and its class structure. What is completely overlooked in such an approach, however, is that the peculiar party system in the United States is the *organizational* side of the absence of a mass labour or socialist party. For, as any student of the emergence of the British Labour Party or any of the continental socialist parties knows, these ideological parties were political expressions of the working-class movement, and embodied a different and for their time radically democratic conception of political participation and party organization. As Duverger has pointed out, the branch or mass party combined for the first time in modern politics formal democratic-membership participation and control and a representative party structure. In this it challenged the old, elitist caucus system under which bourgeois politics had proceeded and, indeed, in time its success forced even the bourgeois parties in search of mass electoral support to democratize themselves to a degree.[30]

In the United States, it was only in the internal structure of the Socialist Party that the democratic and representative type of party organization was developed. Writing in the middle of the Progressive period's mania for 'direct democracy', the University of Chicago labor economist and historian Robert F. Hoxie pointed out that 'it is a fact little known that the Socialists are introducing among us a new type of political organization and new political method very much in contrast with those to which through long usage we have become habituated'. He suggested that the democratically organized convention system of the Socialist Party represented 'a political organization and political methods that are worth consideration on their merits as possible contributions to a more wholesome, more democratic, and more Progressive expression of the social will'. This could not have fallen on deafer ears, at least as far as the leadership of the Progressive movement was concerned. But Hoxie's point remains as valid today as it was at the beginning of the century.[31]

Viewed from the vantage point of the emergence of the participatory branch organization of the European and, later, Australian and New Zealand social democratic/labour parties, and contrasted to the internal democratic organization of the American Socialist Party, the claim that the direct democracy reforms democratized the political system falls of its own weight. To speak of a system which set out to strip individuals of effective organization and which consciously made politics a matter of personality rather than program and party organization as 'democratic', is merely to accept the ideology of Progressivism itself. The degree to which this ideology is still taken for granted may be seen in the way in which the McGovern Commission delegate selection rules in the Democratic Party were justified as maximizing participation. Participation requires sustained membership and a responsible party organization; a herd of delegates who deliver their votes to a candidate who then exercises complete personal control over the party and program may be said to have 'participated' only in the sense that a cow participates in its milking. It is doubly significant, therefore, that the original McGovern–Fraser guidelines also raised, for the first time since the beginning of the Progressive era, the idea of a membership enrolment party, thus confirming indirectly one of the essential points made here: that the hidden issue of the American party system as it evolved out of the Progressive era is the plebiscitarian, non-participatory idea of 'membership' which the Progressive reformers fastened on it. It is not inconceivable, therefore, that when the Progressive-born political system finally breaks up, we shall begin to progress forward by returning to 1912.

To sum up the critical point which makes the individualistic, unorganized politics of progressivism plebiscitarian and undemocratic: democratic participation requires organization (which is not to say that all organization is democratic, even when formally so). However, the mesmerizing of historians and social scientists by what Alvin Gouldner has termed the 'pathos of bureaucracy'[32] – that set of unexamined, metaphysical assumptions which credits Robert Michels' famous 'iron law of oligarchy' as a scientific truth – has led them to overlook the truth of this elementary proposition, one which the contradictory Michels himself also subscribed to: individuals can be powerful in modern society only through organization. Effective democratic participation in politics requires effective democratic political organization. Whatever breaks that down conduces to a plebiscitarianization of politics. If there is an iron law, indeed, it is the iron law of *non-organization*: in the absence of such structures, which in modern society necessarily entails representation, self-selected elites and powerful, wealthy groups dominate the unorganized mass. But this is precisely what the Progressive reformers wanted, while democratic organization of the kind I have described is what they did *not* want and did their best to prevent; they knew, from their class standpoint, that such organization shut out persons like themselves and would encourage the formation of a working-class party. Thus the 'democracy' of the reformers aimed at breaking down responsible organized politics in order to maximize their own role as leaders of 'the people'. They enunciated the ideal of 'classlessness' in politics and society thereby defining their own kind of class consciousness – and class conscious they certainly were when confronted with a militant labour movement which sought the basic democratic right to organize, or which ran its own candidates.[33]

The supposedly democratic reforms, then, which the Progressives advocated were designed to prevent participation: if we understand by participation not the ratification by plebiscite of the policies, programs and candidacies initiated by a well-placed elite, but the possibility of joining organized, mass membership, political parties, democratically structured and committed to ideas and issues rather than to persons. This is the only sense in which we can speak of democratic 'participation' in modern society. Difficult and elusive as the realization of such a goal may be – and Michels' analysis is of inestimable value here – it is not impossible. There is no iron law of oligarchy.

What we are left with, then, when the myth of Progressive democracy is dispelled, is a political heritage of democracy without participation; a democracy predicated on the reduction of parties to their individual atomized constituencies, if not their total legal abolition. The result is a system in which parties are dissolved into a collection of personal factions built around colourful personalities and in which the organization and education of political opinion is virtually non-existent. Organized, democratic, participation – which is a redundancy – is not available in such a system and what is left is the pure essence of plebiscitarian politics: the act of voting which permits a choice between self-selected candidates or the right to ratify or reject issues or propositions manufactured by powerful and well-organized elites.

The subsequent rise of the public opinion poll in American politics, it may be suggested, is a direct continuation of this Progressive notion of democracy through plebiscite. George Gallup wrote in 1940 to propose a 'fourth stage of democracy' through the poll, and the political scientist Harold F. Gosnell hailed the poll as a 'more flexible instrument than the initiative and referendum' because it 'could be used by a legislature to ascertain the unexpressed wishes of the voters'. They were voicing a view of the political process which the proponents of direct democracy would have appreciated if, that is, they could have been assured that this scientific tool would remain in the proper hands.[34]

It has been necessary to grapple with this myth to lay the groundwork for a far more important task: detailing the actual history of this movement which so profoundly altered the structure of American politics. Necessary, because the advocacy of these devices, beginning in the 1890s with the populists and Gompers' AFL, down through the Progressive movement proper after the turn of the century, has seemed completely unproblematic to historians and social scientists. If we were able here to trace this history, we would see how this demand of the populists and the AFL got taken up by reformers who had little in common with them and we would be able to ask why it was that the farmers experienced representative systems and political parties as inherently oppressive. We would then discover the absolutely crucial role played by the idea of direct legislation in Gompers' thinking and see how far it was counterposed to independent labour political action.[35] And we would be able to explore in far more detail the relationship between the restructuring of American politics, which the adoption of these devices entailed, and the formation of the 'administrative state' which was the goal of the Progressive movement. Taken together, the breakdown of democracy through the attack on organized parties, particularly the way in which it short-circuited the emergence of a democratic party of the left, and the creation of the administrative state, constitutes the twin legacy of progressivism to the debasement of the American political system today.

CHAPTER 2

Populism and Direct Democracy

During the 1950s one of the more distinctive strains in the intellectual turn of Cold War liberals to the right arose out of the attempt to explain Senator Joseph McCarthy's appeal to large numbers of Americans. There had been other periods in American history during which civil liberties were threatened or destroyed, other periods of hysteria over the 'red menace', but never one – so it was argued – in which a campaign to enforce conformity and fear became so widespread and received the support of sizeable sections of the population. Even though McCarthy never elaborated a broad program and no organized social movement arose to support him, there were overtones of anti-intellectualism, anti-'Easternism', and even vague expressions of opposition to 'Wall Street' in McCarthy's rhetoric.

In casting about for an explanation of this phenomenon, a number of writers – social scientists, historians, and journalists – reached into American history. The alleged similarity of the rhetoric, the supposedly similar geographical and class basis of McCarthy's support suggest to them that the roots of McCarthyism were to be found in the great agrarian revolt of the 1890s which culminated in the formation of the People's Party or, as it quickly came to be known, the 'Populists'.[1] McCarthy, it was said, denounced the 'Communist conspiracy' and its intellectual fellow travellers in the name of 'the people' – in the same spirit that the Populists called for the rule of the people against the conspiracy of the international bankers, especially against those symbols of financial parasitism, Jews and the Rothschilds, and not least of all, against the corrupt politicians and bosses who were the tools of the 'plutocracy'.

Most important of all, however, these writers argued, the Populists had bitterly resented politicians and organized political parties, and had sought to institute (re-institute, they thought) the will of the people unfettered by the professional politicians and the politicians' own instrument, the political party. In place of these 'excrescences' on democracy they demanded 'direct democracy' – the initiative, the referendum, the direct primary, and other devices designed to break down the conspiracy known as 'party politics'. Lipset writes:

> On the political level they showed a strong mistrust of parliamentary or constitutional democracy and were particularly antagonistic to the concept of party. They preferred to break down the sources of partisan strength and create as

> much direct democracy as possible through the introduction of the initiative and referendum, and through easy recall elections. Parties, politicians, big business, bankers, and foreigners were bad; only the people acting for themselves were good.[2]

In the mid-1960s, Michael Rogin's study, *McCarthy and the Intellectuals*,[3] thoroughly demolished the historical basis of the claim that there was a 'direct line' from Populism to McCarthyism, but it left unanswered a number of questions about the politics and social outlook of the Populists and the broader issues of direct democracy and plebiscitarian politics raised by Lipset and others. Richard Hofstadter's brilliant examination of the 'dark side' of Populism in *The Age of Reform* (1955), from which most of the critics of Populism took their inspiration, was too readily dismissed by historians on the left who, understandably, and on the whole, correctly, comprehended that the impulse behind the argument for the Populist roots of McCarthyism was an attempt on the part of rightward-moving Cold War intellectuals to evade responsibility for President Truman's loyalty-security state and for their support for most aspects of the witch-hunt which ensued. However, in their haste to refute the conservative case againt the Populists, which was, as this essay argues, an attack on democracy itself, not only was the anti-Semitic colouration of the Populists' critique of capitalism too quickly overlooked by the critics but so too was the plebiscitarian nature of the Populist political outlook. This is hardly surprising, however, because it was then and continues to be at the heart of the American view of politics – whether found on the right with its demagogic praise of 'the people' and hatred of politics and politicians, or on the left, with its inability to see the need for political participation through democratically organized political parties rather than the Populist/progressive devices of 'direct democracy' which shut out organized, democratic, political parties.

The major historical reassessment of the Populist-Progressive tradition is to be found in Richard Hofstadter's *The Age of Reform*, published in 1955. Hofstadter saw in the Populist and Progressive tradition 'much that was retrograde and delusive, a little that was vicious, and a good deal that was comic'. Yet, he warned

> ... my comments ... on the old agrarian and entrepreneurial aspirations are not intended to disparage them as ultimate values but to raise some safeguards against the political misuse of them that was and sometimes still is attempted, and perhaps to shed some light on the methods by which that part of them that is still meaningful can be salvaged.[4]

How different Hofstadter's approach is from other critics of 'populism' we shall see shortly. His indictment of the reform tradition is based on its 'moral absolutism'.[5] It is this absolutism that was at the heart of their demand for pure democracy, for such absolutism 'often wanders over the border between reality and impossibility'. Thus, he writes about the Progressives, that

> it is hardly an accident that the generation that wanted to bring about direct popular rule, break up the political machines, and circumvent representative governments was the same generation that imposed Prohibition on the country and proposed to make the world safe for democracy.[6]

This side of Populism-Progressivism – the key American reform tradition – 'foreshadowed' the 'cranky, pseudo-conservatism of our time'. Those 'elements of illiberalism that frequently seem to be an indissoluble part of popular movements' have been ignored by intellectuals, and it is this that Hofstadter sought to correct.[7]

As C. Vann Woodward pointed out, the 'unhappy tendencies' with which the critics are concerned are 'variously described as "mobism", "direct democracy", or "plebiscitarianism", but there is a surprising and apparently spontaneous consensus of preference for "populism"'.[8] The demand of the American Populists for direct democracy is thus made akin to, if not identical with, the developments which preceded the rise of fascism in Germany and which have made societies vulnerable to the cancer of totalitarianism. The demand that the whole people rule, unchecked by parties and politicians, unencumbered by complicated legislation and debate, and the obfuscation which factious and self-interested minorities create to confuse honest men and women, suggests strongly to these critics that the tendency of the 'populist' outlook is to create the 'mass society' of atomized individuals. This society weakening the bonds of old associations and authority and sweeping away intermediate associations as 'conspiracies', or potential conspiracies, prepares the way for movements like McCarthyism, or in times of crisis, for the rise of totalitarian movements.

The most extreme formulation of the last viewpoint is found in the writings of Edward Shils:

> ... populism has many faces. Nazi dictatorship had markedly populistic features in its practice, in its constant invocation of the will of the people as its justification and the good of the people as its end, and in the 'direct' relationship of the people and their leader unmediated by institutions. Bolshevism has a strand of populism in it too, although, like National Socialism and other dictatorships, its practice rejects the will of the people as a guide ...[9]

'Populism', Shils continues 'is tinged by the belief that the people are not just the equal of their rulers; they are actually better than their rulers and better than the classes – the urban middle classes – associated with the ruling powers.'[10] Populism undermines the rule of law, and demands that:

> all institutions be permeated by the popular will or responsive to it – since the validity of the popular will is self-evident – populism inclines towards a conception of the legislative branch which may be designated as 'identity' in contrast with 'representation'. Legislators are expected to be 'identical' with the popular will rather than 'representatives' who will interpret it.[11]

The populist mentality regards politicians with contempt, as 'mere errand boys'. Shils declaims: 'There is a straight line from Ben Tillman to Huey Long and Eugene Talmadge; from Bryan and La Follette to Gerald L. K. Smith, Father Coughlin and Senator McCarthy, Gerald Nye, William Langer and many others.'[12]

Shils' statement is certainly revealing, even apart from the fact that it is a crude amalgam, resting upon a simplification of history and of politics rivalling any of the simplifications which the Populists ever dreamed up. It demonstrates that although Hofstadter sought only to balance an over-idealized portrait of the major American reform tradition, a tradition that has shaped much of the present, the indictment of 'populism' for some of these critics involves a much more thoroughgoing criticism of democracy itself. It is hardly surprising in this connection that Shils' own ideal of the proper place of 'the people' is the forelock-tugging Tory worker, or lower middle-class British subject (a revealing locution), who defers to his masters and knows his place, while the elite controls political affairs free from public observation. Britain, he tells us, is 'democratic and pluralist' while not at all 'populist'. At the same time it is hierarchical: the government is suffused by the symbolism of a hereditary monarch and aristocracy, and the working and middle classes are deferential to the upper classes and their rulers.[13] Using this standard, it is clear how it is possible to form an amalgam between Gerald L.K. Smith, the elder La Follette and William Jennings Bryan. At our charitable best we can only say that such an approach lacks a sense of proportion, not to mention a lack of respect for the truth and betrays a deep contempt for democracy.

The point here, however, is not to belabour Shils. Rather, it is to indicate the dangers of a too facile, too ideological re-evaluation of the Populist tradition and its demand for the direct, unmediated rule of the 'people'. Yet if we are not to be forced to accept his ultra-conservative view of democracy, it is necessary to inquire much more deeply into the reasons for the defects of the Populist movement in order to determine whether or not its manifest failings are remediable in any other way than by the acceptance of a hierarchical, authoritarian society.

Combined with 'mass society theory', this indictment of populism and direct democracy, predicated to one degree or another on the Michelsian thesis of the 'incompetence of the masses' to rule themselves, has led to a redefinition of democracy in terms of the relationship between 'elites' and 'masses'. Democracy resides not in the old ideal of the participation of the intelligent citizen in political affairs and the progressive involvement of larger and larger sections of the populace in such participation, as liberal democrats and socialists of an earlier day had maintained, but rather in the competition of elites for the favour of the masses. As long as balance can be maintained between the elites, through the existence of large numbers of independent centers of power-organizations, different classes, interests, etc., then individual freedom can be maintained and protected both against any 'elite' which tries to monopolize power, as well as against the incursion of the 'masses'. 'Civil liberty', William Kornhauser writes, 'requires considerable social autonomy of both elites and non-elites.'[14]

In short, to demand increased participation by the masses in decision making through the reform of social institutions is not only naive but poses a threat to the stability of the institutions which maintain the precarious balance between freedom and slavery. If it is true that the demand for 'participation' which democrats once took for granted, and not so long ago at that, can be equated with or linked to the 'direct democracy' of the Populists and Progressives and even with the plebiscitarian rule of totalitarian Communist or fascist regimes, then there would have to be some justice to the 'elite theory of democracy'. But, as I want to show in the course of this chapter, this point rests upon a confusion of the 'plebiscite' as used by Hitler or Stalin, or Louis Bonaparte, with the various devices for direct democracy which the Populists and Progressives demanded, as well as with modern democracy itself. To use the term 'plebiscitarian' is not entirely incorrect, as I shall argue, in relation to the Populist and Progressive ideal of democracy, but to the degree that it was truly plebiscitarian, it was a defect which inhered in the political outlook and social position of the people to whom such ideas appealed and *not*, as the indiscriminate use of 'populism' and 'plebiscitarianism' and 'direct democracy' by these critics seems to suggest, in democracy and democratic mass movements.[15]

I would not wish to deny here that the conception of democracy and the program of direct democracy and non-partisan politics which characterized both the Populist as well as the Progressive movements were not defective from a democratic standpoint. There was, without any question, a strand of hostility to politics, political parties and representative democracy, along with bonapartist or caesaristic overtones, in populism as well as in progressivism. There was, I think it can be shown, an underlying attitude of political impotence, especially for the radical farmers who made up the Populist movement, which under other circumstances has made similar petty-bourgeois groupings subject to the manipulation of anti-democratic leaders and movements. Yet, even if this is true, it need not necessarily lead to the kind of disappointed withdrawal from the ideals of democracy which is reflected, for example, in Hofstadter's interpretation of *The Age of Reform*. Nor must it necessarily support the much more conservative views of an Edward Shils, who yearns for a society in which the common people cringe before their betters.

What is required in either case is an historical and sociological specification of the circumstances under which 'populistic' sentiments and theories made their appearance and an analysis of the situation of the social strata or groups for which these politics had its appeal. It is necessary to distinguish between the motives behind the populistic outlook and the actual consequences and objective meaning for democratic processes. Only in this way is it possible to avoid throwing out the democratic baby with the Populist bath-water. To proceed in any other manner is to take the phenomenon of populism out of the world of scientific and political discourse into the kingdom of immutable essences and metaphysical beliefs.

In what follows I wish to take up one of the central strands of the reform outlook: the hostility to organized political parties and politics, and the distrust of representatives or politicians which gave rise to the demand for 'direct democracy' – the referendum, the initiative, the direct primary, and the non-partisan election, etc. Rather than looking for the 'Populistic' mentality, however, I want to analyze the relationship between the capacity for collective class action and the demand for 'direct democracy', unmediated by professional politicians and organized political parties. My aim is to attempt to explain the circumstances and characteristics which determine the relative capacity of a class or stratum to realize its ends through organized class action, and to see how this ability, or lack of it, became translated as it did in the case of certain sections of the rural and urban middle classes, into a general distrust of politics and a demand for direct democracy. When instituted as part of the program of electoral reform by the Progressives, these factors shaped the present-day American political universe.

To open the discussion, it is important first to consider the theoretical side of the issues raised by the critics. In the next section I shall examine Robert Michels' view of direct democracy and the referendum in his work, *Political Parties*, contrasting it to the classical analysis of 'primitive democracy' which Beatrice and Sidney Webb undertook in *Industrial Democracy*.[16] My purpose here is to indicate how Michels' discussion of direct democracy and the referendum, which forms an integral part of his central thesis that 'organization' and its sociological concomitants inevitably lead to the defeat of mass democracy, hinders at least as much as it helps in understanding the dynamics of direct democracy. In a sense, our analysis of the source of the politics of direct democracy involves a specification of Michels' thesis. Rather than assuming an 'iron law of oligarchy', however, it is our task to ascertain why for certain social classes, but not necessarily for others, the organization of a political party or 'politics' as a whole, which involves the functioning of some kind of system of representation, appears to be – and is in fact – a kind of Frankensteins monster which turns upon its creators and subjects them to the very forces which it was designed to overcome.

In the next section I shall examine the phenomenon of 'plebiscitarian' democracy, because, as I have noted, this term is often used interchangeably with 'populism', or 'direct democracy'. There are both important differences between the two ideas as well as critical similarities which must be analyzed, if we are not to end up characterizing all demands for increased participation by the citizens in a democracy as 'plebiscitarian'. It will be shown how in fact when the term 'plebiscitarianism' is understood in its proper historical and sociological sense, that it is the pluralist proponents of 'elite' democracy who are the real plebiscitarians.

In the last section I shall turn to a specific examination of the history and role of the demand for 'direct democracy' in the farmers' movement which culminated in the formation of the People's Party. It will be seen first, how this demand was the natural outgrowth not of the 'Populistic mentality' but of the specific characteristics of the farmers as a class; and second, how, in fact, in different regions where the relationships between the farmers and other classes varied, the plebiscitarian element in populism also varied.

Primitive Democracy *vs.* Democracy

Robert Michels' *Political Parties* is justly regarded as a central contribution to the understanding of the tension between democracy and 'oligarchy' in modern society. Certainly it is correct to view it as the seminal work for contemporary political sociology. Properly modified, its central thesis, summarized although far too simply in the 'iron law of oligarchy', constitutes an essential insight into the dynamics of democracy not only within voluntary associations, but within society as a whole.

And yet, *Political Parties* must be read with a critical eye, for it is a highly tendentious work, written by a partisan of a political viewpoint directly hostile to the Social Democratic movement in general, and to the German party in particular. Though the effect of the portrait Michels draws of the bureaucratized Social Democratic party is in general quite devastating – as chapter by chapter Michels looks beneath the official ideals and claims, beneath the ideology and the formal structure of the organization, into the realities of the relationship between the rank-and-file members and their leaders – it is necessary to understand, as Carl Landauer has pointed out,[17] that his main thesis is 'overstated', and as even Michels admits, one-sided in its emphasis upon the tendencies which reinforce 'oligarchy'.

Many others have dealt with Michels' thesis, and it is not our purpose here to extend that discussion. However it is instructive to examine briefly Michels' views of 'direct' government by the masses and the use of the referendum. A fundamental premise of Michels' entire argument, is a distinction between 'direct' democracy and parliamentary or representative democracy. The latter, according to Michels, is a necessary condition of large-scale mass organizations. It necessarily gives way to 'oligarchy', and hence it is only direct democracy which can be considered real democracy. For Michels anything less than the direct government by the people assembled *en masse* is a sham: thus the abandonment of 'direct government' in organizations is a step away from democracy, directly into the dictatorship of the professional representatives over their nominal masters. In the course of his discussion of the reasons for the impossibility of direct government he draws upon Beatrice and Sidney Webb's account of primitive democracy, set forth in their book *Industrial Democracy*. Yet, as I want to show in a moment, the Webbs' argument is directed to demonstrating that primitive democracy is, as Michels himself agrees, an unsatisfactory method of governing all but the smallest, uncomplicated organizations, and that its maintenance under changed circumstances makes democratic controls impossible. In short, that 'direct democracy' under specified conditions may – and often does – turn into its opposite. In his discussion of the referendum, Michels recognizes this when he notes that the referendum has been 'but little democratic in [its] results'.[18] However, Michels' polemical purpose gets the best of him and a few pages later he directly contradicts himself:

> Now the democratic parties as far as their internal organization is concerned, have either failed to adopt the principles of direct, popular sovereignty, or else have accepted application of these only after prolonged hesitation and in exceptional cases. From the democratic point of view they are therefore inferior to many of the Swiss cantons. For example, the German social democracy does not submit the deliberations of its congresses to ratification by the party as a whole. Moreover ... in Germany the decisions at its congress are determined by the simple majority of the delegates. *Thus we have parliamentarism in the place of democracy*.[19] [Emphasis mine.]

Michels' definition of democracy is thereby limited to one kind of democracy: the primitive democracy of the Swiss canton or the New England town meeting. Representative democracy is thus by definition not democratic. But as an examination of Kautsky's work on direct democracy – a polemic against the simplified notions of Moritz von Rittinghausen, the 'father' of direct legislation – shows, Kautsky's and the Social Democratic Party's opposition to schemes for introducing the referendum stemmed not from an anti-democratic or bureaucratic design but from the recognition of the fact that such 'real' (that is, direct) democracy is in truth undemocratic in the circumstances of modern society.[20]

Michels' argument is misleading – because he ignores the consequences and actual functioning of a given device such as the referendum within a given social setting, and then proceeds to characterize opposition to the use of such devices to 'prove' that its opponents are anti-democratic. Michels' argument is as specious as it would be to maintain that anyone who opposed the dismantling of the city council of a large city (or even a very small one) in favour of setting up a New England-style 'town meeting' to run the city's affairs, was opposed to 'democracy'. Of course, we are here implicitly rejecting Michels' central thesis, that the only possible substitute for such 'direct' government, the representative system, must of necessity result in the complete and absolute domination of the representative or delegate over those who have elected them.

In brief, Michels' approach when applied strictly rules out any discussion of the conditions and circumstances which makes the advocacy of 'direct democracy' in fact, and perhaps even in intention, undemocratic or, for that matter, democratic. At the same time – as his many critics have noted – Michels' approach prevents any investigation of those conditions which determine the degree to which 'representatives,' in private organizations, or in the state, are controlled or guided or are responsive to the people who elect them. And, conversely, it deflects attention from the question which is our main concern in this study: namely, under what conditions and after what specific historical experiences do various classes or strata come to believe (correctly or not) that their capacity for collective action is *diminished* by the organization of a political party or a common association, and to demand as a consequence the abolition of 'politics' and organized political parties because they believe them to mean enslavement of the 'individual' to politicians, oligarchs, bureaucrats, etc.

To ask these questions, of course, involves a rejection of Michels' conviction that democracy is impossible: otherwise the demand for the abolition of political parties, hostility to politicians, etc., is simply a 'natural' reaction to an inherently impossible situation. But to reiterate: even granting the tendencies to 'oligarchy' which Michels points to, it is necessary to enquire why, if democracy in its representative sense is not impossible, it is that this kind of reaction arises. To put it another way: we need an explanation of Michels himself.[21]

It is important to restate here that I have deliberately stressed that side of Michels' analysis which is least defensible. His analysis of the reasons for the tendencies toward bureaucratic degeneration which manifest themselves in mass organizations under capitalism, in so far as it is specific and does not rest upon the false polarization between 'real' democracy and 'parliamentary' democracy, nor upon the assertion of certain innate psychological traits, is of the greatest theoretical value.

Far superior to Michels' discussion of the referendum and direct democracy from a sociological standpoint, is the Webbs' discussion of 'primitive democracy' and its evolution into system of representative democracy in the historical development of the British trade union movement.[22] The Webbs show how in the youthful trade unions, the members insisted on rotation in office, absence of permanent officials and the decision of all members on every issue, rather than the election of an executive committee. Only 'grudgingly' did they delegate any of the functions of the general business meeting to the officers or committees.[23]

Slowly, as the movement spread and local groups were forced to enter into relations with trade unions in other areas, a division of labour arose, and the need for representative bodies made itself felt. Even then, the first representative assemblies were made up of bound delegates.[24] However, since the delegates were only surrogates for the decisions previously made by the local bodies, the introduction of cheap and quick communication in the form of the penny-post brought the replacement of this system by the initiative and the referendum. The defects of the referendum under these circumstances became apparent quite quickly:

> ... however imperfectly the question was framed, however inconsistent the result might be with the society's rules and past practice, the answer returned by the members' votes was final and instantly operative. Those who believe that pure democracy implies the direct decision, by the mass of the people, of every question as it arises, will find the ideal realized without check or limit in the history of the larger Trade Unions between 1834 and 1870.[25]

The referendum proved especially unsound when it came to making decisions about the functioning of insurance funds. In practice the initiative was abandoned, and as the Webbs point out, the referendum 'ceased to provide the members with any effective control'. In a passage which deserves to be read and re-read, the Webbs write

> If the executive could choose the issues to be submitted, the occasion on which the question should be put, and the form in which it should be couched, the referendum, far from supplying any counterpoise to the executive, was soon found to be an immense addition to its power. Any change which the executive desired could be stated in the most plausible terms and supported by convincing arguments, which almost invariably secured its adoption by a large majority ... The reliance of Trade Union democrats on the referendum resulted, in fact, in the virtual exclusion of the general body of members from all real share in the government.[26]

In short, given the atomized state of the membership, the absence of any provision for a system of representation and the monopoly of communication exercised by the executive, the referendum was transformed into an instrument of domination over rather than by the membership. If democracy must mean this kind of 'direct' democracy, the Webbs conclude, then the result will either be 'inefficiency and disintegration' or in reaction to this, 'the uncontrolled dominance of a personal dictator or an expert bureaucracy'.[27]

It was as a result of this historical experience, and only after the *undemocratic* consequences of direct, 'primitive democracy', had become clear, that, the Webbs point out '... we have the appearance in the Trade Union world of the typical modern form of democracy, the elected representative assembly, appointing and controlling an executive committee under whose direction the permanent official staff performs its work'.[28]

Thus, although many factors adduced by the Webbs to explain the failure of primitive democracy are the same as those which Michels mentions – partially on the basis of his familiarity with the argument of *Industrial Democracy* – there is a striking difference in the way in which the Webbs approached the problem. The difference may be summarized in two points. First, they specified the circumstances which made direct democracy in fact undemocratic. These devices, they emphasized, 'proved in practice, utterly inadequate as a means of securing genuine popular control'.[29] Second, the Webbs emphasized the historical evolution of the trade union movement, and the conditions which made it possible for representative democracy to emerge and to secure a degree of popular control.

Even if it is necessary to take the Webbs' conception of democratic control with a grain of salt, given their own well-known bureaucratic proclivities, their discussion provides a basis for further investigation which Michels' work, taken uncritically, does not. On the critical point, the rejection of Michels' absolutist counterposition of 'real' democracy, that is, pure, direct democracy to representative democracy, we find (strangely enough) agreement between Kautsky, the Webbs and Lenin. Writing in *What is to be Done?*, Lenin (who had translated *The History of Trade Unionism* into Russian) took note of the Webbs' findings about the history of 'primitive democracy':

> A long period of historical experience was required to teach these workers how absurd such a conception of democracy was and to make them understand the necessity for representative institutions on the one hand, and of full-time professional officials on the other.[30]

Summarizing Kautsky's work on direct democracy, Lenin notes that 'the conclusions drawn by the Marxian theoretician coincides with the lessons learned from many years of experience by the workers who organized "spontaneously"'. Kautsky, Lenin writes, opposed the 'Socialism of Anarchists and litterateurs', who in their 'striving after effect proclaim the principle that laws should be passed directly by the whole people, completely failing to understand that in modern society this principle can have only a relative application'.[31] This conception of a *relative* application of direct democracy – an idea that entirely escaped Michels – must be the beginning point for any analysis of democratic institutions.

At the end of their discussion of the evolution of trade union democracy, from primitive to representative democracy, the Webbs provide a brilliantly concise statement of the conditions under which the device of the referendum might possibly enhance democratic control in society at large, if not in the trade union. The use of the referendum in trade unions increased the power of the permanent civil service and diminished popular control. However:

> This particular danger would, we imagine, scarcely occur in a democratic state. In the trade union the executive committee occupies a unique position. It alone has access to official information; it alone commands expert professional skill and experience and, most important of all, it monopolizes in the society's official circular what corresponds to the newspaper press. The existence of political parties fairly equal in knowledge, ability, and electoral organization, and each served by its own press, would always save the democratic state from this particular perversion of the Referendum to the advantage of the existing government. But any party or sect of opinion which, from lack of funds, education, or social influence, could not call to its aid the forces which we have named, would, we suggest, find itself as helpless in the face of a referendum as the discontented section in a strong trade union.[32]

The cogency of the Webbs' analysis of the conditions under which the referendum could function as a device of democratic control, is born out amply in Lipset's study of the International Typographical Union.[33] In the ITU, Lipset found that the system of referendums in conjunction with a strong two-party system, functioned as a valuable adjunct to that system, both to correct abuses, and to act as a positive restraint upon the ruling party.[34] Thus far from being an instrument of a demagogic and skilful bureaucracy to elicit democratic legitimation from its members for pre-determined politics, referendums acted as a check upon the membership's elected representatives thereby enhancing democratic control by the union members.

Several important conclusions emerge from this consideration of the Webbs' and Lipset's analysis of organizational democracy which Michels' approach does not permit. First is the necessity of analyzing the specific historical experiences of a class or stratum, in order to understand their capacity for collective action, and their readiness to use one rather than another mode of organization in the struggle to gain their ends. It is this approach which is suggested by Reinhard Bendix, when he speaks of the necessity of studying the 'cumulative historical experience' of a class, especially under crisis conditions: to find out, for example, whether or not there is a 'backlog of success in the use of democratic institutions', the absence of which may predispose a class to undemocratic solutions.[35] It is precisely this experience that the Webbs analyze in their account of the English working-class struggle to create the modern trade union movement and it is, conversely, this lack of success which characterized the social elements who backed the demand for 'direct democracy'. Their opposition to political parties and politicians can only be understood in the context of their experiences: when for a period of time, as we shall see, their experiences changed, their attitudes underwent a sharp change also.[36]

Second, implicit in the proposition which the Webbs formulate to distinguish between the conditions necessary for the referendum to be an instrument of democracy, is the sociological distinction between the referendum and the plebiscite, which had been used most recently in the Webbs' time by Louis Bonaparte. Since the critics of 'populism' use the terms 'plebiscitary' or 'plebiscitarian' quite freely to apply to the demand for 'direct democracy', it is important to examine this point.

'Plebiscitarian Democracy'

It is clear from the Webbs' discussion of the referendum and direct democracy that it is necessary to distinguish between the intentions of those who advocate or institute direct democracy, and its actual functioning. As we saw, the transformation of the referendum from an instrument of democratic control, into an instrument by which a centralized executive could gain support for any proposals it might make, depends on the absence of an organized opposition, with its own press or means of communication, and the concomitant monopoly of communication by the executive matched by the atomization of the membership. Its function under these circumstances is to give democratic legitimacy to the decisions made by the executive. By having the opportunity, in practice if not necessarily formally, to formulate the issues to be voted upon, and to monopolize the means of communication for the purpose of convincing the members to vote for the propositions put to them, the direct or pure democracy of the trade unions was turned by the executive into the opposite of what had originally been intended. Originally designed to give control to the members over their organization's affairs, it became an instrument of bureaucratic domination over the members, in the absence of any effective opposition, and in the absence of any significant secondary organization, which could provide alternative means of communication, so that opposing views could crystallize upon some common platform.

Thus, however 'democratic' the form, in reality the power to make all decisions rested with the executive. It is this use of democratic forms and the relative absence of the necessary conditions for democracy, which combine together to give to the actions of an oligarchy, bureaucracy, or dictator, the quality which can be termed 'plebiscitarian'. In the absence of discussion and, in modern society, in the absence of organized 'publics', through which the individual can participate effectively in shaping the discussion and determining the issues, such devices as the initiative or the referendum tend to be plebiscitarian. The effect is to give the sanction of democracy to the actions and decisions of a minority or even a single individual who are alone capable of effectively presenting their viewpoint.

Only by restricting oneself to the form, thus, is it possible to claim that the use of a referendum or any of the devices of direct democracy under these circumstances can rightly be called 'democratic'. Its actual functioning is to deny the essence of democracy. At the end of the nineteenth century, A.V. Dicey, the noted English constitutional lawyer, in a well-known article on the referendum, wrote that there was an 'essential' difference between the referendum and the French *plebiscite*:

> A *plebiscite* is a mass vote of the French people by which a Revolutionary or Imperial Executive obtains for its policy, or its crimes, the apparent sanction or condemnation of France. Frenchmen are asked at the moment, and in the form most convenient to the statesmen or conspirators who rule Paris to say 'Aye' or 'No' whether they will or will not accept a given Constitution as a given policy ... It is not preceded by debate. The form and the nature of the question to be submitted to the nation is chosen and settled by the men in power. Rarely indeed when a *plebiscite* has been taken has the voting been free or fair ... Grant that in more than one of these cases the verdict of the *plebiscite* corresponded to the will of the nation. The *plebiscite* itself still remains without value, for, at the moment when the nation was asked to express the national will, France was placed in such a position that it would have been scarcely possible for any sane man to form any other wish than to assent to the Government's proposals ... Deliberation and discussion are the requisite conditions for rational decision. Where effective opposition is an impossibility, nominal assent is an unmeaning compliment.[37]

Dicey is reflecting in this passage upon the experience of France under the two Napoleons, especially Louis Bonaparte, who developed the use of the plebiscite as an instrument of despotic rule to an art which only totalitarian dictatorships of the twentieth century were to improve upon. Not only was the opposition effectively prevented from organizing (in the first ten years of the Empire only an official slate of candidates for the Assembly was allowed to run), but Louis

Bonaparte, in the manner of modern totalitarian dictatorships, harped upon the 'democratic' and 'popular' nature of his rule, because it had had the sanction of plebiscites in which the entire male population was able to vote.[38]

The social basis of his support was the French peasantry which composed the vast majority of the nation at that time. It was in connection with the support of the French peasants for Bonaparte, that Marx addressed himself to those characteristics of the peasantry as a class, and those conditions under which it lived at the time, which led to their support for Bonaparte's plebiscitarian dictatorship. In a famous passage in the *Eighteenth Brumaire*, Marx observed that:

> The small-holding peasants form a vast mass, the members of which live in similar conditions but without entering into manifold relations with one another. Their mode of production isolates them from one another instead of bringing them into mutual intercourse. The isolation is increased by France's bad means of communication and by the poverty of the peasants. Their field of production, cultivation, no application of science, and therefore, no wealth of social relationships ... Insofar as there is merely a local interconnection among these small-holding peasants, and the identity of their interests begets no community, no national bond and no political organization among them, they do not form a class. They are consequently incapable of enforcing their class interest in their own name, whether through a parliament or a convention. They cannot represent themselves, they must be represented. Their representative must at the same time appear as their master, as an authority over them, as an unlimited governmental power that protects them against the other classes and sends them rain and sunshine from above. The political influence of the small-holding peasants, therefore, finds its final expression in the executive power subordinating society to itself.[39]

For the purpose of analyzing the phenomenon of the demand for direct democracy, particularly to answer the question of whether or not it is plebiscitarian, Marx's analysis is a model of scientific clarity. Our attention is directed toward the specific circumstances which determine the capacity of a class to 'represent themselves'. Their very inability to do so predisposed them toward the 'direct democracy' of Louis Bonaparte, because, although constituting the vast majority of the nation, the ability of other classes to collectively enforce their interests, which ran against those of the peasants, was greater than that of the peasantry – due to the greater social cohesion or more favourable position of these classes in the economic life of the nation. Under other circumstances, such as the improvement of communications, the peasantry's capacity for representing its own interests might be expected to increase, with the result that Bonapartism would hold less interest for it. Here, as in the case of the British working-class movement, whether or not the referendum is undemocratic and an instrument of a plebiscitarian dictatorship, cannot be determined by the form itself, but by the nature of the class for which it functions, and the specific circumstances under which it functions.

It is important at this point to say that in focusing on the social and historical factors which predispose classes or strata and the movements which express their political views to a plebiscitarian conception of politics, I do not wish to suggest that there does not exist, with a powerful attraction independent of these social factors, ideologies or a politics which can be called 'plebiscitarian democracy' - although, as the foregoing makes clear, I regard this as an oxymoron. In this framework, not dissimilar to the syndicalist views for which Michels himself had an affinity, the only truly democratic political system is one in which all intermediate institutions are absent and the 'direct' will of the masses supposedly asserts itself.

One of the best examples of this is to be found in the biography of Napoleon III by Professor Albert Guerard.[40] Guerard admits that: (1) France under Napoleon III was a 'police state';[41] (2) there was an absence of civil liberties; (3) all elections to the Assembly were a fraud,[42] and (4) Louis Bonaparte ruled unchecked by any other organized power. Guerard nevertheless characterizes and defends Bonaparte's rule as being of the essence of real, that is, 'direct democracy':[43]

> Parties are inconceivable without partisanship, which is the deliberate warping of one's thought ... Worst of all, party rule, if logically carried out, is of necessity tyrannical. The party in power attempts to impose its full program upon the defeated ... These are not the excesses of party spirit, but its very essence. The only legitimate field of government action should be the non-partisan.[44]

Thus for Guerard, Napoleon III's abolition of parties, and his personal rule, with the sanction of 'direct democracy' is the only real democracy: '... if we do not believe in direct democracy now it can only be because we do not believe in democracy at all'.[45]

Similar statements are to be found in the writing of Castro supporters:

> In Cuba today you have a form of direct democracy which the United States press refers to as a Hitler type, or Mussolini type, or Soviet type of democracy. Having been in Cuba this is a hard thing to describe, but it is certainly there. One million people show up at some of the rallies ... Fidel read the [Declaration of Havana] ... and said, 'Do you approve?' And one million people screamed 'Yes!' for five minutes.[46]

Examples of this kind of plebiscitarian outlook, which calls for the abolition of political parties, of intermediate associations, of parliaments, or any kind of representative body, and the substitution of the direct rule of the people as 'real' democracy, might be multiplied almost endlessly. Closely related to it, for example, is the idea which George Gallup seriously proposed in 1940: the use of the public opinion poll as the 'fourth stage of democracy', whereby the will of the people could make itself instantly felt. Conservative writers such as Lindsay Rogers somewhat naively criticized Gallup's idea because they feared that it would lead to the actual rule of the people.[47] In fact, of course, as even Gallup's book suggests, it would be a device that a skilful ruling group would neatly use to justify its actions – in the name of 'the people'.

To summarize thus far: I have insisted upon the need to analyze the actual functioning of a proposal for 'direct democracy' and the circumstances for its institution in order to be able to judge whether or not in fact it is a device that increases the control of the members of an organization over its officers, or of a citizenry over its elected leaders. We saw, thus, that in the ITU, when the referendum was joined with a strong, functioning party system, and an active informed membership, it acted as a powerful force for restraining the oligarchic tendencies of the leadership. On the other hand, in those cases in which the conditions for democratic control were missing (and these themselves have to be specified) then the introduction of the referendum or plebiscite becomes a vehicle for a despotic ruler, casting over the cloak of a spurious 'real' democracy. In general, 'plebiscitarianism' may be said to said to characterize a political system in a given society when the population is: (1) atomized or, in terms of 'mass society' theory, is a mass of unrelated individuals, lacking any associations through which their individual interests can be collectively represented; and (2) lacks an independent source of information or communication with which to discuss issues, and yet is required to render its 'opinion' in response to issues in whose formulation it can have no hand.[48]

The important point is that 'plebiscitarian democracy' is in fact not democratic, does not involve the increased participation of the people in decision making, nor does it give them 'direct' control over their representatives. Its essential quality is that it gives the appearance of control and participation through doing away with parties, parliaments, politicians and 'politics' and all other intermediate institutions which supposedly stand in the way of the participation of the 'people' – but its reality is something quite different. In the case of France, as Marx correctly saw, Bonaparte's plebiscitarian dictatorship appealed to a class that had no way of representing its own interests, and therefore had to be satisfied, in the face of the capacity of other classes to pursue their interests, with abdicating its independence to a single individual, who in return for their support 'represented' them. This is the essence of Bonapartism or 'Caesarism'.

In this context, C. Wright Mills, in *The Power Elite*, makes the distinction between a society of 'publics' and a 'mass society': the former is the requisite for a democratic polity; the latter a prescription for the destruction of democracy.[49] His discussion is a useful starting point for any serious consideration of the difficult problem of constructing a democratic society and a democratic polity in the conditions of modern society; it may be read usefully as a counterpoint to the many variations of the argument for direct democracy, including but not limited to the critics of organized political parties – critics who are, at bottom, critics of democracy itself:

> In all modern societies, the autonomous associations standing between the various classes and the state tend to lose their effectiveness as vehicles of reasoned

> opinion and instruments for the rational exertion of political will. Such associations can be deliberately broken up and thus turned into passive instruments of rule, or they can more slowly wither away from the lack of use in the face of centralized means of power. But whether they are destroyed in a week, or wither in a generation, such associations are replaced in virtually every sphere of life by centralized organizations, and it is such organizations with all their new means of power that take charge of the terrorized or – as the case may be – merely intimidated society of masses.[50]

In such a society, voting and forms of pseudo-democratic participation may exist, but the reality is that they serve as a means of legitimating the rule of a minority over the majority. The form is democratic, the substance is not – which is another way of saying that democracy without organization and effective publics is a spurious or plebiscitarian democracy.[51]

Let us turn now to the largely rural American Populists and the movement for direct democracy which grew up in the 1890s, in order to understand why this type of politics and electoral system appealed to them as well as to sections of the urban middle class who supported the political reforms of the progressive movement. If their demand for direct democracy was plebiscitarian, as indeed it was, it was not due to a mystical 'Populist mentality', nor was it a product of the entry of the 'masses' into political life, but the result of their specific circumstances, composition as a class, capacity for organization and their 'cumulative historical experience' with politics.

Direct Legislation: Politics for the Unorganizable

Certainly it is impossible to cover within the limits of this chapter a movement as complex as the 'direct legislation' movement. Although Richard Hofstadter in *The Age of Reform* cogently summarized the main themes and underlying philosophical assumptions and social outlook that gave rise to the direct legislation movement, and the demand for 'direct democracy' in all spheres of political life, there is as yet no history of the movement itself nor any attempt, beyond Hofstadter's many insights, to relate it to the broader developments of American social structure or to the changes which industrial capitalism wrought in American political life. That this should be so, of course, is hardly surprising; the older generation of historians and political scientists came to intellectual maturity under the influence of the Populist and Progressive reform tradition, and its premises were built into their respective disciplines.[52]

All that can be done here, then, is to take the development of the movement as we now know it, and to attempt to ascertain the reasons for its growth, the course of its development and the variables which determined its popularity.

According to Chester McArthur Destler, whose account of the direct legislation movement and its relation to the People's Party is still the main secondary source of information on this matter, the movement for direct legislation grew up outside of the Populist movement proper.[53] It arose in Eastern urban centers where it was supported by a motley coalition of wage earners and middle-class people who were members of Edward Bellamy's 'Nationalist' movement. In New Jersey, two figures were outstanding in the movement. One was Joseph R. Buchanan who had been founder of the only native revolutionary anarchist movement in the United States. By the 1890s he had broken with his former associates and become a leader in the New Jersey labour movement. He later became an important figure in the Gompers administration. The other figure was a wealthy ink manufacturer, Eltweed Pomeroy. Pomeroy was also a leading member of the Nationalist movement. The major agitational work throughout the 1890s was carried on by Pomeroy through the publication of *The Direct Legislation Record* from 1894 to 1903.[54]

It was Buchanan who, at the behest of the New Jersey 'industrial conference', introduced the resolution calling for direct legislation by the people at the Populists' Omaha convention in 1892, and secured its passage. But, as Destler points out, while the People's Party endorsed the resolution, and in time became more fervent in their support for direct legislation as a panacea, the direct legislation movement itself was organized independently of the Populists, and had strong labour backing. Samuel Gompers warmly supported the Direct Legislation League headed by Pomeroy, and even put J.W. Sullivan, another former Bellamyite, on the AFL payroll to tour the country speaking for this reform.[55]

J.W. Sullivan was a left-wing single taxer and Nationalist whose book, *Direct Legislation*,[56] was the first popular exposition of the new ideas, based upon his investigation of the Swiss use of the initiative and referendum. (His book was published by the *True Nationalist*, a New York Nationalist publication.) It was Sullivan's claim, which seems entirely likely, that in the East the movement to establish the initiative and the referendum had great support from organized workers. The League, it may be assumed, had its greatest impact later on, in the 'Progressive period,' although its role in successfully introducing the idea to the People's Party platform was not at all negligible nor unimportant.

A close reading of John D. Hicks' history of the Populist movement provides a great many clues as to the source of all kinds of direct democracy nostrums, including that of direct legislation and the direct primary. The conclusion which emerges from an examination of who among the farmers opted for 'direct democracy', is one which we have had occasion to make earlier in our discussion of the plebiscite. The demand for 'direct democracy', unmediated by a party or organization and distrustful of 'politicians' and all representatives, arose and grew as a tendency in direct proportion to the real and perceived weakness of a particular group of farmers, and out of the specific situation they found themselves in. It is to be noted that their capacity for common political action, or lack of it, was not necessarily a product of their numerical strength. The situation varied from region to region, and from state to state. Thus, in the case of the Farmers Alliance in North and South Carolina where the demand was strongly made for the institution of direct primaries, Hicks' outline of their reasoning is very revealing:

> Not only was it believed that these primaries would eliminate the jockeying, so disadvantageous to the inexperienced farmer, that characterized conventions, but it was also believed that the primaries would insure a greater voting strength to the rural whites. Under the convention system the number of votes assigned to each county was based on the number of its inhabitants and not on the number of its voters. Consequently a given number of voters in the white up country had less political strength in the conventions than a much smaller number of voters in the black counties of the low country, where the city classes and the great planters were in full control.[57]

In short, the poor white farmers were faced with the opposition of a coalition made up of wealthy planters and urban classes whose greater wealth, social cohesion and homogeneity of economic interests, combined with a higher degree of culture and organization skills, not to mention relative ease of communication, gave to the latter a political weight disproportionate to their actual numbers.

Of course, one critical source of this power was the control by the planter/urban merchant/banker oligarchy over the large number of intimidated rural blacks who were counted for purposes of representation but not permitted to play an independent political role. As long as the white farmers, saturated with fear and hatred for the former black slaves, were as concerned to keep them out of power as to resist the oligarchy, they remained politically helpless. When, as C. Vann Woodward and others have shown, the Farmers Alliance and the Populists began to forge a class alliance with the poor black farmers, the ruling elite reacted with its own form of populism based on segregation and the exclusion of blacks from the suffrage together with an even more virulent form of racist ideology.

Given these conditions, the up-country farmers in the Farmers Alliance sought to make up for their political weakness not by reorganizing the Democratic party and changing its structure, nor even yet of organizing their own party – that came later – but rather to use their superior numbers to institute a reform in the mechanism of the system, a reform which they believed (incorrectly) would strip the black-belt planters and the urban oligarchy of their disproportionate political weight. Since in their view the oligarchy's strength stemmed from their ability to control the organizational mechanism, the solution, entirely understandable from the farmers' standpoint was to do away with the convention system which only (they believed) the sophisticated, upper-class elements could dominate. In its place, then, as Hicks points out, they instituted a system of direct primaries which seemed to suit perfectly their atomized, organizationally unskilled character as a class. Michael R. Hyman's more recent study of 'hill country political dissenters' who opposed the political and economic order created by the 'Redeemers', confirms this conclusion.[58] The unsuccessful struggle of the 'anti-Redeemers' with the Democratic party in the 1870s and 1880s led to support for Populism in the 1890s.[59]

A comparison with the Northwestern states supports this analysis. According to Hicks, ever since the Granger times, in the Northwest,

> ... the farmers had been accustomed to the idea of concerted political action; hence in this region it is not surprising to find that from the very beginning of Alliance agitation Alliance leaders had occasionally attempted to deliver the vote of their followers where it would do the most good. Party loyalties were strong, and in theory they were not to be disturbed, but if one party agreed to the Alliance demands and the other did not, or if a candidate was deemed satisfactory and his opponent was not, Alliance men were encouraged to vote for their own interest rather than for their party. It made little difference whether the concessions came from Democrats or from Republicans ...[60]

Hicks does not explain just what sociological or political variables accounted for the Northwestern farmers' greater amenability to the 'idea of concerted political action', in contrast to the Southerners. In the Northwest, the Alliance had gone as far as it could 'towards taking possession of the regular Democratic machinery'. Among other reasons, 'once nominations had been made, the farmers had considered the matter closed, whether the nominees were satisfactory to them or not'.[61] Such discipline and reliance upon their own organizational abilities was clearly not characteristic of the Southerners. Several explanations of this variation would seem to suggest themselves. First, the absence of a relatively tightly organized coalition of urban upper-class and planter-oligarchs, which characterized many states in the South, and the relatively higher cultural and political development of the independent farmers of the Northwest, especially when contrasted to the poor farmers of the South, made it possible to organize them more easily and ensure a degree of party and electoral discipline. At the same time, the clarity with which the Northwestern farmers could identify their class opponents permitted the development of a relatively high degree of class awareness and cohesion. And, of course, the curse of racial division and racism was not a factor, as it was in the South.

In so far as these Northwestern farmers were similar to the farmers of Saskatchewan, an additional reason for their relatively greater ability to organize, may be found in Lipset's study of the latter. In *Agrarian Socialism*, Lipset points out that the Saskatchewan farmers were especially homogeneous in their social composition: nearly all of them grew wheat. Thus they had little reason to enter into internal competition with each other: on the contrary, they had every reason to attempt through collective action to gain their individual interests. They were able to perceive this easily, Lipset shows, and to formulate a relatively clear-cut program because of the ease with which they could see their dependence on the world market, and hence gain a clearer picture of the forces which determined their individual and collective fate.[62] Because of these factors, the Saskatchewan farmers were able to erect many barriers to the corruption of their leaders by alien class forces, particularly the banking and merchant elite in the urban centres. Lipset acutely observes: 'The "city" is the farmer's functional equivalent for bureaucracy.'[63] Presumably because, unlike the Southerners, they were not divided into sharply antagonistic strata, the power of the 'city' could be overcome through organization, rather than by its illusory dissolution as in the case of the politics of direct democracy.

In the case of the Populist party proper, our conclusion about the underlying reasons for the direct democracy demand is fully borne out; Hicks writes:

> Fully aware of the habits of party bosses in manipulating party conventions, the Populists veered more and more in the direction of direct primary elections, urging in some of their later platforms that nominations even for president and vice president should be made by direct vote ... Direct legislation through the initiative and referendum and through the easy amendment of state constitutions naturally appealed strongly to the Populists, – the more so as they saw legislatures fail repeatedly to enact reform laws to which a majority of their members had been definitely pledged. 'A majority of the people,' said the Sioux Falls convention, 'can never be corruptly influenced.' The recall of faithless officials, even judges, also attracts favourable attention from the makers of later Populist reforms.[64]

'Party bosses' could manipulate conventions, conventions even of their own party, as the rigged fusion with the Democratic party in 1896 was to demonstrate. Such sentiments reveal, once again, the low organizational capacity and self-confidence of these rural middle-class elements, and the relationship of the 'direct democracy' panacea to these factors.

In California, this same antagonism to organized political parties existed. Here too, as in the South, it led to the advocacy of the devices of direct control and to the weakening, subsequently, of partisan organization in California in the Progressive era:

> The Populists [in California] who saw their party 'dissolve in a pool of corruption' ... should not have been surprised. They had accepted political power as infinitely corrupting and had staked fundamental political reform on the transference of political power and responsibility to the people. Thus direct legislation was the great key to unlock all of the other treasured reforms.[65]

Rather than a 'Populistic' mentality, we have the reaction of this class to a situation it could not cope with through engaging in organized politics. Only by doing away with conventions and representative bodies, which placed a premium upon the ability to organize, and by concentrating on their ability to turn out numbers, could they hope to gain their ends. Above all, it was because they saw themselves as 'the people', or at least as its dominant element, could they call for the rule of 'the people' over the parasitical minority.[66]

In addition to these objective factors, stemming from the social position of the small farmers, the demand for direct democracy was also the product of long years of experience, as some of the evidence we have already cited demonstrates. Thus, as we have seen, as their own organization became more and more unmanageable, and finally was 'stolen' – at least in the opinion of many Populists – by party bosses of their own choosing, who had come under the corrupt influence of the Democratic party, the dyed-in-the-wool Populists, after recovering from the shock, turned almost wholly to direct legislation as a panacea. Hicks writes: 'Direct legislation by the people became almost an obsession with the Populists, especially the middle-of-the-road faction, in whose platform it tended to overshadow nearly every other issue ....'[67]

For the farmer supporters of the Populists, Michels' iron law of oligarchy may be said to have been an immutable fact of political life. Mary Elizabeth Lease, a leading Populist orator and organizer, put the Populist political mentality on display in 1896, in an article in the Populist-Bellamyite newspaper, *The Coming Nation*, entitled 'The Next Step':

> The forces of progress are over-mastered in the democratic and republican parties of today. The Populist party, where it has succeeded in obtaining supremacy, has become as corrupt and servile to corporate power as its predecessors. The remedy lies not in a change of party, for history that a new party to become a dominant political factor must enroll in its membership the corrupt and sloughed-off matter of old organizations.[68]

The 'next step' was clear: direct legislation by the people, the whole people, the unorganized people, who could not be bought as could a party or its leaders. The Progressive movement was to build its campaign for direct democracy on the kind of hostility to political parties, even democratic, membership-based ones, expressed in Lease's article. Not able to keep their own party, the Populists turned on all forms of party organization in search of what proved to be an illusion. Direct democracy inevitably became the vehicle for new, and old, elites whose exercise of power was all the greater because of the legitimacy of its seemingly 'democratic' origins.

This same cumulative political experience, particularly in connection with attempts to reform the urban machines, explains a great deal also about the appeal of the Progressive movement's demand for direct democracy to urban middle-class elements. In his brilliant analysis of the American party system, as it had developed in the latter part of the nineteenth century, M. Ostrogorski recorded the endless disappointments which reformers from the 'educated' middle classes had undergone as a result of their attempts to break the 'machine', the 'boss', and the 'ring'. Every organization they created was captured by their enemies and turned against them. Only by opposing the creation of a mass, democratic organization or party, were the reformers able to escape this fate.[69] The middle classes' incapacity for collective action, and their well-founded fear of being dominated by a new 'boss', led Ostrogorski, who shared their outlook, to propose a system of 'temporary' parties, each organized along authoritarian lines, and of such a limited nature, with each person having such a multiplicity of memberships, that no permanent interest could grow up to oppress society.[70]

Thus these devices for direct democracy were intended to return to individuals the powers which were stolen from them by organized political parties which were by definition 'conspiracies'. The form of their opposition to the political oppression of the 'bosses' and the 'machines' – and it is well to remember that they were indeed oppressive, although some of the critics of populism and progressivism tend to romanticize or exaggerate their benevolence – was the breaking down of the organization which sustained the boss, and prevented 'the people' who, they believed, were the majority, from exercising their will. Their paralysis before the 'oligarchical tendencies in modern political parties' led them to abandon organized politics altogether, and even to dream of abandoning politics in favour of so-called 'non-partisan' elections and the creation of a civil service elite to administer government.

Conclusion

It may be seen from the above, how by approaching the problem of Populist politics in historically and sociologically specific terms, the myth of some mystical 'populist mentality' disappears. What we have instead is a particular class or stratum whose circumstances are such that organized political activity appears to be and is difficult or even impossible.

At the extreme, all organization turns into a Frankenstein monster. Thus we find that when such difficulties did not arise, as in the case of the Saskatchewan wheat farmers, there was little or none of the hostility to organized politics and one can trace, as Lipset does, the rise of the Cooperative Commonwealth Federation, an extremely effective farmer-based socialist party, to these factors and this experience with politics.

This variation, this specification, which is entirely ignored by those bent on discrediting the Populists and through them democracy and popular movements, may be traced back in the first place to the difference in social and economic circumstances which the different groups of farmers found themselves. But no less important, and far more subtle and hence unsuitable for those whose purposes are mainly ideological, is the variation introduced by the effect of cumulative political experience: success in organization, the garnering of the skills which are normally believed to be the monopoly of others – the more cultured, the wealthy, etc. – has the effect of undermining or weakening the kind of 'plebiscitarian' attitudes which certain of the Populists did in fact express. Thus it is, as we have shown, the great surge or resurgence of 'direct democracy' sentiment of the kind expressed by Mrs Lease, came only *after* they had experienced failure with organized politics – after the 'theft' of their own party. That such plebiscitarian sentiments did come to the fore, then, is not evidence of some innate, unchangeable mentality on the part of the farmers, nor is it evidence that all democratic popular movements are necessarily plebiscitarian in character. Not unless, of course, plebiscitarianism is wrongly confused with democracy itself – democracy conceived, as it should be, as entailing the direct control and participation by the people themselves over their own lives, rather than the more passive exercise of a check by the governed over their governors.

It is this latter definition, of course, the definition of 'elite democracy' set forth by the most vociferous critics of 'populism' which is the very essence of plebiscitarianism, correctly understood.

CHAPTER 3

Attacking Democracy: State Funding of Political Parties

> We established for the first time in the history of this nation a political police force. You know, everywhere you and I are in society, there are police people watching us to keep us in the frame of what is considered by our society to be the proper framework. We have city police officers, we have sheriffs, we have the security guards in the department stores. We have all way through our society and everywhere you and I are concerned these police people to watch our movements: that is, everywhere except in Washington and Sacramento and other capitals across the nation ... I have heard that it will force good people out of politics. I think the good people will come to the surface even more than is in the present political machinery now and more and better people will want to get involved.
>
> Ed Koupal, Executive Director, California People's Lobby, author of the California Fair Political Practices Act of 1974[1]

Friedrich Burckhardt warned that the twentieth century would be the age of 'the great simplifiers' offering popular panaceas to solve complex problems, whose cost would be the establishment of tyrannies greater than those ever seen before. Mr Koupal was a particularly crude character, cut from the same cloth as many other California demagogues and, in this respect, not at all like his genteel partners, the American political reform organization, Common Cause. Still, he had the gift, or the naivete, of stating simply the underlying spirit of the post-Watergate reforms, which brought the federal financing of presidential elections, set limits on campaign contributions by individuals and groups, established the Federal Election Commission, as well as the passage of 'political ethics' laws purporting to control lobbying in many individual states.

The Federal Election Commission, which was set up in the same year as the California law was passed by an initiative vote, to supervise the Federal Election Reform Act, introduced a new element into the American political system: the administrative regulation of political activity. Ostensibly its purpose was to oversee the contribution and spending of money in federal elections, but because all political activity depends on money, the FEC became, in effect, the political policeman of which Ed Koupal dreamed. An ineffectual one, perhaps, because it is restrained in its actions by Congress and the American judicial system, but a policeman all the same. And one, like police forces everywhere, not independent of the controlling forces in society nor a non-political body. The very act of elaborating regulations is a political act and so is the exercise of administrative discretion – to pursue or to enforce or to prosecute those whom it deems offenders. And, of course, as in the case of all regulatory agencies, as a generation of political scientists has demonstrated, there is an ineluctable tendency for such agencies to become the tools, or at very least the accomplices, of the more powerful of those who they are mandated to regulate.

In an interview some years ago with the Washington lobbyist for Common Cause, I called her attention to testimony in the Irangate affair that some of Colonel Oliver North's money had been siphoned off into the campaign in Maryland of a candidate for the US Senate. When I suggested that this seemed to be a matter which would concern the FEC, she just shrugged her shoulders and told me that the regulatory body which Common Cause had created would never investigate anything so politically sensitive. Common Cause, she admitted, had given up on the Federal Election Commission.

Many years before, in 1976, I had pointed out to the then head of Common Cause, David Cohen, the likelihood that the regulatory body which their legislation had just set up would, in the way of all such regulatory commissions, become the instrument of those of the regulated who exercised power. His reaction was one of surprise at the very idea – not outraged or argumentative, but genuinely surprised. It had simply never occurred to him. In the rhetoric and, I am afraid, the minds, of the reformers, the administrative agencies set up as the Platonic Guardians of the political process would be above politics and ideology, while the administrative process in which the law was actually made and enforced was seen – incredible though it may seem – as merely a matter of applying the law as written. But for the commissioners of one such agency created by Common Cause, the California Fair Political Practices Commission, there were no such illusions. 'I think', said one of them in the second year after its creation,

> that the staff and other members of the Commission have to realise that as the political complecture [sic] of the state may change, the membership on the Commission will change, and the ideology of the Commission will change, since we are appointed by the major statewide elected officials ... If the statewide partisan balance should change ... I'm sure that the ideology of the Commission will change also.[2]

The simple-minded reform tradition is strongest in the United States, because the politics of this great country is, to be polite, so underdeveloped. Mechanical solutions to complex political problems and an inability to ask questions about their root causes flourish in a nation which lacks an opposition political party and a sophisticated political culture and one whose existing parties are centered around the candidates and the politics of personality as conveyed in the electronic media.

When asked how a man of high moral character and courage like the former oppositionist and now President of Czechoslovakia, Vaclav Havel, would fare in the American system, one American congressman could only comment, bitterly, that it would depend on how much money and what consultant he had and, whether, 'he would be willing to shave his mustache'.[3] Senators and congressmen could only stand in awe before the wisdom and vision of a man so recently in prison – an awe (mixed with not a little shame, I suspect) which was deserved, of course, but his words and presence were felt to be a devastating commentary on the political culture of which they are a part.

To the undoubtedly all-pervasive and ever-growing role of money in American politics the answer seems quite obvious to the great simplifiers of reform: control money and substitute state financing of candidates for private money. This is, I would submit, another of those panaceas which have afflicted American politics and is itself, however good and honourable the intentions, and however descriptively correct the view of the destructive and corrupting role of money, a reflection of the very debased political culture it seeks to revive in the name of democracy. Like other reforms which fail to go to the root causes, it would compound the problems it seeks to correct, make the role of money (even if not in the form of campaign contributions – as if this were the only form that unequal wealth takes!) more important than ever, and undermine the democratic institutions and values which at least some of its advocates genuinely favour.

Still, the role of money in the politics of capitalist parliamentary democracies is not a peculiarly American problem, nor is the solution of state financing of candidates or parties an uncommon one in the electoral systems of the parliamentary democracies. Common solutions in countries whose political cultures are so diverse, even though we correctly group them under the label of 'parliamentary democracies', suggest that we are dealing with a powerful institutional trend which is independent of the political culture or dominant ideologies of individual nations.

This trend, to put it in a nutshell, involves the breaching of the barrier between political parties and the state and raises profound questions about the future of democracy in modern society. If the classic liberal model of the political party as a private, voluntary association independent of the state is undermined by state funding, as it clearly is, then we have moved toward an illiberal and undemocratic political order in which society – or civil society – is permeated by the state, and the state becomes the master and not the servant of society.[4]

This autonomous role of the state – or the 'government' as Americans, who have a strong democratic tradition which obscures the distinction between state and government, like to say – is the subject of an important contribution by one of the most perceptive students of political finance, Herbert Alexander.[5] In focusing on the state and questioning what has far too frequently been ignored or taken for granted in the vast literature dealing with state funding of politics, Alexander has drawn our attention back to the larger philosophical issues which are my concern in this chapter and to the fact that the discussion of these questions cannot be free of political values, however we may rightly strive for scientific objectivity in our study of the way in which particular electoral systems or systems of political finance impact on political institutions and behavior. These are not technical matters. Any serious consideration of these questions requires a discussion of very profound issues about the fate of democracy in the world of the twenty-first century.

Looking at the Record

In this chapter, therefore, I wish to focus on these issues of value and democratic theory rather than the questions of mechanics, which are, in my view, important, but derivative. In any case, as I think is amply borne out in the evidence presented in the latest compilation considering the issue of comparative political finance, any idea that state funding is a cure for corruption is manifestly absurd, while the other main argument for adopting such a system, that it improves the quality of political life and strengthens democracy, is equally unsupported by any evidence.[6]

Limitations on financial contributions or expenditures are also largely a futile task, although it is possible to pass laws and even to enforce them to a degree, affecting the right of corporations or unions to make contributions, but it will not affect, if there is a need for it, the uses of large amounts of money, legal or illegal, in politics without far more fundamental changes in the political culture and basic economic institutions of society. Unenforceable laws lead to evasion and contempt for the law. Thus, the political scandals which 'appeared to threaten the liberty' of several hundred and perhaps several thousand French politicians, who extorted illegal kickbacks for their parties, was resolved by a presidential amnesty in June 1989. Enforcement would have required 'mass jailing of guilty politicians' – one estimate went as high as 5,000 or even 10,000 politicians from all sides of the political spectrum.[7]

The fact that the passing of laws does not necessarily result in their observance may come as a surprise to political reformers and even to some academic specialists, but even more important than this is the fact that they are, like most laws, enforceable only on a selective basis. In the realm of the regulation of politics, this can mean the use of political criteria: there is a very fine line between this and outright political persecution of minority or unpopular views.

Moreover, in the case of political money, the definition of what is 'political' or a contribution to a party or a candidate is not obvious. No zealous reformer – not yet, at any rate – proposes to stop newspapers from discussing public matters in a partisan fashion, but these are as much a political intervention involving the command of large amounts of money as any direct contribution or expenditure. In Britain, the popular newspapers of Mr Murdoch, which reach twelve million readers every day, are little more than Tory propaganda leaflets. In neither case does anyone yet propose to control them or count them as a financial contribution to, or expenditure on behalf of, the Tory party, which they are. The Tory government runs huge advertising campaigns for the privatization of public enterprises which are, at the same time, advertising campaigns for the government. Institutional ads for the virtues of the enterprise economy inundated the media during the 1987 election; not a word about politics but still they were highly important in setting the tone of the campaign at the subliminal level.

Crucial civil liberties questions are raised by state funding and the control of contributions and expenditures. Although the US reformers and their academic friends may curse the Supreme Court for its decision in *Buckley v. Valeo*, which recognized the free-speech issue in allowing independent expenditures, the decision was undoubtedly an important victory for free speech and, no matter what the reformers and their sympathizers may think, for good democratic politics as well. The same issue was raised in Canada and it is interesting to note the way in which the Buckley decision was attacked on anti-civil libertarian grounds in the testimony of a number of academic specialists, thereby demonstrating conclusively that these questions are basically political ones involving important philosophical issues rather than mere technical issues.[8]

The American Case

Certainly the case of the United States is not one to give comfort to the advocates of 'public funding' (to use the euphemism for the state which advocates have adopted) or of limitations on contributions. The reformers may have persuaded themselves, but they have not persuaded the American public whose 'confidence' in government was supposed to be restored by the Watergate reforms governing the use of money in elections and establishing the use of state money for presidential elections. In 1964, a poll conducted by the University of Michigan showed that 64 per cent of voters believed that government is 'run for the benefit of all', and only 29 per cent thought that it is 'pretty much run by a few big interests looking out for themselves'. In 1988, according to the *Wall Street Journal*, '24 years and innumerable Washington scandals later, the same survey group found the proportion reversed: 63% believed that America is run by a government of the few and for the few, while 31% thought it is run for the greater good'.[9]

It may accurately be said that in this matter the majority of American people are showing good sense and an appreciation of the true state of US politics, although the cynicism and civic malaise which it reveals is potentially dangerous. No less an expert on political cynicism than Mr Lee Atwater, campaign advisor of the Republican Party, has said that

> the public's attitude toward politics is very much in concert with their attitude about all institutions ... the American people are cynical and turned off about all the institutions and politics is one ... Bull permeates everything. In other words, my theory is that the American people think politics and politicians

> are full of baloney. The think the media and journalists are full of baloney. They think organized religion is full of baloney. They think big business is full of baloney. They think big labor is full of baloney. To single out politics is making a big mistake in terms of understanding the attitude of Americans.[10]

Coming from someone so immersed in this subject, as the infamous Willie Horton campaign demonstrates, it is a damning indictment of American politics and society today, whose accuracy cannot be doubted. This all-pervasive cynicism, particularly as it touches politics and politicians, is an important factor – some think it is the main cause – explaining why a smaller and smaller proportion of Americans bother to vote in presidential, state and local elections.[11]

Given the dimensions and depth of the crisis, even if one limits it only to the political realm, it is ludicrous if not bizarre to think that the solution which every editorial writer and many of those genuinely concerned for the health of American democracy seems to pull out of their hat is legislation to control or abolish the use of private money in election campaigns and politics. More of the same medicine of state money and control over the contributions of political action committees (PACs) which the Common Cause reformers succeeded in instituting after Watergate will not cure what is a political and, one must add, moral problem, which is exacerbated by the absence of a civic culture in which politics is not a synonym for corruption and self-seeking. The role of money in American politics is the symptom of a deeper malaise, as Mr Atwater's statement reveals.

The source of this obvious decay in American political institutions is to be found in the strong anti-party political culture and in the lack of an opposition political party on the left with genuine oppositional politics. The creation of the latter, however improbable it may seem to some, would act to erode the powerful anti-partyism which is the legacy of progressivism. Only in this way is it possible to restore the health of civil society in America. Not a 'third party' but a second party, given the similarity of the Republicans and Democrats. It is interesting that this hitherto unrespectable view of the essential identity of the two parties, although not the solution proposed here, is shared by Felix Rohatyn, the wealthy Democratic financier, who has said that the Democratic Party echoes the Republican's 'conservative if not reactionary' stands on a wide range of critical issues: 'What does the Democratic Party stand for as an alternative to this program? It is exceedingly hard to tell, because the Democrats are not an opposition political party. The Democrats share power, they do not seek it.' In Congress, 'they are part of an existing power structure, almost a coalition government with a Republican administration'.[12] Powerful words, and given Rohatyn's respectability, they are perhaps destined to become a respectable opinion and thus to penetrate the mainstream of American political science where such obvious truths have been long derided as radical poppycock. Or, although it is even less likely, perhaps Rohatyn's words may penetrate the heads of the political reformers who have systematically ignored or explained the similarity of the political views of the two parties away on the grounds that the sinister interests of big money have bribed and bought the politicians of both parties or that competition is absent in campaigns because of huge election expenditures.

If the situation is as I have described it, then it is best to understand the large amounts of money spent in American campaigns as a result rather than a cause of the condition of American politics. A candidate-centered politics; an absence of membership political parties and an undemocratic plebiscitarian electoral system of 'direct primaries' invented by Progressive reformers in place of membership parties; the absence of a democratic party of the left which can challenge the prevailing political ethos, in which politics is a business just like any other: these are, among others, the causes for the large amounts of money which inundate the American political process. Proposals for reform, which would extend state funding to other federal offices, in order to increase 'competition', will not improve anything, and will undoubtedly, if effective, create new problems, including the weakening of the legislative branch. 'Competition' between individual candidates running in the existing parties is beside the point: it is something like the competition between different brands of toothpaste and testifies to the Common Cause-type reformers' addiction to the status quo of a plebiscitarian electoral system rather than grass-roots democracy through organized parties and political movements with alternative political programmes.[13]

Democratic politics in the US or anywhere else require membership parties, which are not, as most Americans have been taught to believe, a 'European' invention, but a fundamental necessity of democracy. In this respect, as James MacGregor Burns has shrewdly observed, Americans may have much to learn from the example of Eastern Europe where the crucial role of the political party is being rediscovered.[14] Legal barriers to political contributions or controls over expenditures – police tactics, as it were – and public financing of campaigns can only compound the problems of democracy in these circumstances and everything that has happened since Watergate has proven this to the hilt. The 'Irangate' episode, for example, demonstrates that there are even deeper sources of the corruption of American democratic institutions – sources found in the security state created by the Cold War – which reforms of the order of campaign spending legislation cannot touch. Who is to say that the use of public money by the Executive branch to subvert the will of the elected Congress and to win, secretly, public support for its policy in Central America, is not connected indirectly to the breaking down of the autonomy of the political process through state funding? In an earlier, more democratic America, both would have been unthinkable.

Fundamental problems require fundamental changes. The reformers – and surely this ought to be no surprise, since the function of 'reform' is to head off more fundamental and radical changes – have prepared the ground for increased public cynicism about politics through their systematic miseducation of the public about the causes of the catastrophic state of American politics and democracy. There is a long and well-grounded tradition of contempt in American political thought for 'goo-goos' which the role of modern-day reformers has proven is well-deserved.

The situation of the American parties has been for most of this century one of legal regulation by the state.[15] It is not possible to go into this most important aspect of the American political party system in any detail here, but it is significant that one of the most astute students of political parties, Leon Epstein, can, partly as a matter of analysis and partly as a matter of advocacy, speak of American political parties as 'public utilities' and oppose the right of freedom of association as an instance of 'privatization'.[16] This is, in my view, as clear, if unthinking, a repudiation of democratic values as anything to be found in the thought of anti-democratic theorists, although it has deep roots, it must be said, in the anti-party (and equally anti-democratic) history of American liberalism.

Fortunately, there is a challenge to this view embodied in a number of legal cases before the American courts, based on the claim of freedom of association. It may well be that a conservative, Reagan-appointed, Supreme Court will restore the political parties to their proper position as private associations independent of state regulation, free to choose their candidates as they wish and free, too, to be controlled by their members rather than by the members of the various state legislatures. This challenge to deregulate the parties can be seen as an alternative to the anti-party, anti-democratic political police approach of the Common Cause-style reformers.[17]

Funding Politics in Britain

If we take the case of Britain at the beginning of the 1980s, where there was a meteoric rise of a multi-party challenge to the two-party system and an equally meteoric decline of one of the newest ones, David Owen's Social Democratic Party (SDP), there is not the slightest evidence, and no one I know bothers to argue it, that money had anything to do with the demise of the Social Democrats. What occurred was a political default combined with an electoral system which denied fair or proportional representation to the new party. The SDP lost its members and electoral support. As a result it found itself in a financial crisis and vanished from British politics.

Had a system of state aid been in place before the founding of the SDP, as the Houghton Committee advocated in the mid-1970s, it might well have led to a situation where, despite its catastrophic political leadership, the SDP would have continued on with the support of public money but not of any substantial membership, a kind of life-after-death situation freezing the political situation in a new unpopular mould. The recent emergence in Britain of the Green Party and its possible replacement of the SDP as a new third force in British politics, which may, indeed, break the mould, is, in my view, confirmation of this argument. How would this have occurred if state funding had embalmed the center parties in British politics? The members and voters voted with their feet and with their money. This is elementary democracy and why, although money talks, as the Americans say, it is important to remember that private, voluntary money sometimes talks in support of democracy.

If anything, it is more convincing to argue that British democracy is far healthier without state funding than it would have been with it. Certainly the other democratic aspects of the British electoral system, such as the ease with which new parties can run candidates (in contrast to the US) together with the highly developed democratic political culture which characterizes the British political system, were crucial to the emergence of the SDP and the potential which it had for 'breaking the mould' of British politics. And it is certainly true that had state funding existed, allowing it to be, as the SDP's founder David Owen earnestly wished, an American-style party controlled by the politicians rather than the members, then state funding would have guaranteed that Owen would have been able to dispense with the members or, at very least, relegate them, as he proposed to do, to the role of doorbell ringers and envelope stuffers.

The British system, for all its many faults, has proven to be remarkably flexible and open, allowing parties to rise and, as the result of their own efforts, to fall as well. Surely, not all of the money of the trade unions would have saved the Labour Party from extinction had it not been for the political incompetence and personal ambitions of the leadership of the center parties and the widespread antipathy to the leader of the Tory Party, combined with unpopular policies such as the poll tax. And, conversely, not all of the unequal money and access to resources, including newspapers reaching millions of readers, will necessarily insure the survival of the present Tory government.

This point is reinforced if one notes that one of the key arguments of the proponents of the Houghton report on financial aid to the parties (a point taken up by its minority members) was that it would allow Parliament to set the rules for the internal procedures of the parties. This would have ruled out, of course, the remarkable upsurge which resulted in the internal democratization of the Labour Party (a mixed result, to be sure), and opened the way for a government, such as the present one, which dominates Parliament so thoroughly and which has demonstrated its authoritarian and anti-democratic proclivities, to pass legislation governing the internal life of the opposition political parties. From not being 'recognized in law', as at present (although this was to some extent breached by the use of the party labels on the ballots), to being licensed by the state, is not a very long step for a government which dissolves democratically elected local governments it cannot control.

Note that the same issue was faced by the British trade unions when they were offered state money to conduct ballots; their fear that the taking of state money would breach the barrier between the state and the unions and lead to a loss of their autonomy is not an unfounded one. Certainly a government which can by executive fiat outlaw union membership with the excuse of 'security' would not hesitate to use the excuse of a state element in trade union funding to argue that there is a state interest in other aspects of trade union organization, as indeed it already has. And, if not this government, then perhaps the next one, perhaps even a Labour government.[18]

It only remains to be noted that the present leadership of the Labour Party calls for state funding in order to free itself of the trade unions and to reduce the role of the membership in the affairs of the party. This would hardly be a victory for democracy, in my view, desirable as it would be, from a democratic standpoint, to change the role of the bloc vote in the Conference. But the two issues are not necessarily connected and the result of state funding would be the political weakening of the unions, which are a powerful force for democracy in Britain, and the 'modernization' of the party into an undemocratic American (or Spanish) -type party, which is undoubtedly what the leadership is aiming for.

I have touched upon the US and Britain here to illustrate the point that campaign contribution limits and the infusion of state money into the parties and campaigns of parliamentary democratic systems, provide no evidence of the beneficial effects which its proponents have claimed for it. British democracy is, with all the flaws which the major new reform movement, Charter 88, has shown, much healthier without state funding than with it. It is significant that Charter 88's proposals for democratization of the electoral system are confined to proportional representation: state aid to the parties was seen, at least by many of those who formulated its demands, to run counter to the democratic and pluralistic politics required to restore civil society to its proper place in the face of an enlarging authoritarian state. This is a point of view and a temper which, although representing a wide part of the British political spectrum, from liberal to libertarian left, would, of course, be utterly incomprehensible to the advocates of public financing in the US. In any case, with a well-working party system, state aid to the parties has simply dropped off the political agenda and finds few advocates today although it remains on the Labour Party's agenda.

Thus, if the comparison between the US and Britain is a convincing one, we can hardly say, as the advocates of state political finance do, that not all of the evidence is in, unless our purpose is to provide continuing employment for political scientists or we are intent on ignoring all evidence. If the latter, as I think is the case of the the US reformers, then we would do well to recall Santayana's definition of a fanatic as one who advocates a course of action against all evidence that it can achieve the goal set for it. If the jury were to be called in today, the verdict would certainly be one of failure – and worse, as I shall argue.

International Comparisons

Consider a few more examples: Italian politics is awash with money and corruption and the interpenetration of the party machines with the state is well known. Public financing is just one more source of money and no one can seriously say that democracy is healthier because of state funding.[19]

Spain's party system has been established from the top down (with, in the case of the Socialist Party, generous dollops of money from the German SPD) and has been able to avoid, because of the availability of state funding, a grass-roots membership or ties to mass organizations such as trade unions which can exercise effective control over the party leadership. The Spanish Socialist Party, with its large proportion of state employees, is a particularly extreme case of party–state interpenetration. Germany has not been immune to financial scandals and the generous amounts of state money available have undermined internal party democracy in the SPD and assured that parties without significant membership, such as the Free Democrats, could play a disproportionately important role in German politics. Only the emergence of the Greens, who introduced a fresh, democratic element into the Federal Republic's politics, might be cited in support of the system of state finance, but there is no evidence that without it the Greens would have been unable to survive and play a signficant role. And, last but not least, Japan's system of public financing did not prevent the festering corruption which resulted in the scandals of 1989 that engulfed the LDP. Moreover, the system of restrictions on political activity by the Ministry of Home Affairs, which, as Professor Rei Shiratori notes, 'controls the police system also' has resulted in a 'great sacrifice of the freedom of election campaigning'.[20]

The only possible exceptions are Sweden and Holland. In the latter, as Ruud Koole has shown, a very strong democratic political culture rooted in the peculiar history of Dutch society has minimized the role of money in politics. The strength of Swedish democratic culture is, I think, a factor in the way in which state funding has worked, but whether the all-pervasive role of the state is a guarantor of democracy or a cover for a powerful economic and political establishment must be left to another discussion. Certainly there is a feeling that state funding has, in the case of the Social Democratic party, made the party more bureaucratic and centralized and less dependent on its members than it ought to be from a democratic standpoint. In the case of its main conservative opposition, its leader told me in the early 1980s that state funds meant that the membership is a bit of an unnecessary bother for the leaders. The democratic ethos of Swedish society and the need for campaign workers stands in the way, presumably, of jettisoning the troublesome membership altogether.[21]

Toward a Democratic Politics

If the claims of the advocates of state funding of politics and legal controls on contributions and expenditures cannot be sustained, it is also true that these measures have important if not entirely intended consequences for the health of democracy in so far as they break down the wall between the state and political institutions and rights which ought to be independent of and superior to the state and not the reverse.

To deal intelligently with these issues we must have a vision of what a democratic political order ought to be in a world increasingly dominated by large bureaucratic institutions and a powerful state which dwarfs the individual.

We also must not divorce, as is so often done, the political order from the economic and social order. The point of view which underlies the discussion in this essay is one of a profound belief in the value of democracy and of the necessity of economic and social equality as a condition of political democracy.

Mechanical fixes for ailing democracy which ignore the economic and social dimension, particularly great inequalities of wealth and power, lead everywhere except where their designers intend, usually reinforcing or even worsening the problems they are designed to cure. And the same must be said for tinkering which ignores the political dimension: a corrupt political order in which the parties and politicians are literally for sale to the highest bidder cannot be cured by an injection of state money or even by the total banning of private funding, and certainly not by a political police in the form of a supervisory administrative agency. The cure is worse than the disease or, more accurately, becomes part of the disease.

Nor can that ephemeral but all-important quality of a democratic political culture which encourages civic morality and responsibility be ignored, but this too is rooted in social and economic realities. A society whose highest value is each for himself and whose standards are set by the marketplace is no more a fertile field for high civic and personal morality than bureaucratic totalitarian societies which proclaim their devotion to collective good in order to mask the tyranny of a new class who hold the reins of political and economic power.

The importance of these concerns to the study of money and politics and electoral systems has been underlined by the experience of Eastern Europe, the Soviet Union and China as the forces of democratization have gathered force in recent years. By looking at the problem of establishing a democratic political order in societies where the state has absorbed society, one can see with greater clarity the problem of the relationship between political parties and, indeed, all forms of associational activity, and the state. Democratic pluralism requires that groups, including parties, be autonomous of the state. In Eastern Europe and the student and worker movement in China, the idea and ideal of democracy has once again come into its own: only old Cold Warriors and cynics could fail to be moved by the students and workers in Tiananmen Square as they demanded democracy from the rulers who gave them the only answer they could give if they were to preserve their power.

Civil Society and Parties in Eastern Europe

The political earthquake which shook all of Eastern Europe and the Soviet Union and redrew the map of Europe during 1989 is not yet over, even if a period of settling down has occurred in some countries where elections have been or are about to be held at the time this is being written.

In Eastern Europe and the Soviet Union, the key to the final demolition of the system was, and still is, the full re-emergence of civil society from the crushing weight of the state which had outlawed all forms of autonomous activity. In the collapsed social order, after a long, still unresolved, struggle to emerge, may be seen the appearance of the central and most important institution of any democratic political order: a multi-party system. Not only political parties, and certainly not political parties as narrow electoral groups or merely factions of parliamentarians, but also a proliferation of groups, broad and narrow, voluntary associations and 'clubs', and 'civic forums' which call for the restoration of 'citizenship', are needed to deal with the host of questions confronting modern society on the edge of the twenty-first century. The most important of these are the trade unions, legally and financially autonomous of the state, and the 'new social movements' such as the environmental and women's movements – all of which impact upon and intertwine with the political parties, and in the case of the environmental movement even emerge as significant political parties in their own right.[22]

All of these, and more, go to make up 'civil society'. The fundamental requirement is their *autonomy* from the state and, conversely, the subjection of the state to democratic control. Surely the future of democracy in the next century depends upon whether there can be meaningful participation, as opposed to passive plebiscitarian-style 'democracy', in and through a plurality of groups and parties in the modern state. These states' own boundaries, it must be said, are themselves being eroded by the forces of the global economy, leading to the emergence of transnational corporations and parties and movements, the democratic control of which pose the most profound and difficult questions of all to those who value democracy.

Consider now the moral and intellectual position in which Eastern European democrats are placed by the proposition, which has indeed already arisen in Poland and Hungary, that the state ought to fund the new political parties or that there needs to be a law giving legal status to political parties. It is not only that the state long funded one political party, or that in the case of the Soviet Union, not to mention, as of this writing, Albania, Romania, and to some extent Poland, the state remains in the hands of the Communist Party or its heirs, which continues to monopolize the means of violence (which rules out in itself the acceptance of such a proposition for any democrat long used to the domination of the state over society). It is that the very idea of creating parties which are financially dependent on the state, any state, is contrary to the conception of 'civil society' which has been the guiding concept of Eastern European democrats. The idea of state control over politics – the 'regulation of politics' about which American reformers so naively chirp – is precisely what they have only so recently overthrown.

Consider too the ambiguity, from the standpoint of a truly democratic constitution, of the legalization of political parties: a kind of licensing by the state of this central political function. Licensing or legal recognition of the parties by the state, an important element in most systems of state political financing, is diametrically opposed to the idea of freedom of association. Freedom to form a political party or engage in political activity by permission or by state license is not freedom at all. The idea of the political party as a 'public utility' is, in both the American context as in the East European, to see political parties as extensions of the state.

Let us return for a moment to the idea of funding political parties in the parliamentary democracies: there is no reason, either in logic or in the underlying philosophy of the proponents of state funding, why a line ought to be drawn between funding parties and funding any other voluntary association with broad (or narrow) political or social ends: trade unions, environmental organizations, women's groups, peace organizations, in other words, the new social movements. Why not give them state aid as well, for certainly they play an important part in the political process? Such proposals have been made from time to time in the United States, and in Sweden the state does subsidize such organizations, including newspapers, in addition to the parties, contributing, depending on your point of view, to the strengthening of democracy or to its ossification.

If state funding and accompanying regulation of political parties and electoral activity is acceptable, why not legal control over other forms of organized political activity which are known as 'lobbying'? Or of newspapers, to solve the well-known problem of monopoly control of the print, not to mention the electronic, media? Here too, the logic has been played out by reformers, at least in the US where the single- and simple-mindedness of reformers is unmatchable. The repeated attempts of Common Cause to pass 'lobbying reform' legislation which would have, at least in its first versions, required virtually anyone who engaged in associated political activity to register, and have given the Federal Election Commission (the same one which Common Cause now finds a tool of the existing government) supervisory powers over them, underlines the manner in which ordinary democratic rights – especially First Amendment rights – give way to the zeal of the reformers to stop 'corruption' whose true causes they can hardly imagine.[23] As the US Attorney General argued before the Supreme Court in one of the early tests of Watergate legislation, a defense in which they were joined by Common Cause, 'any adverse impact on individual rights is overridden by governmental needs'. Political action is regulated by an agency of the state: the agency is the 'political policeman' advocated by the California political reformers. In Japan, state financing and the excuse that there is a need to control campaign costs have been used to legally prohibit (or inhibit) a wide range of political activity.[24]

Now, return again to Eastern Europe whose experience has led those of their leaders who are genuine democrats rather than just exponents of the free market, to reject these statist ideas and to reassert, indeed to insist upon, the crucial importance of the boundary between the state and civil society and the subordination of the state to society through democracy. If democrats in Eastern Europe were to be presented, as they may be, with the proposition that democracy depends upon the state funding of political parties or of trade unions and newspapers, they will face a crisis of political philosophy with momentous practical implications for democratic institutions in their respective countries. The upheaval which we have witnessed originated in the idea that the restoration of individual freedom and democracy had required the re-establishment of the wall between the state and society and the subordination of the state to society. The idea of state funding of parties and the legal recognition of parties which accompanies it would breach that wall and once again make independent associational activity potentially subject to state control.

The point is made crystal-clear when we consider the position of the trade unions in the Soviet-type societies. Progress toward democracy requires either their replacement by new, independent unions financed by their members (with assistance from the international movement) or, at very least, cutting the existing unions off from state funding and making them dependent upon their members' dues, together with a change in the leadership. Only such unions, free of state funding, can be said to be democratic. It is hard to see how the same point does not apply to political parties.

Lack of money is a problem, to be sure, for the new parties struggling to be born, but the method of financing must not undermine the need to create a genuinely democratic political party culture – and this includes money from abroad.[25] The top-down nature of the Spanish Socialist Party, with its lack of internal democracy and heavy reliance on a membership which holds political appointments should be a warning about the consequences of foreign assistance and state funding in the transition from totalitarian or authoritarian regimes.[26] In the case of the 1990 East German elections, one cannot, strictly speaking, describe the huge sums of money from West Germany as foreign, but it was a substitute (justifiable, in my opinion, in the circumstances) for the creation of a genuine grass-roots party structure which if not quickly corrected does not augur well for democratic political life in the new united Germany. In any case, money is not the problem in Eastern Europe: lack of democracy and the need to destroy remnants of the Communist Party-state is the real dilemma. 'Pluralism' will not, as the experience of Poland demonstrates, evolve gradually out of the decay of the old order until the Party's hold on the army and the police are eliminated along with the *nomenklatura*. Nor, as in the critical case of the Soviet Union, would the declaration of a multi-party system in itself create a democracy whatever the formal status of the Communist Party.

If, in response to the foregoing, a proponent of state funding were to argue (as they frequently do), that a 'democratic state' need not be feared, then it would be necessary, although probably useless, to point to the experience of the leviathan state in the twentieth century. More importantly, the argument must be joined around the common threat to democracy, East and West, of the ongoing bureaucratic statification of society and economy. The possibility of the convergence in the twenty-first century of the two competing social systems, into some common form of 'managerialist' society hardly augurs well for the future of global democracy.

State financing of the political parties is part of this trend. When we are told by the Parliamentary Secretary of the German Free Democrats that political parties are 'state executive bodies and function as such', there is cause for alarm and reason to question motives as well as consequences.[27] This is not in substance different from the idea of the parties as 'public utilities'. Nor is it reassuring to hear from Professor Samuel P. Huntington that

> the bureaucracy now does not just administer things, but it makes most of the demands for new resources, new policies, new programs and new ideas.

It performs many of the functions which private-interest groups and the political parties used to perform. Political parties, Huntington writes, are in decline and although they are unlikely to disappear altogether,

> their function and role will change ... Political parties no longer provide a bridge between private groups and individuals on the one hand and the Government on the other in terms of pushing new policies. *The bureaucracy and expert groups closely associated with it have taken over that traditional party function.* [My emphasis][28]

This is a piece of advocacy, of course, and one can hardly be surprised that Professor Huntington is one of the main authors of a Trilateral Commission Report advocating the introduction of state funding of parties as a part of the cure for the 'democratic distemper' of the times. Still, it is also an analysis of something which is happening to political parties in the West and of one possible – but only possible – outcome of developments in modern society. That it points directly at the absorption of all of the key institutions of society into the state bureaucracy underlines the importance, from a democratic standpoint, of resisting proposals for statification of the parties through state money and of reasserting the centrality of civil society and its autonomy from the state.

From our discussion of the rebirth of democracy and of civil society in Eastern Europe, we come to one of the great ironies of the last decade of the twentieth century: that ideas about democracy and the state, which were common to the liberal and socialist movements before the age of totalitarianism, and before they were eroded in the West by the institutions and ideologies of the Cold War, are being rediscovered or reinvented in Eastern Europe (and in China) as the bureaucratic totalitarian regimes crumble and the Cold War sputters out. And the greatest irony of all: that their rebirth may reinvigorate the idea of democracy in the West – and perhaps even lead Americans to reinvent the voluntary political party as a vital link between citizen and state.[29]

Looking Forward: Democracy and the Future of Political Parties

I have undoubtedly raised more questions than I have answered. But, to go back to the starting point, when we consider questions and proposed reforms about the role of money in democratic politics, we are not considering dry technical matters which can be separated from issues of values and political commitment.

I have addressed these issues from the standpoint of a belief that the leviathan state will continue to loom up in the twenty-first century as the great problem for those who understand that the future for humankind and civilization depends on the establishment of political, economic and social democracy. Even if we can take heart from the visible crumbling of communist totalitarianism and see that the desire for individual freedom and human dignity is as much a need as a set of values which cannot be extinguished by the forces of state repression and terror, we still have a choice to make as we contemplate the alternative roads which humankind may follow.

The choice I advocate rests upon this premise: that the individual in modern society can neither have the dignity nor the freedom which he or she requires without the right and the capacity to freely associate with others for social and political purposes. Individual freedom requires organization. There is no 'iron law of oligarchy' inherent in organization. There is only one iron law: that without the right to belong to effective political parties and other groups and social movements which are autonomous of the state and internally democratic, oligarchs, both state and 'private', will rule. And without this right, the state and, to anticipate the twenty-first century, transnational corporations and political entities whose shape we can only speculate about, will rule society. Individual freedom within society, which must mean the capacity to participate in and to make choices about the entire range of social and economic issues through democratic politics, will wither if these aims cannot be realized.[30]

Is this a replay of Edward Bellamy's *Looking Backward*, or of Huxley's *Brave New World*, or of Orwell's vision of *1984*? If it is, I would certainly not want to suggest that it is inevitable. There is no 'wave of the future' carrying us inexorably toward the leviathan state. But it is certainly a step in that direction to breach the barrier between political parties and the state through the state funding of political parties and the creation of administrative agencies to regulate political-finance abuses, however modest and benign it may appear at first.

One final word: I have borrowed the term 'civil society' from Eastern European democrats to summarize what I think the requirements for a democratic political order are. It is curious and touching (in the same way that the Chinese students' 'Goddess of Liberty' was) for anyone familiar with Tocqueville's great study of American democracy, that the role of such independent, voluntary citizens organizations, independent of the state, which Tocqueville rightly found to be the genius of American democracy, should be reinvented in this way. And sad, too, that so many people, including Americans, seem to have forgotten it.

We owe a profound debt to the oppositional democratic movement in Eastern Europe for reminding us of an important heritage. One can only hope that their rediscovery of some old ideas will help to drive out the new ones which the Western advocates of reform through the statification of political parties have put in their place.

PART II

After Watergate: Reform *Redux*

In the wake of the Watergate affair, Progressive-style political reform reappeared in the form of the self-styled 'citizen's lobby', Common Cause. In 1974, Common Cause placed an Initiative on the California ballot – 'Proposition 9' – which created a 'Fair Political Practices Commission' which was to 'clean up' California politics. Having written about old-fashioned Progressive reform, I was fascinated to see the same ideas resurrected nearly 60 years later. For nearly two years, between 1974 and 1976, I observed the workings of the Fair Political Practices Commission and interviewed the reformers, the Commission staff, as well as the villains of the piece, the professional lobbyists. Chapters 4, 5, 6 and 7 were written contemporaneously. Even at this late date, the Common Cause ideology continues to have a powerful hold on American politics and the kind of criticism contained in these pieces is still rare.

CHAPTER 4

Political Reform as a Danger to Democracy[1]

Although the California Political Reform Act has been in operation for only seven months, it is important to examine some of the basic questions raised by the statute and its administration. The act is among the most far reaching of the many laws either being proposed or enacted throughout the US under the banner of political reform. Its impact upon politics in California and the way in which its unique features are administered will undoubtedly have an important bearing upon the content and direction of the entire movement to alter American political institutions. One measure of the need for a critical look at the law is the recent call by David Cohen, Common Cause president, for passage of a national 'Proposition 9'. Given the source, the words are not to be taken lightly.

We should be primarily concerned with the consequences of the law, especially its implications for democratic political rights, rather than with the stated purposes or the rhetoric of its advocates. The test of a law as broad and as sweeping as this is its actual impact and implementation, not the sincerity or high purposes avowed by its proponents.

Political 'Poison'

As for the purpose of the law, it is sufficient to recall that at the heart of the argument favouring the passage of Proposition 9 was the view that almost all of the major problems in the American political system could be traced back to one source: the 'poison' of money in politics. The new law was designed to control the size and secrecy of political spending, thereby restoring to 'the people' control over their government. Watergate, of course, became a crucial element in the campaign. The lesson of Watergate, according to advocates of Proposition 9, was the need for a law to 'help put an end to the corrupting influences of secrecy and special-interest money in government'. The California Political Reform Act of 1974 provided, its advocates said, a 'simple, direct, [and] democratic' solution to these problems.

The reformers' analysis of the deep crisis through which American politics has been passing for more than a decade is, to be charitable, an over-simplification. Their explanation of the cause of the present state of the American political system as the result of its corruption by 'special-interest' money would not merit serious attention, however, were it not for the dangerous practical consequences. Even in the case of the Watergate affair, such a view does little to explain the real causes and significance of the widespread political rot exposed in the course of the investigation. As a diagnosis it confuses the symptoms with the disease. It goes without saying that if the disease has not been correctly identified there is not much hope that the cure will work.

Reform – A Problem?

This is not meant to be an alternative analysis of the origins and nature of this crisis, except to point out that not one of the great issues of the last ten or 15 years can be intelligently understood in terms of covert corruption or lavish financial contributions to politicians and parties by the 'special interests' – an ideologically loaded term used promiscuously in American political discourse which equates organizations of working people with multinational corporations. Would anyone seriously argue, for example, that the war in Vietnam began and was prolonged over more than a decade because of the 'poison' of money in American politics? Or that the problems of widespread poverty and unemployment have not been effectively addressed because our political leaders have been flooded with special-interest campaign contributions? Such an analysis reflects an inability and unwillingness to come to grips with the political roots of these problems.

Money is only the symptom of a far deeper and more serious illness in American politics. It is an illness that is political in character; no series of mechanical devices will do anything except exacerbate the situation. In the absence of an effective party of opposition which stands for social justice and economic equality against the big corporate interests which run *both* of the existing parties, there is no cure for the curse of money in American politics. Mechanistic solutions in the absence of a recognition of this basic fact change very little except to increase public cynicism when they fail, as they must inevitably, to change the practice of politics. This is especially true of such legislation as the Political Reform Act, no matter how sincere its sponsors may have been. Sincerity, unfortunately, is not equivalent to political wisdom.

In fact, political reform itself may well be one of the greatest political problems in the United States today. In the name of reform, vast changes have been made in the political system and even greater ones are being proposed in the form of the public financing of elections. These changes will radically affect democratic institutions and political freedoms. However, there is no evidence that the advocates of these reforms understand the long-term consequences of their proposals.

Reform, it seems, is a word before which all critical thought must stop. The political damage resulting from this inhibition of thought is only now becoming apparent. Recently, for example, the realization has begun to emerge, even among some of those who originally supported it, that the new Federal Election Campaign Act is a disaster. Among other things, it provides for campaign-expenditure limits that protect incumbents. Yet, like Proposition 9, the federal law was hailed as a reform, and never has a law of its magnitude and impact – with the possible exception of the California law – been passed with so little critical discussion and attention to its consequences. The reason: it has become unthinkable or, more importantly, politically dangerous, to criticize anything given the label of 'political reform'.

Boomerang Effect

After studying the California law and following the deliberation of the new Fair Political Practices Commission for six months, it is clear that its operation will have a seriously damaging effect upon political activity, especially upon the very grass-roots groups and individuals who were supposed to be its main beneficiaries. Is the cause of democratic participation served by requiring that the identities and the employers of all those who make contributions of $50 or more to candidates or ballot-proposition campaigns be disclosed? What it will actually do is inhibit those persons who would like to contribute to unpopular causes – or to causes unpopular with some segments of society, and especially to their employers. In an ideal world, no one ought to be intimidated but in the real world, social, economic and political pressures are real. Do we have a right to make that judgement for someone else whose livelihood is at stake or who believes that it is, however unrealistically? Certainly, it violates the democratic right of privacy – no different in principle or in consequence than the right to a secret ballot – to compel such disclosure by law.

Consider for example, what will happen to the rights of the homosexual community, whose individual members may want to contribute money to defend the recently enacted sexual rights law against the drive to repeal it. Who is to say that homosexuals – indeed, anyone hesitant to risk the opprobrium that association with this cause may bring – must, under penalty of law, reveal their names to the public and to their employer in violation of their democratic right to political anonymity and secrecy? What about the bank or utility employees, including highly paid executives, who may privately support gay rights or sympathize with the goals of the environmental movement and wish to contribute money to a candidate or an initiative campaign that goes against the interests of their employers? Or the frequent cases of the independent businesspeople who support causes and candidates that would horrify their bankers and their customers? It's no secret that a great deal of money for liberal causes has come from just such individuals. The anti-Vietnam War movement was bankrolled by wealthy persons who were not willing, especially in its early stages, to go public. It will not be the 'fat cats' and their causes who will suffer, but the popular causes with whose goals the proponents of reform claim to sympathize.

The Lawyer's Mind

From those who defend this and other aspects of the act come assurances that such requirements are constitutional. And, indeed, they may be found constitutional and not in violation of the First Amendment. If so, it will be a sad day for the First Amendment and the basic political freedoms it represents. Only a lawyer's mind bent on finding justifications for a particular political course would so approach these basic questions of political freedom. The Supreme Court recently upheld for the first time the government's right to exercise prior restraint over publication – censorship – in clear violation of the guarantees of the First Amendment.

So much for constitutionality. The advocates of forced disclosure repeatedly say that only people who have something to hide – people skulking around corridors and exerting 'improper influence', whatever that may be – have anything to fear from such disclosure. When the elementary democratic right to hold opinions and to act upon them collectively in the political arena without being required to subject oneself to governmental scrutiny or to social and economic pressure is so viewed, then there has been a dismaying erosion of the very idea of democracy.

In the name of controlling lobbyists, the law infringes upon the basic right of citizens to petition the government and to do so in an organized fashion, which is the only way most individuals can hope to be effective politically. For ordinary people, who cannot be full-time organizers or political volunteers because they must work for a living, this means the democratic right to join together with others, pool their financial resources and hire someone to act on their behalf. While the new law doesn't forbid this outright, it does set up requirements for registration and reporting that cannot be effectively met without the nagging fear of investigation or prosecution. The reporting requirements can only be met by organizations already well-established and able to spend large amounts of money on skilled lawyers, accountants and clerical staff. In other words, compliance is easiest for those very same groups, especially the professional lobbying firms which the advocates of reform claimed would be checked by the new law.

Those who doubt this conclusion are invited to do the following:

- Examine the forms and detailed accounting requirements developed by the Fair Political Practices Commission.

- Study the complicated regulations (after having learned which are currently operative) and the equally complicated opinions drafted by the commission's legal staff.
- Attend the commission hearings and take in the conflicting interpretations of the statute and interminable discussions of the existing, revised and draft regulations and opinions.
- Watch the well-paid lawyers and representatives of the special interests at the meetings do what they are paid so well to do: protect the interests of their clients by trying to understand the meaning of the law and attempting to bend the commission's interpretation of it in a 'reasonable' direction.

Most of this requires the financial ability to travel to Sacramento and spend days on end in hearings, although it is also possible (for $250 per year) to subscribe to the *Campaign Law Reporter*. Thus, what turns out to be at worst an expensive inconvenience for the big lobbyists and rich corporations – not to mention a bonanza for rich corporations, lawyers, accountants and professional consulting firms – can easily break the back of many small groups and organizations. This will be especially true for those forced to defend themselves in the course of an investigation or prosecution, no matter how baseless the charges may turn out to be. And the above describes only the requirements for *lobbying*: the effect upon candidates for office – except the very well-heeled – will be of the same kind, only multiplied many times.

Class Legislation

There is another and even more obvious and direct infringement of civil liberties: Section 86108(b) of the law. In Washington State they call this the 'grass-roots lobbying' provision, and the idea has been copied in the California law in the name of reform. It is safe to say that few people know of its existence. In the words of the commission's own publication, this section specifies that 'persons who do not employ a lobbyist are required to file periodic disclosure reports [Form 650] if they expend $250 or more in a month for the purpose of influencing legislative or administrative action'. Thus, a demonstration on behalf of labour legislation organized by the United Farm Workers and held on the steps of the Capitol becomes subject to the filing requirement because the money (likely to exceed $250) must of necessity be collectively expended. Are these the nefarious lobbying activities that the proponents of Proposition 9 were talking about? Meanwhile, a group of wealthy growers, each spending as individuals $50 or $100 or $200 to come to Sacramento and buttonhole legislators, need not fill out Form 650, even though the total amount spent may exceed $250 by far.

This is just one example of the kind of class legislation and bias against organized groups that is built into the Political Reform Act. The other and potentially just as damaging one is the control over democratically structured associations such as the AFL–CIO. Section 86108(b), together with the complicated lobbyist registration and accounting procedures, constitutes a grass-roots control law.

Arbitrary Power

The examples cited could be multiplied. The issue they illustrate is not of these particular commissioners or the current chairman and staff. The law may be administered today by persons who have a due concern for political rights and their interpretations may conserve those rights. But tomorrow there will be different commissioners and a different political climate. The same powers can just as easily (indeed, more easily) be made use of by those who are today the targets of so-called political reform or by those who are not sympathetic to democratic political rights.

If there is any one lesson that Watergate ought to have taught, it is this: civil liberties are indivisible. The rights of some cannot be infringed without potentially infringing the rights of all. The point is that even lobbyists' rights must be protected – as well as those of a number of people or organizations with whom the majority may not agree. Create a weapon to be used against your enemies today and tomorrow it may be used against you. A bad law remains a bad law even if administered today by well-intentioned officials.

This brings up what may be the most important issue in the Political Reform Act and the key to understanding why the direction of the entire present movement for political reform poses a danger to democracy in the US. The very existence of an independent commission charged with the *regulation of politics* is an extraordinary assault on First Amendment rights and political democracy. This is perhaps the most difficult point to grasp about the law and its practical operation, particularly for people who are, quite properly, used to calling for strong government regulation over broad areas of economic life. One does not have to be a defender of *laissez-faire* in economics to defend it in politics.

The power given to the Fair Political Practices Commission (as well as to the new Federal Election Commission) is unprecedented. It cannot be equated with the regulation of economic activity. To attempt to do so, as the present-day proponents of political reform have done, is to be led inexorably to the most anti-democratic conclusions. Speech and its effective use in politics is constitutionally protected, or ought to be. It cannot be arbitrarily regulated or subjected to administrative rules by an agency of the state without trampling on democratic rights.

Through the exercise of its statutorily conferred power to interpret and implement the law by issuance of administrative regulations and opinions – thereby, in effect, writing the law – the California Fair Political Practices Commission, as also the Federal Elections Commission, can oversee, control and investigate as well as prosecute broad areas of political activity hitherto beyond the purview of any governmental body and with very few effective limits on its discretionary powers. The commission, in other words, is an arbiter over political activity and has the power to determine what is and is not permissible in this broad area. In itself, the possession and exercise of such arbitrary power is an invasion of basic democratic rights. Given the nature and range of the activity – politics and the organized expression of opinion – over which the commission exercises control, its decisions and interpretations cannot be non-political and objective nor, in any meaningful sense, independent. When, for example, we are told by the present chairman that in 'defining lobbyists so far we have been applying some common-sense tests that have proven very successful', we are witnessing an admission that the foundation of the commission's operation rests upon the exercise of arbitrary administrative power. It is also, in the most basic sense of the term, an example of a political judgment.

With the creation of a commission whose power to regulate politics is based on the discretionary authority of appointed officials to say what constitutes common sense or what are reasonable forms of political activity, the political reformers have led American politics into a new and dangerous age.

CHAPTER 5

Regulating Politics[1]

Speaking in December 1974 to a gathering of top California lobbyists, State Senator James Mills wisecracked that the new Political Reform Act which was about to take effect might well be renamed 'The Lobbyists' Relief Act of 1974', in so far as it would provide a legal shield against the incessant demands of certain politicians for financial assistance.

Had an advocate of this particular piece of reform legislation overheard him, they would have undoubtedly accused the senator of political cynicism. That the new law might not have the consequences claimed for it by its chief backers and, indeed, that its consequences could be quite other than the 'purification' of politics and the end of 'special interest' influence would have been indignantly denied.

The test of any piece of legislation, of course, is to be found in an examination of its consequences and not in the intentions or rhetoric of its sponsors. This is especially important when the legislation rests on a faulty and rather simple-minded understanding of the situation which it is designed to change. Over two years have now passed since the implementation of the California Political Reform Act of 1974 – 'Proposition 9'. As might be expected, at least by those familiar with the history of 'good government' reform groups in America, very little is to be heard from its original backers by way of a serious evaluation of its impact, apart from ritualistic claims that the law has cleaned up politics in Sacramento and 'equalized access' to legislators and administrative agencies for 'public interest' groups, as opposed to the various 'special interests' who had previously monopolized the attention of the lawmakers. Thus to the executive director of California Common Cause, the new law has put

> lobbyists – us, and Pacific Gas & Electric – all in the same bag, so that we have to deal with the people who make the decisions on the basis of the merits of the issue – on the ability to convince people that our position is meritorious, rather than on the fact that we are such good friends that it would be unseemly to vote against the bill.

And, in response to the many Doubting Thomases who apparently abound in California, not to mention Sacramento, other leaders of Common Cause have proclaimed that 'the lobbying regulations have changed the way business is done in Sacramento. The social and fraternal links between the Legislature and the third house, links that give the well-heeled lobbyist an extra edge, are breaking down.' For the first few crucial months of the existence of the Fair Political Practices Commission itself, a period during which regulations were drafted to cover lobbying activity, Common Cause was unable to mount a sufficient organizational effort to present its views before the commission. Even when it was finally able to muster a volunteer to attend these hearings, it was unable to effectively oppose the drafting of administrative regulations which substantially softened the impact of the law on the lobbyists. At the same time, the professional lobbyists were, not surprisingly, able to make their views known and played an important role in shaping the regulations and the enforcement of the law. As a final comment at this point it should be noted that of the two organizations which originally sponsored the initiative measure, one of them, Peoples' Lobby, is now in a state indistinguishable from death, while Common Cause is experiencing a severe organizational crisis. (See Chapter 7.)

In this chapter, I am primarily concerned with the impact of the Reform Act on lobbying, although much of what can be said in this respect can be applied to the other major sections of the law dealing with conflict of interest and campaign disclosure. There seems to have been massive compliance with the requirements of the law. The result has been a blizzard of paper, a flurry of press releases from the commission, and, after some initial interest in the not surprising news that powerful and wealthy groups gave money to politicians (frequently on both sides) and spent money to influence legislation, there was a rather disenchanted yawn from the public.

Over the past two years I have attended the meetings of the Fair Political Practices Commission, interviewed its members and staff, and spoken to dozens of lobbyists and political activists about their experiences under the Act. Some things have changed, but not in the way the proponents of Proposition 9 intended or would have ever predicted. More important, most of the ways of 'doing business' in Sacramento have not changed, except for their surface manifestations, most of which were unimportant for the 'special interests', with the exception of one particular group whose views are represented by the contract lobbyists. Even here, there is no evidence that substantial damage has been done to lobbyists' ability to influence legislation. Indeed, it would seem that the greatest burden of the law has fallen on the groups who were most adamant in their support of the law – the so-called 'public interest' lobbyists and the representatives of the various non-profit charitable groups.

In this respect the evaluation I made in Chapter 4 has been fully borne out. 'Compliance is easiest,' I wrote, 'for those very same groups, especially the professional lobbying firms we were told would somehow be checked by the new law.' This judgement is supported by the lobbyists' own lobbyist, Allen Tebbetts, who observes that as the result of the law 'a group has to hire a high priced lawyer or accountant, and fund the expenses of someone who will sit through these proceedings to find out how to comply with these regulations'. 'The greatest irony of all,' Tebbetts concludes, 'is that the "endangered species" is not the lobbyists per se, but the so-called "good-guy" lobbyists, the ones without the bankroll.'

To review briefly the provisions of the Political Reform Act as they relate to lobbyists and lobbying:

- Under the law, lobbying is defined as any attempt, direct, or indirect, to promote, support, influence, modify, oppose or delay any legislation or state administrative action of a 'quasi-legislative' nature.
- The expenditure of $250 by a person, business or association in any one month for this purpose constitutes lobbying and a report must be filed.
- For an employee to become a lobbyist he or she must, under the terms of the original statute, be compensated and the activity must be a 'substantial and regular' part of duties.
- A person required to register as a lobbyist is forbidden to expend more than $10 in any one month on a legislator, or to make personal political contributions.
- The statute forbids the lobbyist to 'arrange for' the making of political contributions. This provision, now substantially overturned by the California courts, was, according to the law's proponents, a crucial check on the power of the 'special interests' because it provided a way of 'breaking the connection' between lobbying and campaign contributions. Presumably if lobbyists could no longer 'arrange for' the making of contributions – a term which the commission defined very broadly to include recommendations to an employer based on a particular legislator's record – a particular piece of legislation would be judged on its 'merits' rather than being (directly) linked to an offer of a campaign contribution.[2]
- Lobbyists and employers of lobbyists are required to keep records of all lobbying-related expenditures and these records are to be fully and completely audited on a yearly basis by the State Franchise Tax Board.

The Administrative Process

Much of the Fair Political Practices Commission's attention over the first year was directed to formulating the regulations spelling out the statutory provisions dealing with lobbying. To say that the regulations and the process by which they were arrived at were confusing is an understatement. Understanding the avalanche of draft regulations and being able to intervene effectively in their reformulation, not to mention the difficulty of knowing what they meant and being able to comply with their terms, required the efforts of individual lobbyists and the formation of a protective association of private lobbyists, the Institute of Governmental Advocates (IGA), which itself hired a lobbyist and retained one of the most knowledgeable lawyers in the state to guide its individual members.

Extensive record-keeping and extremely detailed audits conducted by the Franchise Tax Board, resulted in the expenditure of money and time by the lobbyists. For those unable to hire accountants and pass along the charges to clients or to absorb the costs in corporate budgets, it meant the expenditure of a great amount of time, which, in the nature of things, meant the same thing as a great deal of money. Certainly the experience of the lobbyist for one small state-wide union was not untypical: he found that three to four days per month were necessary to keep the records and fill out the required forms.

Auditing requirements apart, the net effect of the regulations which emerged from the hearings of the FPPC was to soften the impact and scope of the law. This was largely the result of the assiduous and very effective lobbying effort of the lobbyists and other representatives of the 'special interests', to borrow that highly misleading term which the proponents of reform apply to everyone but themselves. Thus, for example, the meaning of 'regular and substantial' were given time and/or monetary measurements, although, of course, the original statute had no such standard built into it.

How the commission arrived at these judgements, such as the conclusion that one would have to spend 40 hours in any two months (of which ten hours has to be in direct communication with legislators) to be required to register as a lobbyist, had its amusing side but one which also underlines the entirely arbitrary nature of the process. After some discussion in which a few of the members of the FPPC wanted a higher standard (60 hours) and others a lower one (20 hours) it was decided, in the words of one of them, to 'cut the difference' at 40 hours. The serious side of this, of course, is that the commission could easily decide tomorrow, with as little reason apart from the 'common sense' of the chairman, to cut the matter a different way in order to placate whatever transitory pressures might be brought to bear on it. This illustrates what is the most dangerous aspect of the new law, and indeed of the entire 'political reform' movement in the United States today: the arbitrary regulatory powers of a commission over political activity. I want to return to this last point in my conclusion because it is the least examined and least understood aspect of these laws. How effective was the softening process carried out on the FPPC is demonstrated by the decision in the beginning of 1976 of the IGA lobbyist to deregister as a lobbyist before the FPPC. The regulations had been adopted and, with some exceptions, the lobbyists were home free.

One important legal action undertaken by the IGA must be mentioned in this connection: its successful challenge to the very broad definition of the term 'arrange for', in connection with a lobbyists' activities, struck a death blow at one of the elements in the law which the reformers regarded as crucial. The FPPC's construction of this provision was enjoined by a lower court from enforcement and this decision was later upheld by the State Supreme Court. It can now be said that short of making a direct approach to a legislator, the lobbyist is free to make such recommendations to his or her employer. The employers of lobbyists, on the other hand, are not under any such constraint, nor, for that matter, need they be concerned about wining and dining legislators. Thus it was something of a shock to the proponents of the original statute, who had focused on the lobbyist alone, when apartment-house owners were able to descend on Sacramento *en masse* for the purpose of supporting a bill denying local control over rents, in the course of which they entertained and, apparently, freely mentioned the kind and size of campaign contributions which they were prepared to make – or not to make. This incident also demonstrates the class bias of the law since only a relatively affluent group of individuals could undertake the kind of effort and the offers of contributions which the apartment-house owners were able to make in this case.

Consequences of Reform

To evaluate the consequences of the law, in summary, it is useful to divide the lobbyists into three groups: the contract lobbyists; the lobbyists for major corporations and financial interests; and the 'public interest' lobbyists, together with the numerous representatives of tax-exempt, charitable organizations who seek to influence legislation. It will then be necessary to mention, briefly, the impact of the law on administrative lobbying and the 'grass-roots' lobbying provision.

Contract lobbyists

There are some 80 to 100 of these lobbyists in Sacramento. They contract with one or several clients to represent their views to the state government. Such contract lobbyists probably make up the bulk of the membership of a group like the IGA. I said earlier that some things have changed. There is no question that the stringent limit on entertainment has made life more difficult for the lobbyists who speak for relatively marginal economic interests with small constituencies. They have been forced to rely on the 'social and fraternal links' which obsess the Common Cause-type reformers. The president of the IGA, William Keese, formerly the lobbyist for the California Dental Association, put the matter in this way: 'The breakdown of the social situation is happening and over the years will continue to do so. I see a bad side to that. I feel that in knowing legislators, they know whether I'm telling the truth and the degree of conviction I have.' How much more difficult and whether the changes are substantial or cosmetic, and whether things will go back to normal as the routine builds up are other matters. Ways can be found to circumvent the entertainment rules, for example. There is an unverified rumour now circulating in Sacramento that a private club (or clubs) has been organized at which members of the 'third house' and members of the legislature can gather to engage in a little friendly gambling. On the face of it there would be nothing illegal about such an arrangement assuming that all 'members' paid their own dues and liquor and food tabs; if the winners were all on one side of the table, there would be, of course, reason for suspicion of a relationship verging on bribery. But such things are, in their very nature, difficult to prove and there is no doubt that a weary public would probably shrug its shoulders in any case, knowing what 'politicians' are like.

For the contract lobbyists, the major problem has been and is the fear of being cited either as the targets of an investigation by the FPPC or as the authors of an incomplete or incorrect financial report. Even if such reports later prove to be entirely false, it is possible – even likely – that their business relationship with a client will be irreparably damaged. There already have been several such instances and the fear that there will be more has made many of these lobbyists extremely cautious.

Major corporate and financial interest lobbying

In a law filled with ironies, perhaps the most ironic aspect of all is the fact that those lobbyists who represent or work for major corporate interests or groups with substantial financial impact have probably been greatly helped by the very provisions which have hurt the contract lobbyists. Able to maintain a large legal department and research staff, with access to large amounts of money to be contributed either by individual officers or out of corporate and/or association funds, the access of this element of the lobbying community to the legislature and the administrative agencies has been made 'more equal than others' in all likelihood. As one lobbyist for a large national corporation told me recently,

> Proposition 9 has been terrific for the corporate lobbyists. We've always tried to keep a low profile in Sacramento and never went in for the wining and dining of legislators. Now we have greater access to the legislators because we can present our case to them on its merits. It's the contract lobbyists who have been the big losers.

It is interesting that this statement coincides on the face of it with the Common Cause rationale for lobbying regulation. The meaning of it, of course, is somewhat different than they would admit to.

Money and financial power still talk, but not in the way in which the advocates of reform understand. When the representatives of big national corporations speak they are listened to because they do so in the name of jobs and the health of the economy, with the premise, stated or not, that what is good for their company or industry is good for the economy of California or the nation. This is a powerful argument and it is one which the legislators and the executive basically accept because they genuinely agree with it. It is this commonality of social and economic beliefs which makes them susceptible to the arguments directed to them by large economic interests: they are, within their framework, genuinely 'meritorious'.

The recent efforts on the part of Governor Jerry Brown and the leaders of the legislature to 'improve the business climate' in California, in the wake of the Dow Chemical Company's withdrawal of a major project because of environmental red-tape, is direct evidence of how little the influence of big business has been eroded since the passage of Proposition 9, while the rather futile (increasingly so) protests of the environmental lobby testify that the 'equality of access' which the law was to bring about was largely an illusion. The threat to withdraw jobs or not to invest in the California economy is a very persuasive and 'meritorious' argument to those who see society through the same lens as the major economic interests.

In this connection, it is necessary to mention the role of labour lobbyists, although they do not, properly speaking, belong in the same category as those lobbyists we have been discussing. It would require a separate article to fully comprehend the impact of the new law on labour. The California AFL–CIO was in the forefront of opposition to the initiative measure and it joined in a coalition with groups like the Chamber of Commerce for this purpose. There is some evidence that the vehemence of labour's opposition made their traditional enemies in the Chamber somewhat less militant in their opposition to the law than they might otherwise have been. After all, they reasoned, could a law denounced so furiously by labour and described by the Peoples' Lobby as one designed to 'get John Henning' (Executive Secretary Treasurer of the California AFL–CIO) be all bad? In any case, labour was probably the chief beneficiary of the successful IGA suit seeking to overturn the prohibition against lobbyists 'arranging for' contributions to politicians. At the same time, it seems clear that except in those cases where labour allies itself with big business, as it frequently has in the case of environmental issues, it is politically weak and growing weaker all the time. However, this is not directly assignable to the impact of the Political Reform Act, except in so far as the passage of the initiative was linked, politically, with an attack on the power of 'big labour' as a 'special interest'.

'Public Interest' lobbyists and tax-exempt organizations

Every week in Sacramento, a small group of registered, humorously self-designated, 'good guy' lobbyists, meet for lunch (appropriately brown-bag) to exchange views and information. Included are lobbyists for environmental causes, consumer groups, multi-issue social concern organizations such as the Friends' Committee on Legislation, the American Civil Liberties Union, and a few of the smaller and more liberal trade unions. Most of them, with the exception of the ACLU and the unions, strongly endorsed passage of Proposition 9. Most of them today say they wish they had never heard of it. Many of this group have received fines from the Secretary of State for late filing of their lobbyists' reports. Secretary of State March Fong Eu's statement to the IGA deserves to be quoted in this connection:

> With all due respect to the initiative's sponsors and proponents and with all due respect to the assumptions which have no doubt governed their thoughts, the bottom line to date [the end of 1975] is that the big fish are getting away and an awful lot of little fish are going to be caught. ... The vast majority of lobbyists who have been late [filers] ... have been the little guys, the inspired amateurs who are perhaps registered even though they do not fall under the mechanical definition adopted by the Commission. The really professional lobbyist ... and the people who in some instances have fleets of accountants and attorneys backing them up ... are quite rarely late in a filing ... and if they are late and they are fined, they can afford to pay.

Although these groups have apparently learned to cope with the complexity of the forms they are required to file and the detailed record-keeping which is entailed, none of them that I know of have any illusions left about the way in which the Reform Act 'helps' them in their work. Says one lobbyist for an environmental organization,

> I feel that large organizations that are well funded and many special interest groups who are provided with a battery of lawyers, or have subscriptions to the *Campaign Law Reporter* at $250 per year have an advantage over groups like ours. It is the small groups who are caught.

It should be noted that many of these groups pay their lobbyists salaries amounting to as little as $250 per month: time spent filling out the forms is, in effect, a financial contribution to the work of the commission to be deducted from the main purpose of the organization. As for the supposed 'equality of access', the testimony is equally negative. The lobbyist for one of the oldest and most effective of these groups, the Friends' Committee on Legislation, states that the law 'hasn't affected my access to legislators at all', although 'at lunchtime you do see more of the legislators in the (Capitol) cafeteria and that means you can buttonhole them there.' And yet another lobbyist for an old-line citizen's group:

> I would say that there has been little or no effect of Proposition 9 on our operations because we never did contribute to campaigns and we were never involved socially ... Those legislators to whom we had access before Proposition 9 in the office during business hours, we still have access to; and those legislators we did not have access to, we still don't. I have often been asked if Proposition 9 puts us on an equal basis with other lobbyists because now that they are reduced to our level ... I do not feel we have been put on the same basis. I am not sure that at the present time Proposition 9 has done much to reduce their influence.

Another entirely unforeseen consequence of the law was, and is, as far as I know, the crippling of the tax exempt, charitable organizations who are not permitted to lobby without loss of their tax-exempt status. Being required to register as lobbyists subjects them to an immediate challenge by the IRS. Thus, in one case

I am familiar with, that of a major community chest-type organization, a complete withdrawal was made from legislative involvement on issues such as aid to crippled children.

Administrative lobbying

The California Political Reform Act expanded the definition of lobbying to include the lobbying of administrative agencies with regard to 'quasi-legislative' actions. Here too, as in the case of the legislative lobbyists, the Fair Political Practices Commission was forced to develop regulations spelling out the meaning of the statutory provisions. It soon became apparent that the drafters of the legislation, including the chairman of the commission, had not had the slightest understanding of the relationship between regulatory agencies and regulated industry. The fact, for example, that employees of the Public Utilities Commission are required by law to spend large amounts of time in direct contact with the utilities they regulate, and that the utilities are required to supply information which is obviously used in 'quasi-legislative' hearings, threw the FPPC into a tailspin since it seemed to mean that large numbers of utility employees would be required to register as lobbyists and that the output of paper would be even more prodigious and self-defeating than in the case of the legislative lobbyists.

Common sense, and the powerful arguments of the lobbyists, not to mention those of the regulatory agencies themselves, dictated a separate and even more generous standard for defining what constituted a lobbyist in these cases. Precisely what the result of all this has been, no one knows, and it seems that no one cares. Certainly there is no evidence that the registration and disclosure and limitations on entertainment have changed in the slightest degree the influence of those who were influential before the legislation passed.

Grass-roots lobbyists and lobbying

One of the most intriguing and dangerous provisions of the law was the one providing for the reporting by anyone who spends $250 or more in a month to influence legislative or administrative action. For all practical purposes this provision has not been enforced, with the exception of one case I know of: Gallo Winery was required to report their expenditures of more than $100,000 to influence the outcome of pending farm labour legislation. At the same time, dozens of demonstrations – perhaps hundreds – have been held on the Capitol steps in the last two years, many of them costing far in excess of $250 to the organizations sponsoring them, and yet few if any have been reported as the law requires. Nevertheless, as the chairman of the commission told me, it is only a matter of time before the commission attempts to enforce this clause in the law. Given the liberal leanings of the staff and the chief officials of the commission at the present time (both were officials of California Rural Legal Services), it is not surprising that the first group which came to the FPPC's notice and was required to file was Gallo Winery. Under another set of commissioners and with a different staff, leaning in a different political direction, it will be a different type of group or cause who will be 'noticed' by the commission, although the 'reminder' in-lieu-of-prosecution given Gallo may not be so friendly in the future. The point is that this element of the law can only be enforced selectively.

Audits

The greatest number of complaints have centered about the audit and disclosure function. The State Franchise Tax Board has taken the position that it is required to undertake a full audit of all lobbyists on a yearly basis, rather than a mere sampling. The audits conducted thus far have been very time-consuming affairs. Here too, then, the burden of the audit falls most heavily on those least able to afford the time and/or money necessary for compliance. Moves have been made to simplify and consolidate the reports themselves and undoubtedly other reforms will be made.

From a civil liberties standpoint the audit poses some interesting questions of privacy, particularly for those organizations which employ lobbyists and themselves have numerous members. The Northern California ACLU when ordered to submit 'all of its records' refused to do so, demanding in response that the Franchise Tax Board specify the documents required and specifically refusing to turn over membership records and records of special contributions. At this writing the inaction of the Franchise Tax Board and the studied avoidance of the issue by the commission has meant that the test case which the ACLU wishes to provoke has not yet developed.

Civil liberties of lobbyists

The provision of the Reform Act which forbids lobbyists to make political contributions has not yet been tested in court. One lobbyist has openly made regular contributions to the Sacramento Democratic Party Central Committee and has so informed the commission as well as its enforcement arm of this fact. The commission has failed to charge him – rather they have once again ignored this attempt to mount a test case. One can only suspect that apart from the fact that he is a liberal democrat, the commission fears the results of a court test of its powers. By not acting in this case the chilling effect of the law remains and the clear violation of the First Amendment which is entailed here continues.

Enforcement

This is the area which is least understood and which, in my opinion, holds some of the greatest dangers from the standpoint of democratic institutions. Having made a whole range of political practices subject to civil penalties and criminal prosecution, it has been necessary to create an apparatus to enforce the law. The FPPC has hired investigators who use normal police techniques in the course of their work, including, presumably, the gathering of files on politicians, lobbyists and other persons suspected of violating the law. There is no reason to think that other techniques, including the use of informers and wiretapping will not be employed, if they have not already been. One of the recently resigned members of the FPPC told me, when questioned on this point, that he saw no principled reason why paid informants should not be employed. There is good reason to believe, indeed, that in an early stage of the commission's activities, a tail was put on a lobbyist employee who was meeting with state officials and legislators.

Dangers to Democracy

Much more could be said by way of evaluating the impact of the California Political Reform Act. At this point, however, I think it has been made plain that the law has not had the consequences claimed for it by its proponents and that some of its erstwhile supporters may have been its chief victims. The powerful are still powerful and if everyone is equal it is only true in the Orwellian sense. Some and perhaps all of this would be quite funny when viewed from the vantage point of the political cynic. After all, this is not the first time in American history that a political reform movement has made its enemies more powerful and, in effect, helped to cut its own throat. The legendary Boss Tweed, the symbol of nineteenth-century urban corruption, is said to have told one interviewer that the attainment of his goals had been aided immeasurably by the 'stupidity' of the reformers of the day who, like their present-day counterparts, failed to understand the realities of power.

However, despite the temptation to dismiss this law and the spate of similar laws which have been passed in other states as yet another example of the limitations of the reform mentality, I think it would be a mistake to do so. The regulation of lobbying – not to mention the proposal for state subsidies of political parties and candidates – is a challenge to democratic institutions. I say this not because I like or defend the organized forces who now dominate our political process – on the contrary, I do not. But lobbying, if one can strip it of the pejorative connotations which the reformers have given it, means nothing more than the right to petition the government – in short, politics carried out by organized means. The regulation of lobbying means the regulation of politics and this means, in turn, nothing less than the direct infringement of First Amendment rights. It is revealing of the anti-democratic, totalitarian mentality that stands behind the current reformers' proposals that time after time it has been proposed by Common Cause that all attempts to 'influence' government, even those *not* involving any expenditure of money (although this would make no difference) be considered 'lobbying' and that such efforts come under the guidance and control of an administrative agency. This fact, together with the creation of such an administrative agency which may, at its discretion, regulate political activity indicates that one of the greatest dangers to democratic institutions may be the reformers themselves.[3]

CHAPTER 6

Democratic Rights and the Regulation of Politics[1]

Even more remarkable than the speed with which the current wave of comprehensive political reform laws have been enacted in over 35 states is the virtual absence of any critical attention to the implications of this legislation. I have in mind the regulatory commissions such as the California Fair Political Practices Commission, the Washington Public Disclosure Commission, and, of course, the Federal Election Commission. These commissions have been given power to enforce, through regulation, the statutes governing campaign expenditures, contributions, lobbying, disclosure requirements, conflicts of interest, etc. If the drive for public financing of elections at all levels of government is successful, these regulatory commissions, upon which the supervision of the subsidies will fall, will become key institutions in the 'statification' of American politics.

In arguing for the need to tie reform to the creation of such commissions, the advocates of political reform point to the many earlier abortive attempts to legislate against 'corrupt practices'. They were ineffective, it is claimed, precisely because of the absence of a specific enforcement agency which would be removed from the day-to-day pressures of partisan politics and which would have broad regulatory powers. The particular model, of course, for these new agencies is the so-called 'independent regulatory commission' whose chief role is the regulation of economic activity. The power granted to the new agencies and the procedures under which they operate are comparable to those of the older commissions.

Power of the Commissions

In California, for example, Proposition 9 mandates that the law be 'liberally construed' and gives the Fair Political Practices Commission power to adopt such regulations as it deems necessary to implement the law. At the same time, it provides for a system of formal opinions which in time will themselves constitute a substantial body of precedents of no small legal weight. In the recent Michigan reform law, modelled on the California statute, but passed by the legislature rather than through the initiative process, the same broad grant of power is to be found. In the case of the federal law, the ability to issue regulations is checked by the right of either house of Congress to exercise a veto power.

What makes these newest forms of regulatory commissions – and the ideas advanced to justify them – unique is the subject matter with which they deal: politics and political action. Put very simply, it is a matter, as one reformer told me, of government regulating politics just as it does economic activity. It is true that boards and commissions have existed before which have dealt with particular electoral arrangements. New York is one example. In these cases, the frequent harassment of minority parties or dissident candidates of the major parties may be remedied by court action – assuming that the particular court is not (as it frequently is) the creature of the same partisan policy as the board itself. In any case, damage resulting from abuse of power, although considerable, was limited by the board's fairly narrow domain. In contrast, the new commissions are given powers which cover virtually the entire range of politics and especially organized political activity.

Controlling Money or Controlling Organized Political Activity?

The major justification advanced for these laws and their enforcement by a regulatory commission is the need to effectively control the use of money in politics. However, whatever the reformers may say, it is a fact that the ability to collect and expend money in the pursuit of a political objective is indissolubly linked to the very possibility of effective politics. Effective politics, particularly for those who are neither wealthy nor notable or who lack leisure time, requires organization. And organization, alas, requires money. The impact, therefore, of such regulation is primarily upon organized political activity. What is excluded from such regulation are the isolated, atomized, unorganized and hence, ineffectual actions of ordinary people. At the same time, those individuals whose occupations, notability (or even notoriety), or personal wealth give them influence or permit them free time to participate in politics also remain largely untouched by the law.

Favouring the Leisure Class

This class bias of the regulation of politics is very clearly illustrated by the *amicus curiae* brief filed by the California FPPC and three other state commissions before the Supreme Court in *Buckley v. Valeo*. The brief argues that the giving of money to a candidate is not speech but 'conduct' and as such is not protected by the First Amendment. What then is left to 'speech' or 'pure speech' as it is termed? The answer given by the FPPC brief clearly reveals the tacit bias toward wealthy and well-connected individuals and others whose occupations (or non-occupations) allow them the leisure or freedom from the constraints of the office or the factory: 'The friends and supporters of the candidate or party are not restrained by the disclosure requirement from communicating their ideas: they may give speeches, write articles, and distribute pamphlets without disclosure under the Act.'

Precisely how any of them can be accomplished effectively without either the expenditure of personal money or, more likely, organized money, is not dealt with by the authors of the brief. Speech in a closet is hardly free speech, which is why money is a necessary and inseparable component of free speech. The important point, however, is that the range of actions described here as permissible without regulation are those actions that are typically engaged in, if at all, by individuals, although not just any individuals, but those of a certain social-economic background.

This point is made even more explicitly when the authors of the brief note that 'private support, personal assistance (such as the donation of the supporters' labor), and the contribution of ideas, position papers, and draft speeches are not infringed nor is disclosure required'. In short, what is *not* regulated, in the ideal world of the reformers, are the kinds of political activities engaged in by people like themselves: lawyers, publicists, journalists, intellectuals, professors and ladies and gentlemen who customarily write position papers, draft speeches, or merely offer their ideas and who are in a position to be listened to. The contribution of money, especially the pooling of small contributions to be used by an organization, and the kind of political pressure brought about by a mass demonstration or the ability to employ paid representatives (which is the only way most people can be politically effective) is thus left to the regulatory mercy of the commissions.

To see how this perspective works out in practice, one need look no further than the limitations of expenditures in ballot proposition campaigns. On the one hand, newspapers are exempt from regulation, although, as former Senator Eugene McCarthy has recently pointed out, there is no reason why in logic or fact they should be excluded from the coverage of such a law given their impact on the electorate, and certainly not under a doctrine which distinguishes speech from conduct. At the same time, the expenditures of organized groups in connection with the circulation of petitions are strictly regulated.

Newspapers are free to editorialize and print articles written by the kind of people who agree with their owners and who are able to write articles, or have them written for them. Thus, we have the example of Richard Tuttle, a member of the California Energy Commission, who points out why the nuclear initiative is a bad idea. Mr Tuttle's article in the Los Angeles *Times* must seem to the writers of the commission brief to be a wonderful example of 'pure speech'. That it was made possible through the generosity of the *Times* and, more than likely through the generous help from Energy Commission staff may bother them for a moment, although I doubt it. So much for 'pure speech'.

The Myth of the 'Non-Political' Commission

We are assured by the advocates of these commissions that they are 'independent' by virtue of being free of either the legislative or executive branch and are, therefore, responsible only to 'the public'. It is also held that the commissions are capable of being 'non-political' and 'non-partisan'.

Of the latter claim it is enough to note that without exception the commissions are composed of members of one or another of the two major parties. Only someone whose political ideas and partisan loyalties are firmly rooted in the dominant political system could so blandly term such bodies non-partisan. It is true that the members are prohibited from participating directly in partisan politics; but it is inconceivable that the underlying attitudes, political ideas, loyalties, etc., held by such individuals would simply be blotted out. Narrow partisanship can perhaps be eliminated, at least when it comes to the two major parties, although the case of the New York Election Board which has regularly split along direct partisan lines indicates what the future holds in store for political regulatory bodies such as California's Fair Political Practices Commission.

As for being 'non-political': impossible, given the kinds of issues the commissions are asked to resolve and the quite open recognition by the members of the commission of the political climate within which they must operate. Hence, we note the constant and open recognition of 'policy' questions, such as is reflected, for example, in California's lobbying regulations. And it is this concern with 'policy' that lies behind the use of administrative discretion so dear to the hearts of the reformers. Only in the ideology of the reformers which divides the world into the 'public' and the 'special interests', could the illusion of a non-political commission be maintained for long.

As for the 'independence' of such commissions, one can only marvel at the ability of the human mind to believe in the existence of such an animal in the face of over 75 years of experience with just such 'independent' regulatory bodies. In the case of the Fair Political Practices Commission, for example, it is obvious that they have been very effectively lobbied by the wealthy, powerful forces whose influence was, we were told, to be destroyed by this law. The rules on administrative lobbying – a particular concern of the big utilities and large corporate law firms – is just one example. The rule is undoubtedly very 'reasonable', especially inasmuch as it serves the function of preserving the law, but it is largely the result of the ability of such affected parties to represent themselves, very ably and very effectively, to the commission. The commissioners are, after all, hardly immune to an appeal which points out the disruptive effects of a given regulation on, for example, an important segment of the business community like the utilities. And they are no less sensitive to the reasoned appeal of the Bar Association – that segment of 'public opinion' whose views so perfectly mirror those of big business in California.

Political Reform: An Assault on Basic Rights

There is much more to say about the political regulatory commissions, especially about their enforcement and investigatory functions. For the present, however, I would like to conclude by pointing to what I believe is the larger significance of the creation of such regulatory agencies in politics.

The existence of an independent commission charged with the regulation of politics is an assault on First Amendment rights and political democracy. Interference by the state in political organization and activity is a step toward the practical negation of freedom of association.

The power given to the Fair Political Practices Commission and the Federal Election Commission is unprecedented and cannot be equated with the regulation of economic activity. To attempt to do so, as the present-day proponents of political reform have done, is to be led inexorably to the most anti-democratic conclusions. Speech and its effectuation in politics through freedom of association is constitutionally protected, or ought to be. It cannot be arbitrarily regulated or subjected to administrative rules by an agency of the state without trampling on democratic rights.

Using their discretionary powers, these commissions can oversee, control and investigate political activity hitherto outside the scope of any state regulatory body. Through administrative sanctions, based on often arbitrary or politically motivated rule-making powers, or through the prosecution of those who do not accede to their findings of wrong-doing, the penalties for which often entails substantial heavy fines, these commissions become arbiters over political activity (a kind of 'political police' as one reformer termed them) over a broad range of political activity. The possession and exercise of such arbitrary power is thus an invasion of basic democratic rights associated with the First Amendment.

The regulatory commissions created in the name of 'political reform' are a very large and very dangerous step toward the day when all political activity will be conducted under the supervision of an agency of the state. Such a development is consistent with the legal regulation of political parties which one proponent, Professor Leon Epstein, correctly describes as turning them into 'public utilities' – although the term 'public', in the Progressive-inspired lexicon of the reformers, conceals the reality that it is the *state* which is thereby brought into the political process.

Real political reform, in my view, requires the rejection of this anti-democratic strain in American politics. The task of those who understand how democratic rights in America are threatened by the encroachments of the military-bureaucratic state and by the all-pervasive power of big business, is to build the kind of mass-based, member-controlled political party which alone can offer a democratic alternative to the prevailing social and economic system.[2]

CHAPTER 7

'Common Cause': The Dangerous Lobby[1]

In the June 1974 primary election, Common Cause[2] showed itself to be a potent force in California politics. As a key sponsor of Proposition 9, the Political Reform Act, Common Cause could justifiably see itself as a Hercules cleansing California's political stables. San Diego attorney Michael Walsh, who as chairman of Common Cause headed the campaign for Proposition 9, was hailed by the Los Angeles *Times* as 'one of California's most influential political leaders'. After all, the Common Cause-sponsored Political Reform Act was the most sweeping law of its kind passed in any state, and it passed despite opposition from business, labour and most of the political establishment with the exception of Governor-to-be Jerry Brown.

To the leadership of Common Cause it seemed as if the organization's horizons were virtually unlimited. Its most important goal, the public financing of elections in California – toward which Proposition 9 had been seen as the preliminary step – appeared to be attainable. Common Cause's assets were impressive: more than 60,000 members in a state in which organized political parties are notoriously weak; a budget of nearly $200,000; an eight-person paid staff working out of its San Francisco headquarters; scores of volunteers, many of whom devoted full time to the organization; and the political capital gained from the Proposition 9 campaign. It was hard to fault Common Cause for its optimism.

Today, three years later, that optimism seems to have shrunk, as has Common Cause's membership, which is down to 45,000. The self-proclaimed citizens' lobby has seen its budget reduced by 25 per cent, while the entire state-wide organization has undergone a radical shake-up. Michael Walsh is no longer chairman, although he remains active on the national Common Cause board. His place has been taken by a relatively unknown Oakland attorney, Gary Sirbu. Scott Fitz-Randolph, the executive director hired in the wake of the 1974 victory, quit; long-time staffer and lobbyist David Arthur has resigned, and the board of more than 20 members has been replaced by a 'streamlined' group of eight. Most of the volunteers who made the San Francisco state headquarters a beehive of activity have disappeared with the closing of that office. The congressional district organizations, which some had hoped would develop into important local power bases for Common Cause, have been relegated to the more limited purpose of serving as the national organization's network to lobby Congress. Amid such turmoil, some of the top leadership now admit that prospects for the passage of public financing legislation in California are cloudy.

Walsh and Sirbu assert that the changes in Common Cause's operation in California, as well as in other states, are the result of a decision by Common Cause's national board to focus the organization's energies on the passage of federal legislation, such as public financing of congressional campaigns. There can be little doubt that the candidacy and election of Jimmy Carter were regarded by Common Cause leaders as an opportunity to secure national reform legislation which had not been possible during the Nixon–Ford years. Thus the triumph of an 'outsider' like Carter – which Common Cause hailed as proof of the success of its presidential finance law – was also seen as a victory for the policies of Common Cause, even though the organization did not and could not formally endorse him.

The emergence of Carter undoubtedly played an important role in the national Common Cause decision affecting the California organization, but the evidence at hand indicates that California Common Cause was already in decline. And there is some evidence that the whittling-down of the state operation was not at all unwelcome to the national leadership, which has always regarded Common Cause primarily as a national lobbying organization and which found itself worried about the possibilities of a runaway state or local leadership. For example, the attempt of California Common Cause to endorse Proposition 15, the anti-nuclear initiative, was aborted by the strenuous objections of the national staff.

The rapid reversal of fortune, which California Common Cause seems destined to share with a host of bygone political reform organizations, is rooted in the nature of such groups. First, their heterogeneous membership is unified and motivated behind a narrow range of clean-up-the-process issues. When such issues cease to be compelling – for whatever reason – the membership loses interest. As one wag commented, Common Cause is like a would-be surgeon who vigorously scrubs himself and his patient to ensure the highest standards of hygiene before surgery, but who, once the scrubbing is completed, is immobilized because he doesn't know how or where to operate.

Common Cause has manifested a second weakness characteristic of political reformers: the inability to grasp the connections between political cause and effect; a failure or unwillingness to think through the consequences of their proposed reforms. Proposition 9, the centerpiece of the recent reform movement, was hastily drafted by a coterie of attorneys from Common Cause and then-Secretary of State Brown's office. Uninformed about the history of reform in California, they drafted an initiative which would ostensibly clean up California government. However, as Ken Smith, director of the Proposition 9 campaign for Common Cause, later said, the drafters' overriding concern was for a statute that would stand up to a court challenge; the implications or consequences of the initiative measure were rarely discussed or considered. 'We wanted to get it out,' said Smith, because of the opportunity which Common Cause felt Watergate had given them to secure passage of reform legislation.

One major result of this haste is that Proposition 9, as one might expect with any extremely complicated measure drafted without benefit of the legislative process, has had a number of consequences which many of its sponsors did not anticipate. Judging by testimony before the Fair Political Practices Commission, a strong case can be made that the Political Reform Act has hindered grass-roots campaign activity and the activities of small, non-commercial 'public interest' lobbyists, while exercising negligible restraints on the well-financed candidates and lobbyists over whom the Reform Act was to have had control. There is bitter-sweet irony in the statement of a lobbyist for a large national corporation who notes, 'Proposition 9 is the best thing that ever happened to us because it gives us the opportunity to present our case on its merits to the legislators.' Proposition 9 may have curbed wining and dining by some lobbyists, but as one top former Common Cause staffer, who had himself played a key role in its passage, admitted in a recent interview, it has done little to affect the substance of political influence in Sacramento. What Proposition 9 did establish, much to the dismay of some of its initial supporters, is a large, sometimes unwieldy bureaucracy which operates as a kind of benevolent czar over California politics, but which could become a full-blown political control commission – a 'policeman' in politics, as Ed Koupal, the late chairman of the Peoples' Lobby, once described it.

The third flaw in the organization is structural. Common Cause might have been able to redirect some of its strength had it been able to more effectively tap the energy of some of its more active members. In addition to the short leash on which the national organization has always tried to keep the state organization, the most important factor preventing the emergence of a powerful organization has been its organizational character. The blunt truth is that despite its preachments about 'democracy' and 'participation', Common Cause is not itself an internally democratic organization. Even the chance for members to disagree with the organization's position on key issues is greeted negatively by some leaders. One top Common Cause staff worker suggests that any member who has significant policy differences with the reform group should quit, rather than try to work within the organization to change its direction. Another activist and board member acknowledges, 'You have to run this organization in a very autocratic way to make it function.' Rather than a functional strength, however, this lack of internal democracy has been an Achilles heel for Common Cause.

The Common Cause state board is not elected but is chosen by a selection committee appointed by the board chairman. In theory the board is guided by the issue preferences of California members who respond to a national Common Cause poll. In fact, some board members have never seen the poll results and state frankly that such results might well be ignored if they conflicted with what the appointed board members felt were their own priorities for the organization. In any case, a poll is not a substitute for democratic decision making. There is a contradiction in the fact that Common Cause, on the one hand, battles to open up the system and make democracy function through greater public participation and, on the other, runs its own organization as a benevolent autocracy with a very limited kind of participation for its own state members.

A fourth important factor associated with the decline of Common Cause surfaced some three years ago but was masked in the euphoria surrounding Proposition 9. Common Cause was the group most closely identified with the victory of Proposition 9 and essentially ran the campaign after the initiative qualified for the ballot. But with all of its presumed clout, Common Cause was unable to obtain even half of the signatures needed to qualify the political reform initiative. This role was assumed by the now semi-moribund Peoples' Lobby, an organization with only a handful of members but a mastery of the techniques of qualifying ballot initiatives. Common Cause, with a far larger membership, could not mobilize its own upper middle-class people, most of whom saw their 'memberships' as limited to an annual $15 contribution.

Given this litany of assorted but not well-recognized limitations, the Common Cause state leadership began, in 1975, to pursue its goal of partial public financing of elections. It already had lost six months in an internal reorganization which saw the departure of its competent director, Ken Smith. Partly because of strong opposition from various liberal groups, and partly because many legislators believed the proposed public financing bills were far too complex and unwieldy, the campaign stalled. Common Cause was even forced to oppose one bill for public financing because it contained strong pro-incumbent features.

Some members of the Common Cause leadership, like Robert Girard, the Stanford law professor who was chief drafter of Proposition 9 and the public financing bill, believed that the legislature would never pass a satisfactory bill. They began in late 1975 to press for a Common Cause initiative campaign which would go over the heads of a recalcitrant legislature.

The issue came to a head at a crowded board meeting at a San Francisco airport motel on 14 February 1976 – a day which some Common Cause members later called the 'Valentine's Day massacre' because of the stunning defeat which the leadership was dealt. The proposal was simple: Common Cause would put all of its energies into a petition campaign to qualify a public financing bill for the November 1976 ballot. Then came the shocker. Because time was short, it would be necessary to hire circulators or, as coordinator Al Haas sheepishly termed them, 'paid volunteers'. Someone shouted, 'You mean, "mercenaries",' and the battle was on. Haas, in a statement which must be rated as one of the most ironic admissions for an organization used to praising 'volunteers', put the case for the paid circulators:

> There must be no chance to fail and the only way to avoid the possibility of failure is to be … prepared to hire a corps of people who will work not when it is convenient – not the eight and a quarter hours per week that our volunteers will … Money can't buy everything, but I think that it's important

> for us to realize that there are some things that can't be achieved without money. That's particularly germane to us talking about campaign finance …

The phrase 'paid volunteer' became the battle cry of the opponents of the initiative campaign. Clara Link of Pasadena, a long-time member of the board, stated the case in terms consistent with the Common Cause ideology:

> I'm totally opposed to paying for signature gathering. As I understand it, Common Cause is a volunteer organization. We have paid staff, which we need, but I'm certainly against any mercenaries going out to gather signatures, and one of the main reasons is that it simply wipes out our vision of ourselves as a volunteer organization … Keep it volunteer, keep us clean. I don't want to be contaminated with paying any volunteers.

The clearest statement of the issue, from the standpoint of organizational necessity, was voiced by state board chairman Mike Walsh:

> I don't think if we are going to be a meaningful organization we are ever going to be anywhere but in the middle of high risk propositions … When I became chairman of this organization … we were into Proposition 9 and we had gotten into it without any kind of rational thought put forward … and what we did was, we said, 'we're going to scramble and we're going to do it' … If we pass a public financing omnibus measure in 1976 … we would in fact be an organization to be reckoned with politically in this state … I invite you to think long and hard about where in the hell this organization is going, and what we're going to do to really be worthy of the position we find ourselves in nationally and in this state, and that we don't succumb to the kind of thinking that requires 90 percent certainty in order to take substantial risks. Because we ain't going nowhere if that kind of philosophy is the essence of our being.

Despite Walsh, the board rejected the public financing initiative campaign by a vote of 15–6. His warning turned out to be prophetic: in 1976, a general election year, Common Cause's membership, income and activities declined. An unsuccessful public financing initiative campaign might well have turned out to be more disastrous for the organization; but without it there was nothing left for the California organization and membership to do, except to wait for a new opportunity in the legislature in 1977 or to return, once again, to its earlier subordinate role as the agent of the national organization's lobbying effort. Some indication of what might have happened if California voters had had the opportunity to vote on the question of public financing of elections can be seen in the overwhelming defeat of a public finance initiative in Oregon in 1976. One top Common Cause leader admits candidly that Common Cause made a conscious effort to keep news of the defeat, which was not widely reported, from their own members and the California public, not to mention the legislators.

Common Cause now faces a crisis. In the backlash of Watergate, the group essentially fulfilled its limited agenda of ostensibly increasing the openness and accountability of our legislative institutions. But openness or 'sunshine' issues are relatively non-controversial. As Watergate recedes into history, finding new issues will be no easy task. Already the California board is groping amidst a potpourri of 'process' issues, such as judicial reform, many of which have been bandied about by reformers for decades. It is doubtful whether a new agenda to hold the membership and attract media and public attention can be developed in the absence of a new series of scandals.

Political bosses of an earlier era rarely worried much about the impact of reforms. The bosses knew the reformers would get bored or disillusioned by their crusades and return to their upper middle-class pursuits. The bosses were eventually able to circumvent many of the reformers' roadblocks and even, frequently, turn them to their own advantage, because politics and the influence of what reformers call the 'special interests' is a more complex phenomenon than the good-government advocates realize. There are no old-fashioned bosses battling political reform in California or preventing Common Cause from pursuing its goals. Indeed, Common Cause tends to subvert its own reform ideology by confusing regulation of politics with correction of the fundamental problems of the political system.

So historians will probably remember Common Cause as that well-intentioned organization whose 'reforms' imposed a bewildering system of bureaucratic regulation upon the political process. It may be that a subsequent generation will have to undo these reforms, as the early twentieth-century California 'reform' of cross filing had to be undone in the 1950s.

In reacting to the malaise of American politics, Common Cause may have contributed to the problems it attempted to overcome, by imposing additional bureaucratic rigidity upon government and thereby further reducing its responsiveness to the people. As the distinguished political scholar Theodore Lowi noted, the legacy of reform is the bureaucratic state.

PART III

Theorists and Advocates

CHAPTER 8

Karl Mannheim: Turning Marx Upside Down

Karl Mannheim's ideas may not be as well known today as they were in the 1940s and 1950s, but as one of the most influential social thinkers and sociologists of the twentieth century his ideas are well worth reviewing today. Mannheim's contributions to the 'sociology of knowledge', the field most often associated with his name, provided if not a satisfactory systematic theory, provocative and suggestive ideas for much of the subsequent work in this area. His political sociology deeply influenced C. Wright Mills, reinforcing the deep political pessimism of *The Power Elite* while the theories of mass society and elites which dominated political sociology in the 1950s and 1960s also owed much to Mannheim. As a refugee in Britain in the late 1930s and throughout the war, Mannheim's intellectual influence was not inconsiderable, especially in the conservative 'Moot' group which had been inspired by T.S. Eliot's *Idea of a Christian Society* to seek ways to create a new elite in post-war Britain.[1]

In this chapter I focus upon Mannheim's intellectual development, particularly his contributions to the sociology of knowledge, in order to show how it underpinned his advocacy of a managerial or bureaucratically planned society presided over by a meritocratic elite which would combine intelligence and knowledge with power.[2] In this respect, Mannheim, like Clark Kerr, whose advocacy of 'the new slavery' is examined in the next chapter, is one of the key thinkers whose ideas fall, broadly speaking, into the ideology of bureaucratic, as contrasted with democratic, socialist, collectivism.[3]

Mannheim had a varied intellectual background, ranging from Marxism and 'left-wing Hegelianism' to the neo-Kantian tradition and historicism. The diversity of his intellectual forebears was, however, '... reflected in his eclecticism, and in a fundamental instability in his conceptual framework'.[4] For the purposes of a critical analysis of his theoretical framework, this eclecticism and lack of conceptual stability pose difficult problems. In seeking to lay out the essentials of Mannheim's thought, there is a danger either of presenting his concepts in a form far more consistent and logical than they really are, or of simply following Mannheim's various subtle twists and turns (many of them contradictory) to the point where logical analysis completely gives way and is replaced by mere description. Certainly Mannheim's own conception of 'methodology' aided this confusion. At one point, he noted that 'this instability in the definition of the concept is part of the technique of research, which might be said to have arrived at maturity and which therefore refuses to enslave itself to any one particular standpoint which would restrict its view'.[5]

In addition, while Mannheim did not completely reject the idea of formal theory, his overwhelming tendency was to regard his theory as an attempt to comprehend certain distinct, historically specific phenomena, and all of its propositions were attempts to deal with these. Even his abstract philosophical categories are socially and historically grounded. For this reason, it is difficult to deal with Mannheim's theory systematically without reference to substantive propositions.

Whatever consistency can be found in Mannheim's sociological theory, therefore, must stem from an awareness of his continuing concern with a substantive problem. The aim of this chapter is to show how Mannheim's successive theoretical positions posed difficulties for the understanding of his central problem, and how he attempted – successfully or not – to overcome these difficulties as his work developed.

Louis Wirth aptly characterized the main problem with which Mannheim tried to deal throughout his work when he wrote that, as a practical matter, Mannheim's sociology of knowledge had as its task that of 'inquiring into the prospects of rationality and common understanding in an era like our own that seems so frequently to put a premium upon irrationality and from which the possibilities of mutual understanding seem to have vanished'.[6]

The problem of rationality and of the conditions for the exercise of reason have been, of course, a main concern of Western social thought since the Enlightenment. Whereas the Enlightenment philosophers expressed their faith in unlimited progress based on increasing rationality, later thinkers came to question this Enlightenment faith, and to look into the specific social or moral conditions which affected the possible growth of rationality in the mass of humanity.

At the heart of the problem of the prospects for rational behaviour and thought is the question of objectivity and its possibilities. For if ordinary humans are unable – for whatever reason – to acquire an objective knowledge of the world, then the Enlightenment's vision of reason coming to rule in the affairs of society and democratic self-rule becomes a utopian vision. Various thinkers have attempted to resolve this problem. Among the greatest of them were Marx and Freud, who, each in their own manner, sought to establish the specific conditions under which either social or individual rationality was possible.[7]

Mannheim's attempt to provide an answer to the problem of rationality in the modern world led him to formulate a sociological theory of knowledge which aimed at the replacement of traditional epistemology. While we cannot deal fully with the epistemological questions which Mannheim posed, we will attempt to show why he posed them, and what kinds of solutions he attempted, from the standpoint of sociological theory.

In his later work, Mannheim came more and more to concentrate his attention upon the characteristics of modern industrial society and its social structure which affect the exercise of rationality and influence the possibility of an objective science. Gradually, Mannheim moved from a consideration of the problem of rationality on a philosophical level to one on a cultural and social level, but only in his later work did he attempt to assess the sources in the social structure of the process which had come to characterize the modern world. In short, what he had taken as a given in his earlier work, became a subject of analysis in what might be called Mannheim's 'political sociology'. One of our central concerns is to show how the 'sociology of knowledge' is inextricably linked to Mannheim's later political sociology.

The sociology of knowledge, in its most general form, raises the question of the existential bases of knowledge. The very raising of the question implies a view about reason and its functioning which is contrary to the simple rationalistic views of the Enlightenment. If social relations affect the ways people know the world, then the sources of error and of truth in idea systems are to be sought in the characteristics of groups and social strata, and not in the malfunctioning of an abstract 'reason'. Even the possibility of attaining objectivity in science becomes problematic, if not impossible, because the views of all individuals are necessarily rooted in different, and sometimes conflicting, 'frames of reference'. The seriousness of the problem depends, in large part, upon one's conception of the validation of knowledge.

To summarize: the direction in which Mannheim's successive theoretical solutions to the problem of rationality moves is from the philosophical plane to the sociological. By tracing the philosophical positions in Mannheim's theory it is possible to show they work into his 'sociology of knowledge', that is, the study of the source of the ideological superstructure in the 'underlying social reality'. The problem of objectivity in social thought, and in social science, comes into focus within Mannheim's political sociology as the problem of a 'scientific' and 'impartial' politics. Linking his theory of the sociology of knowledge with his specific ideas about the characteristics of modern society leads to a consideration of Mannheim's views of the problem of rationality and the possibility of democracy in modern society. Ultimately, it is to a new elite, whose final definition is ever elusive, that Mannheim looks for a way out of the impasse in which modern society finds itself. Democracy requires planning by a bureaucratic elite: 'planned freedom'. But the advent of this new kind of freedom 'does not mean that all earlier types of freedom must be abolished'.[8] Mannheim leaves open just which freedoms will have to go, thereby fully meriting Hayek's view of Mannheim as a collectivist ideologue on 'the road to serfdom'. As we shall show of Clark Kerr's ideas in Chapter 9, the advocacy of a 'new freedom' which 'goes hand in hand with the new slavery' is the hallmark of a deeply authoritarian and anti-democratic point of view, one for which Mannheim's ideas provide both theoretical clarification as well as political justification.

The Sociology of Knowledge

Mannheim's attack on the problem of objective perception of truth started not in sociology but in philosophy. Traditional epistemology, according to Mannheim, errs in assuming that it was possible to separate the acting, participating human being from the object of his perception.[9] To Mannheim, the problem is to search for a theory of knowledge which would take into account the fact that the individual is a member of society and of particular groups, which affects his or her way of looking at the world. Each group, or class, is possessed of a particular *Weltanschauung* which determines its particular mode of thought and its view of 'objective' facts.

Mannheim made a fundamental distinction between the problem of objectivity in natural science and that in social or cultural sciences. The error which Mannheim attributed to positivistic sociology, Paul Kecskemeti has written, is that it

> ... neglected the 'phenomenological' difference between the inanimate and the cultural historical world ... [Mannheim] was impatient to penetrate beyond the phenomenological surface to the very core of things, to the substance of historical reality which only the active fully committed subject was able to reach. This is the essence of Mannheim's sociology of knowledge ...[10]

Mannheim maintained that cultural objects cannot be treated by the methods of natural science because 'meanings' are involved in cultural objects which cannot be observed. Meaning can only be grasped within the total *Weltanschauung*. And, meaning itself is composed of three distinct strata: 'objective meaning', by which is meant the simple objective consequences of an act; 'expressive meaning', the interpretation of which '... always involves the task of grasping it authentically – just as it was meant by the subject, just as it appeared to him when his consciousness was focused upon it', and 'documentary meaning', which is not an 'intentional object' for the actor, but can only become an object for the observer.[11]

Thus throughout his criticism of the application of the methods of natural science to cultural matters, and throughout the elaboration of these distinctions, Mannheim was concerned with the problem of the interpenetration of the subject with the object of his perception. Yet, because of his rejection of the distinction between the two, he could not solve the problem of meaning, except in a relativistic fashion.

The conception of 'documentary meaning' brought Mannheim directly back to his critique of the application of natural science methods to cultural science, and illustrates the relativism inherent in his position:

> Unlike the other two types of interpretation, documentary interpretation has the peculiarity that it must be performed anew in each period, and that any single interpretation is profoundly influenced by the location within the historical stream from which the interpreter attempts to reconcile the spirit of a past epoch. This, however, does not mean that knowledge of this kind is relative and hence worthless. What it does mean is that the type of knowledge conveyed by natural science differs fundamentally from historical knowledge ... We should try to grasp the meaning and structure of historical understanding in its specificity, rather than reject it merely because it is not in conformity with the positivist truth-criteria sanctioned by natural science ... In historical understanding the nature of the subject has an essential bearing on the content of knowledge, and some aspect of the objects to be interpreted are accessible only to certain types of minds – the reason for this being precisely that historical understanding is not timeless like mathematical or scientific knowledge but is itself shaped by the historic process in self-reflection.[12]

The problem of 'meaning', the subjective motivations of the actors, was also faced by Max Weber, whose concept of *Verstehen* was elaborated to meet precisely this problem. Mannheim could not accept Weber's solution because of his radical relativistic position which stemmed from his criticism of traditional epistemology. He remarked, in a different context, that Weber's solution for the problem of impartiality in politics 'suffers from the assumption of the separability of theory and evaluation'.[13] That Mannheim himself rejected the possibility of such a separation has already been made clear.

It is important to note that at this stage of his intellectual development, Mannheim's terms have not yet become sociologically precise. However, the use of *Weltanschauung* and the 'spirit of the age' – even without reference to their 'connections', so to speak, to society – attests to the point that although Mannheim's starting place was on a philosophical plane, the direction his theoretical development carried him was toward the development of more concrete sociological concepts.

In Mannheim's theoretical structure, 'truth' itself becomes relativized. Mannheim rejected the idea that the individual is capable of attaining objective detachment from his or her social milieu. For Mannheim, this conflicted with his view that in cultural life there was an indivisible connection between the subject and object. His 'dynamic conception of truth and knowledge' and his rejection of the 'absolutism' of the method of natural science, led directly to the relativism which was to remain, no matter how much it was reformulated, at the core of his sociology of knowledge and was to influence profoundly his political sociology.

At this early stage, Mannheim had not yet developed the idea of 'relationism' through which he was later to attempt to escape the charges of relativism made against his sociology of knowledge. Yet, he was clearly groping in this direction, for he preferred a relativism 'which accentuates the difficulty of its task by calling attention to all those moments which tend to make the propositions actually discoverable at any given time, partial and situationally conditioned' to traditional epistemology which overlooked the 'way in which this situational condition enters into the structure and the evolution of knowledge'.[14]

To summarize thus far: Mannheim rejected the application of the methodology of natural science to historical and cultural knowledge and events. His alternative was to adopt a position in which truth was 'dynamically and historically determined' and the 'situational' determinant of propositions affected their validity.

It may be seen, for analytical purposes, that Mannheim confused two points in his theory. One is the question raised in his sociology of knowledge as to the existential bases of ideas, ideological systems and 'knowledge' in general. The psychological and sociological situation of the subject can be taken into account under this point, and the validity of the old, individualistic psychological assumptions of traditional epistemology can be questioned. The other question is whether 'truth' is an attribute of propositions, and not of 'things', and concomitantly, whether the 'logic' of scientific method can be separated from social and psychological influences. Had Mannheim not persisted in tying these two questions together, his sociology of knowledge as a theory might have escaped many difficulties. Merton notes that 'Mannheim acknowledges that the substantive results of *Wissenssoziologie* – which comprise the most distinctly rewarding part of the field – do not lead to his epistemological conclusions.'[15] True as this may be, it would still appear that his epistemological conclusions led to theoretical difficulties in Mannheim's sociology.

Mannheim's rejection of traditional epistemology and of the positivist method of natural science, and his counter-formulation of a theory of 'dynamic truth' led him directly to his concern with the sociology of knowledge. The sociology of knowledge was to replace epistemology as a way of assessing the truth-value of cultural and social knowledge. It would be a technique for overcoming the bias inherent in every point of view. Later on, in *Ideology and Utopia*, in trying to get out of his relativistic impasse, Mannheim saw the sociology of knowledge as a supplemental element to epistemology.

It is important to understand that the sociology of knowledge was itself, in Mannheim's view, a historical product, emerging at a particular time, under specific conditions. Thus, in a paradoxical manner, by a kind of 'dialectical' development, the very social conditions which set the problem of objectivity and challenged the simple Enlightenment view of the role of reason also made possible the sociological approach to knowledge and its problems. Sociology was the product of the development of modern society, for the breakdown of the feudal order brought with it a breakdown in the caste organization of knowledge.

Historically, then, Mannheim argued that the sociology of knowledge emerged as a result of:

> (1) the self-relativization of thought and knowledge; (2) the appearance of a new form of relativization introduced by the 'unmasking turn of mind'; (3) the emergence of a new system of reference, that of the social sphere, in respect of which thought could be conceived to be relative; and (4) the aspiration to make this relativization total, relating not one thought or idea, but a whole system of ideas, to an underlying social reality.[16]

The very process of relativization which made objectivity a problem produced its opposite in a Hegelian fashion. The sociology of knowledge as a historical product was based on 'previous stages' of development. As Merton notes, Mannheim derived certain of his basic conceptions of the sociology of knowledge from an analysis of the concept of ideology.[17] In *Ideology and Utopia*, Mannheim begins by distinguishing between the 'particular' conception of ideology and the 'total' conception. The 'particular' conception includes 'all of those utterances the "falsity" of which is due to an intentional or unintentional conscious, semi-conscious, or unconscious, deluding of one's self or of others, taking place on a psychological level and structurally resembling lies'. This conception of ideology is 'particular' because it does not attack the 'total mental structure of the asserting individual'. This is the 'unmasking turn of mind'. Subsequently, in an extension of the particular conception of ideology, the sociology of knowledge emerges

> ... and takes as its problem precisely this mental structure *in its totality*, as it appears in different currents of thought and historical social groups ... One sidedness of observation, which is not due to more or less conscious intent, will constitute the subject matter proper of the sociology of knowledge.[18]

A further refinement of the concept of ideology brought Mannheim to the 'general form of the total conception of ideology' which is distinguished from the 'special' form by the 'decisive question [of] ... whether the thought of all groups (including our own) or only that of our adversaries is recognized as socially determined'.[19] Thus, in Marxian thought, only the opponents' thought need be subjected to ideological analysis: this is the 'special' form of the total conception. But if one has the 'courage' to subject one's own viewpoint to ideological analysis, one arrives at the 'general' form. The general 'total' conception, Merton points out, 'leads at once, it would seem, to radical relativism with its familiar vicious circle in which the very propositions asserting such relativism are *ipso facto* invalid'.[20] Mannheim's endeavour to escape this dilemma led to his formulation of 'relationism'.

'Relationism,' according to Mannheim,

> does not signify that there are not criteria for rightness and wrongness in a discussion. It does insist, however, that it lies in the nature of certain assertions that they cannot be formulated *absolutely*, but only in terms of the perspective of a given situation.[21]

It should be obvious that Mannheim here was simply returning to his original epistemological starting point. For what is the opposite of the 'absolute' formulation if not some kind of 'relativistic' one?

The inescapable conclusion is that Mannheim, try as he might, could not escape a relativistic position. When he asks, as an example of the application of 'relationism', whether or not the 'truth or falsity' of a statement is established by its being imputed to 'liberalism or Marxism', his answer comes full circle to a relativistic position:

> Every complete and thorough sociological analysis of knowledge delimits, in content as well as in structure, the view to be analyzed. In other words, it attempts not merely to establish the existence of the relationship, but at the same time to particularize its scope and the extent of its validity ... The relational process tends to become a particularizing process, for one does not merely relate the assertion to a standpoint but, in doing so, restricts its claim to validity which at first was absolute, to a narrower scope.[22]

All of the references to 'absolute' claims to validity and to 'particularization' come down to the same thing. That is, Mannheim was unable to see statements as either true or false, and was forced to an untenable position in his sociological theory of knowledge. His conception of validity, at this point, is very close to a pragmatic one which posits that truth-value is an attribute of action and its fulfilment.

Thus far, Mannheim had established that the 'sociology of knowledge' is itself a historically determined product. In a dialectical process, the very forces which make objectivity and rationality problematic in the modern world also produce the sociology of knowledge which would enable men to overcome the partial views of particular groups or strata. With his concept of the 'general' form of the total conception of ideology, Mannheim saw all modes of thought – even one's own – to be socially determined and hence susceptible to partiality. His efforts to extricate himself from the relativistic implications of this idea, through the concept of 'relationism' came to very little.[23] The consequence is that the realization of an objective knowledge of the world would seem to be even more improbable.

The Existential Bases of Knowledge

How Mannheim attempted to solve the problem brings our analysis, at the point, to a consideration of the 'existential bases' of knowledge. In the course of this discussion, it will be possible to see how Mannheim was forced to resort to, in his later work, the *deus ex machina* of the 'socially unattached intellectuals' in order to rescue objectivity from its hopeless position.

There are two interrelated propositions about the 'existential determinants' of knowledge which, when considered, will enable us to better understand how

Mannheim early laid the theoretical groundwork for the emergence of the special role of the intelligentsia, and to see how his political sociology was a direct function of his concerns in the sociology of knowledge. The first proposition concerns the location of the 'existential bases' of mental products; the second concerns the relationship between the mental productions and their existential bases.[24]

To the extent that he participated in the Marxian tradition, Mannheim took as a basic point in the structure of his theory the view that social class based upon the relations to the means of production was the decisive source of variation in the ideological or mental superstructure. While he gradually came to modify his position greatly, social class remained the ultimate source of ideational differentiation.

In *Ideology and Utopia*, Mannheim postulated that in tracing the 'origin and diffusion of a certain thought-model' one would find '... the peculiar affinity it has to the social position of given groups and their manner of interpreting the world'. He rejected the idea, which a 'dogmatic' Marxism would hold, that class *alone* is the existential foundation of 'thought-models'. Rather, he stated,

> By these groups we mean not merely classes ... but also generations, status groups, sects, occupational groups, schools, etc. Of course, we do not deny that of all of the above mentioned social groupings and units class stratification is the most significant, since in the final analysis, all the other social groups arise from and are transformed as parts for the more basic conditions of production and domination.[25]

Thus, even while extending the existential bases to vaguely-defined groups, Mannheim clung to the Marxian view of the class structure as the fundamental social datum of a sociology of knowledge. Yet, the second query forces itself upon Mannheim's theory at this point; it becomes imperative to discover the 'connections', the precise ways, in which the mental products are related to the existential base.

In his earliest work, as we have seen, Mannheim had tried to make the vague notion of *Weltanschauung* do service as a way of getting at the connection between ideation and social base.[26] *Weltanschauung*, in one form or another, never disappeared from his conceptual apparatus; yet it always remained at the level of assertion without a demonstration of the concrete mechanisms whereby social groups could be related to their particular forms of knowledge.

In his first attempt to apply concretely his conception of the sociology of knowledge, Mannheim utilized, from art history, the notion of 'styles' of thought. He contended that in human thought, as in art, 'there are different schools of thought distinguishable by the different ways in which they use different thought patterns and categories'.[27]

At this point, however, Mannheim introduced a distinction which was of crucial importance in the development of his entire theoretical structure – both in the sociology of knowledge and political sociology. Thus far, Mannheim had not succeeded in solving the problem of the 'connections' between group and idea. As we pointed out previously, the Marxian solution was unsatisfactory to him because he felt it simply deduced the 'connections' *a priori* from the position of a social class in the relations of production. The distinction has importance not only for the problem of 'connections' but also for the understanding of the origins of his concept of the role of 'the socially unattached intelligentsia'. Mannheim stated that:

> ... in establishing correlations between products of the mind and social strata, we must distinguish between intellectual and social stratification. We can define social strata, in accordance with the Marxian concept of class ... but it is impossible, in our opinion, to establish a historical parallelism between intellectual standpoints and social strata defined in this fashion. Differentiation in the world of the mind is much too great to permit the identification of each current, each standpoint, with the given class. Thus we have to introduce an intermediary concept to effect a correlation between the concept of 'class' defined in terms of roles in the production process, and that of 'intellectual strata'. We mean by 'intellectual stratum' a group of people belonging to a certain social unit and sharing a certain 'world postulate' (as parts of which we may mention the economic system, the philosophical system, the artistic system 'postulated' by them), who at a given time are 'committed' to a certain style of economic activity and of theoretical thought.[28]

It may easily be seen how Mannheim's 'intermediate concept' seriously affects his theoretical structure. For if there is 'intellectual stratification', what is the meaning of social stratification? And what is the relationship between intellectual and social stratification? In any case, it can be seen how it was easy, later on, for Mannheim to utilize the intelligentsia – the non-class – as a *deus ex machina* to solve the problem of objectivity. The significance of the whole idea of the 'intermediate strata' of intellectuals for the query about the relationship or connectors between existential bases and mental production is obvious. By one stroke, Mannheim attempted to answer the question: the link resides in a special group of men whose *function* is the production of ideas for various classes, parties and groups. If it is the intellectual's product with which we deal, then to know how the product is related to the base, we can examine their relationship to it and come up with a satisfactory answer.

In the essay, 'Conservative Thought', written immediately after the essay from which the previous statement is quoted, Mannheim made it very clear that he was dealing with the intellectual strata which emerged with the rise of the bourgeoisie. These are the 'ideologues'. The romantic movement, he asserted, had as its chief exponents, the 'socially unattached intelligentsia'.[29]

Mannheim used the term 'committed' to link the intellectual strata with a particular style. 'Committedness' is contrasted to vulgar Marxian 'economic determinism' which directly associates 'the most esoteric and spiritual products of the mind with the economic and power interests of a certain class'. Motivation by interests is valid 'only where interests actually can be seen at work, and not where mere "commitment" to a *Weltanschauung* exists'.[30]

What links the intellectual standpoint with a particular social class? This is achieved, according to Mannheim, by finding out '... the correlation between a "style of thought" underlying a given standpoint, and the intellectual motivation of a certain social group'.[31]

The obvious difficulty is that the use of such terms as 'committedness' and 'correlation' simply do not go beyond the level of a figure of speech, and give no clue as to the sociological or socio-psychological relationship between the intellectual strata, the style and the social group or class. Merton, in a detailed analysis of the different kinds of 'connections' between society and knowledge which Mannheim developed, comes to the conclusion that Mannheim completely failed to specify the 'type or mode of relations between social structure and knowledge'.[32] The foregoing analysis, as can be seen, is in agreement with Merton's judgment. But by tracing the development of Mannheim's attempt to solve this theoretical problem, it has been possible to lay the groundwork for an understanding of the emergence of Mannheim's political sociology and his attempt to ground his study of the problem of rationality in the social structure of modern society.

In *Ideology and Utopia*, this aspect of Mannheim's work first emerged. He evaluated the role of 'ideology' and 'utopia' as two contrasting orientations to the world, and their meaning for objectivity. He concluded that neither the 'ideological' not 'utopian' points of view hold promise for objectivity, and that no one social class, in contrast to Marx's view, is the bearer of reason within the modern world. It is in this context that the role of the 'socially unattached intellectuals' is clearly related to the function of the sociology of knowledge.

The ideological outlook is one which 'conceals the present by attempting to comprehend it in terms of the past',[33] while the utopian outlook 'transcends the present and is oriented to the future'. Both 'ideology' and 'utopia' are 'situationally transcendent' or unreal ideas 'because their contents can never be realized in the societies in which they exist, and because one could not live and act according to them within the limits of the existing social order'.[34] Thus, the 'attempt to escape ideological and utopian distortions is, in the last analysis, a quest for reality'.[35] Ideologies never succeed *de facto* in the realization of their projected goals, while utopias are not ideologies to the extent that they 'succeed through counteractivity in transforming the existing historical reality into one more in accord with their own conceptions'.[36] Mannheim noted that ideas which are 'adequate' (that is, correspond to the existing social order) and which are 'situationally congruous' (that is, do not transcend reality) are 'relatively rare and only a state of mind that has been sociologically fully clarified operates with situationally congruous ideas and motives'.[37] Note the role assigned here to sociology – and sociologists. Sociology embodies the consciousness of its own relativity and is thus capable of objectivity.

Since the term 'ideology' as commonly used implied 'falsification' – although for Mannheim it had no such 'moral or denunciatory intent' – Mannheim concluded that it would be best to instead 'speak of the "perspectives" of a thinker. By this term we mean the subject's whole mode of conceiving things as determined by his historical and social setting.'[38] The important point here for our purposes is that Mannheim related his categories to specific classes or groups in society and made their 'perspective' process. This was a much more explicitly sociological way of approaching the problem than, say, in terms of the subject's 'world view'.

Mannheim Against Marx

Once having disposed of the idea that either the ideological or the utopian mentality were capable of being the bearer of reason in society, Mannheim needed only to come to grips with the position of one of his central intellectual progenitors, Marx, in order to clear the way for the central role of the socially unattached intelligentsia in modern society.

For Marx, the dilemma of relativism is shattered by a decisive historic event: the appearance in society of a class whose angle of vision is precisely that of the universal, rather than that of the fragmentary, which is driven by the conditions of its class existence to represent, not a distorting self-interest and self-image of reality, but the needs, the interest, of humanity as a whole. In Mannheim's system, the Marxian view represents the 'special' form of the total conception of ideology, for it refuses to relativize itself.

Mannheim rejected Marx's way of solving this theoretical dilemma. In the 'general' total conception of ideology, as was shown earlier, all points of view are relativized. The working class, for Mannheim, does have some of the historical attributes at the beginning of its historical struggle, which Marx attributed to it. At this point, the class is literally without a self-interest since it is excluded from a significant participation in society. Because of this, it gives rise to radical critiques, to utopias, which are a fundamental challenge to the status quo and which call for the total transformation of political and economic relationships and the establishment of a classless society. But this process does not, according to Mannheim, continue to deepen and develop toward an actual revolution in the interest of humanity as a whole. Rather, '... to the extent that Marxian proletarian groups rise to power, they shake off the dialectical elements of their theory and begin to think in the generalizing methods of liberalism and democracy, which seek to arrive at universal laws'.[39] That is, their ability to perceive truth and the mechanism of social knowledge alters in correspondence with a shift as a class within the social structure. Partial victories lead to the incorporation of the working class and make the ultimate victory much less imperative. It is only those national working classes who still have to resort to revolution who cling to the 'dialectical' element.

Mannheim argued against Marx that the working class becomes more of a class in the traditional sense (narrow self-interest; functional self-delusion) as it carries on its battle. Rather than becoming a bearer of an eventual classless 'objectivity' and the goal of a rational society, and thereby overcoming its alienation, it becomes just another class among classes with its own need for justifying its gains against other elements in the society. Consequently, the problem of transcending the relativism of a truth which develops in history through social classes remains unsolved.

Mannheim attempted to resolve the dilemma through reference to the position of the intellectuals in the social structure. He takes as a fact the intellectual's own claim of their classlessness in order to distinguish between intellectual and social stratification, thereby giving to the socially unattached intelligentsia the role of an 'intermediary concept' between class and style. For Mannheim, the classlessness of the intellectuals is not incipient or eventual (as was Marx's vision of the classlessness of the working class), but immediate and realized. Their existence opens up the possibility of discovering an objective angle of vision in society, here and now. Intellectuals exist within the interstices of the social structure, which allows them a peculiar 'perspective' toward the world. They are a platform, so to speak, upon which society can stand in order to achieve an objective view of the real world and to create rational social order.

Rationality in the Age of Equalization

How did it come about, Mannheim asks in *Ideology and Utopia*, that in the modern world people 'talk past one another'? His answer is that as the masses of the people enter into public life, there has occurred an 'age of equalization'. People talk about concrete issues with one another, but while they believe they are concerned with the same subject matter, actually the very meaning which they assign to it differs according to the various 'frames of reference' within which it is viewed. This is an 'inevitable phenomenon of the age of equalization'.[40]

In previous ages there were only closed groups which came in contact with each other; each recognized its particular place in the hierarchical social structure. In the age of equalization, however, the formal barriers between groups have disappeared, giving rise to the illusion of a commonality of existence. But such commonality is only an illusion which only the development of the sociology of knowledge can address.

The role of the sociology of knowledge in an 'age of equalization' is to seek to

> overcome the 'talking past one another' of the various antagonists by taking as its explicit theme of investigation the uncovering of the sources of the partial disagreements which would never come to the attention of the disputants

> because of their preoccupation with the subject matter that is the immediate cause of the debate.[41]

Mannheim's faith in the sociology of knowledge and its ability to overcome bias and to resolve disagreement and conflict is very much like the belief of the rationalistic Enlightenment philosophers in the efficacy of education as the means for overcoming irrationality, and as the way for reason to rule in the affairs of men. The sociology of knowledge and the socially unattached intellectuals who are its bearers, are, in Mannheim's theory, what education by an elite and the model of naturally rational man are to Enlightenment social theory. In short, they are an effort to escape the relativistic premises of his theory, and to offer a way out of the dilemma in which rationality and objectivity are placed by its implications. It is interesting to note that it is Mannheim's assertion of the role of the sociology of knowledge which leads otherwise critical commentators like Kecskemeti to conclude that Mannheim's sociology of knowledge is misunderstood as a variety of 'scepticism and illusionism', and that his

> purpose was not to demonstrate the inescapability of a relativism and scepticism, but rather the thesis that in spite of the inescapability of certain relativist conclusions, genuine knowledge of historical and social phenomena was possible ... participation in the social process ... renders one's perspective partial and biased ... [but it] also enables one to discover truth of deep human import.[42]

Be this as it may, the adequacy of the solution is not established by reference to Mannheim's purpose. The creation of the *deus ex machina* of the sociology of knowledge and the social role of the intelligentsia does not extricate Mannheim from the sceptical implication of his theory. That Mannheim himself recognized this dilemma and its unsatisfactory solution is demonstrated by the later stages of his theory (and political program) in which the socially unattached intellectuals and their role are replaced by a theory of 'elites' which (desirably) are, if anything, firmly attached to the social structure.

In *Ideology and Utopia*, Mannheim stressed that the 'decisive fact of modern times' is the emergence of a 'free intelligentsia':

> Its chief characteristic is that it is increasingly recruited from constantly varying social strata and life situations, and that its mode of thought is no longer subject to regulation by a caste-like organization. Due to the absence of social organization of their own, the intellectuals have allowed those ways of thinking and experiencing to get a hearing which openly competed with one another in the large world of the other strata ... In this process the intellectual's illusion that there is only one way of thinking disappears.[43]

A new 'synthesis' is called for because of the nature of the times; the lack of agreement among people and the partial nature of all views threaten to break down whatever remains of concord and reason in society. But, for the first time, a science of politics is possible. It will not be just a 'party science, but a science of the whole'.[44]

The political and social bearers of this synthesis must have an 'experimental outlook' and be 'unceasingly sensitive to the dynamic nature of society and to its wholeness'. Such an outlook is not likely to be developed by a class occupying a middle position, but Mannheim noted, only by a '*relatively* classless stratum which is not too firmly situated in the social order'.[45] The 'socially unattached intelligentsia' (from Alfred Weber) constitute such a class. At this point Mannheim returns to a discussion of the Marxian theory of social class in order to point out the phenomenon of the unattached intellectuals cannot be comprehended within the framework of that theory. In Marxian theory, intellectuals are either members or appendages of a class.[46] In Mannheim's view, there is, instead, a 'new basis of association' which, while it does not overcome the class and status of the individual, does result in a class placed between classes but not forming a middle class.[47]

Note how this last formulation is a development of Mannheim's earlier distinction between 'intellectual' and 'social' stratification. Then, 'intellectual' stratification was a way of creating an 'intermediary concept' between social class as a role in the system of production and 'intellectual standpoint', or the products of the mind. Now, however, what was an abstract 'concept' becomes a concrete sociological phenomenon – a 'relatively classless stratum'. From the standpoint of systematic theory, the fact that Mannheim did not abandon or even revise his essentially Marxian theory of social class, but simply let it rest side-by-side with a phenomenon which does not fit into its framework and perhaps even contradicts its basic premises, is evidence of his inconsistency. It suggests that the concrete sociological phenomenon remained more of an abstract, metaphorical concept than Mannheim would have liked to admit.

Mannheim's conception of a 'relatively classless stratum' is contrary not only to his version of the Marxian theory of social class, but also, as we have pointed out, to his relativism. That is, the intelligentsia are simply exempted from the operation of relativism and bias. Mannheim's elaborate explanation of this solution was apparently unsatisfactory to him, for in an essay written just before he departed from Germany in 1933, and after the German edition of *Ideology and Utopia* had appeared, he subjected the concept of the 'socially unattached intelligentsia' to sociological scrutiny and found that the 'main drift' of modern society has its effect upon them just as upon all other groups.[48]

This conclusion is developed in his once influential, but now largely forgotten, book, *Man and Society in an Age of Reconstruction*, in which Mannheim moved to a consideration of the changes in the social structure which made for the very conditions that he, in a sense, had taken for granted at the beginning. The lack of communication, the prevalence of ideological thinking had been a given in his sociology of knowledge. The proclivity of modern society for irrationality and bias had remained, analytically speaking, more or less at the level of assertion.

The discussion of 'scientific politics' in *Ideology and Utopia*, however, foreshadowed this concern.

Rationality in Bureaucratic Society

In his essay on 'The Problem of the Intelligentsia', Mannheim returned to his thesis about the special role of the intelligentsia. Its rise, he reiterated,

> marks the last phase of the growth of social consciousness. The intelligentsia was the last group to acquire the sociological point of view, for its position in the social division of labour does not provide direct access to any vital and functioning segment of society.[49]

Mannheim's explanation of the intelligentsia's characteristics is essentially the same as his earlier one. The intellectual's 'tendency to question and seek rather than to affirm becomes its permanent trait', once its compact organization is abandoned. In a dialectical fashion, the same process – the self-relativization of thought – which gives birth to the problem of objectivity and relativism (thesis), also gives rise to the sociology of knowledge based on the 'growth of social consciousness' (antithesis). Its resolution (synthesis) is through the intelligentsia and their role in 'scientific politics'.[50]

However, Mannheim pointed out, the inevitable tendency of modern society toward bureaucratization and large-scale organization *also* affects the socially unattached intelligentsia: 'The existence of the outsider in a highly institutionalized society, such as ours is, is more precarious and more trying.'[51] Even the very intellectual and educational training which makes the intelligentsia an independent and relatively classless group, even when 'attached' to some class, is itself becoming more and more a mass education and fitted to the needs of modern bureaucratic society. The narrow training received in educational institutions leads to a 'bureaucratic mentality' which does not seek and question.[52] In *Man and Society*, Mannheim explains this in terms of the 'proletarianization' of the intellectuals. He asserts that this development is dysfunctional even for bureaucracy, and that it should be possible to educate officials so as to allow them to retain their 'initiative and capacity to invent'.[53]

Whatever the effectiveness of an improved educational system (and Mannheim was to lay great stress on education in his later political work) Mannheim's theoretical dilemma is complete. He recognized that there was rationality and objectivity in the modern world – indeed, if he was to assign any objective validity to his own work and not relativize it to the point of meaningless, he had to admit this. Yet, the postulate of the socially unattached intelligentsia as the bearers of a new synthesis, simply had not held up under 'empirical' examination. It was necessary for Mannheim to come up with a new kind of theoretical explanation.

In *Man and Society*, Mannheim turned to the problem of considering how the social structure of modern bureaucratized society affects rationality. As at the very beginning of his work on the assumptions of traditional epistemology, he challenged the psychological assumptions of the 'Age of Reason'.[54] The very question raised by the Enlightenment about the role rational reflection and irrationality play in human affairs must be re-opened. The 'recent experience with the power of the irrational' can give little support of the Enlightenment's belief in the inevitable progress of reason.[55]

The crucial event in the modern world, according to Mannheim, is the entrance of previously excluded classes into public life.[56] It is this shift from a closed, static society to a mobile, dynamic and democratic one, which undermines even the special ability of the intelligentsia to be relatively bias-free. The term which Mannheim used to designate this process – 'fundamental democratization' – is obviously essentially the same as his 'age of equalization'. The consequence of the fundamental democratization of society is that the irrationality of the masses is injected into public life. In the old, limited democracies, rationality and power had co-existed within the same elite groups. The irrationality of the masses is due to their exclusion from power and the lack of proper training, but also to changes within the social structure itself.[57]

Mannheim postulated yet another 'principle': the 'fundamental interdependence' of modern society. The greater interdependence of the parts of society means that the whole of modern society is much more vulnerable to outbursts of irrationality in any one area.[58]

These, then, according to Mannheim, are the central characteristics of the modern social structure, of 'mass society', which are the setting for the problem of the exercise of rationality. Mannheim then makes a basic distinction between types of 'rationality':

1. *Substantial rationality* – an act of thought is substantially rational if it '... reveals intelligent insight into the inter-relations of events in a given situation'. 'Substantial irrationality' refers to everything else, which is either false or not an 'act of thought at all'.[59]

2. *Functional rationality* – in this type of rational action, a

> series of actions is organized in such a way that it leads to a previously defined goal, ... Whether a series of actions is functionally rational or not is determined by two criteria: (a) Functional organization with reference to a definite goal; and (b) a consequent calculability when viewed from the standpoint of an observer or a third person seeking to adjust himself to it.[60]

Anything which disrupts the relationship between the series of actions and the goal is functionally irrational: 'The term ... never characterizes an act in itself, but only with reference to its position in the entire complex of conduct of which it is a part.'[61]

Substantial rationality corresponds to the ideal of 'reason' in classical liberal political theory. Functional rationality, on the other hand, simply refers to a kind of means–end chain, a purely technical relationship, which has no normative content. It is in this sense that we speak of the 'rationalization' of industry.

The bureaucratization of society and the growth of large-scale economic enterprise, underlie the tendency toward increasing functional rationality. However, in contrast to both liberal and Marxian hopes, functional rationalization works to paralyze, and not foster, substantial rationality.[62] The individual who lives his or her life now within functionally rationalized organizations loses the capacity for intelligent insight into the overall structure of relationships within society.

The net effect, then, of functional rationalization or the bureaucratization of society is to deprive the individual of the capacity for rational judgement, while at the same time making this capacity the exclusive property – potentially – of the elites who direct or organize this process of rationalization and who stand at the very pinnacles of society. They are enabled by their position in the society to see the 'major structural connections', the *Gestalt*, of modern society. Substantial rationality comes to reside, more or less exclusively, in the persons of the managers or elite of society.

But note now: it is the characteristic of being firmly anchored, so to speak, in strategic or key positions in the social structure which allows the individual to exercise rational judgement. The socially unattached intelligentsia who played a central role in Mannheim's theory, are now subjected to the same forces which make for an inability to exercise intelligent insight into the structure of society, for other groups. The estrangement of the intellectuals from major social groups turns out to be a characteristic of a particular historical period – that of liberal democracy.[63] Of course, this shift is due not to any theoretical re-evaluation on Mannheim's part, but an assessment of the actual state of present-day society. As such, this empirical question does not concern us here. Yet it is important. It allows us to see that as Mannheim turned to an analysis of actual social forces, he was compelled to locate rationality within specific social institutions and structures; this is the significance of his distinction between substantial and functional rationality. With this distinction, the rejection or critique of the naive views of the 'Age of Reason' and of liberal philosophy need not rest upon a relativistic notion of validity, but upon an appreciation of the actual sources of rationality or irrationality in society.

Conclusion

Mannheim in his later work no longer explained the dilemma of reason and the problem of objectivity in modern society in terms of a theoretical position which made the validity of all propositions and points of view relative to the time and place of their origins, hence making them necessarily biased. The explanation of these phenomena in terms of specific institutional and structural characteristics of society constituted, it would seem, an advance over Mannheim's previous theoretical position. It now became possible to explain the sources of irrationality or rationality within society without reverting to a class or category essentially outside the workings of society. Given this approach, the problems of objectivity and the role assigned to reason in human affairs become sociological and scientific ones, unencumbered by a dubious relativistic conception of validity.

Viewed from the standpoint of the latter, as I have tried to show throughout this essay, there is only one solution to the problem of bias and partiality: the creation of a *deus ex machina*, in the form of a new ruling class, one which is excluded from the very operation of the laws which have been postulated as fundamental or basic to the system. Mannheim's solution is of a piece with utopian thinking throughout the ages: a class of Platonic Guardians is needed who transcend, whether because of their innate characters or because of the special nature of their upbringing, the societal forces which shape ordinary people. In this respect, the title of 'bourgeois Marxist' given to Mannheim is well deserved. For Mannheim change can only come from above, from an elite, while for Marx, the anti-utopian, the key is a movement from below in which the self-activity of the working class allows it to transform itself even as it transforms society.

But from the point of view of the former – the sociological and scientific approach – it becomes possible to treat the problem as one which has determinate social and historical roots. Thus, the partiality and bias of different social groups, and the irrationality which characterizes modern society is located not in a theory of knowledge – even a 'sociological' theory of knowledge – but in the features of mass society with its vast bureaucratic structures. Specific propositions about the effect of these features on rationality are amenable to empirical sociological investigation, and may be accepted or rejected according to their validity.

Mannheim thereby abandoned, though not explicitly and not in a systematic manner, the relativism of his earlier work. By subjecting what he had taken as given or had merely asserted to sociological assessment, he was able to make a more substantial contribution to the theoretical understanding of the sources of reason and un-reason and the possibilities of objectivity than his earlier work had given promise of.

Theoretically and politically, Mannheim's development of the concepts of functional and substantive rationality provide a fertile framework for characterizing the bureaucratization of society and an insight into the premises of those who are its advocates. The intersection of these concepts with Marx's theory of alienation is taken up in Chapter 9.

CHAPTER 9

Alienation and the New Slavery

Any serious student of Marx who attempts to discuss the idea of 'alienation' finds him or herself in the curious position of writing about a term so widely and variously used, even (or especially) in connection with the name of Marx, that the temptation to avoid the task altogether is, at times, almost overwhelming. 'Alienation' has become the latest academic cottage industry and even an official government report has proclaimed the 'alienation' of the American working class which it proposes to solve in a manner consistent with the greater productivity and profits of American capitalism.[1]

What then can be the possible value of yet another essay on alienation? The market has been flooded with books and essays, a few of which are serious contributions to social theory or the history of social thought, but the overwhelming majority of which are filled with maudlin, often incoherent, cries about 'the human condition'.[2] One cannot help but fear that whatever is written on this topic will only add to the confusion and perhaps even be co-opted by the busy entrepreneurs of Alienation Alley.

Nevertheless, it would be intellectually and politically irresponsible if the idea of alienation were to be left to its present academic exploiters who, although they may genuflect in the direction of Marx, have succeeded in stripping it of its original revolutionary meaning and analytical value and transformed it into a harmless sigh about the alienation of everybody, everywhere, all of the time.

The reason for the resurgence of interest in the idea of alienation is, of course, more serious than the careerist designs of academics. The rise of an anti-Stalinist opposition in Eastern Europe, the revolutionary working-class upheavals against the self-styled Communist regimes and the development of a new interest in Marxism in the West all have led to a search for a political and theoretical basis for a democratic and genuinely humanist socialism and it is in the course of this that 'alienation' has come to the fore. However, neither the radicals who adopt alienation in order to depoliticize Marx out of a well-intentioned but misguided belief that the 'old' Marx is somehow responsible for the authoritarian anti-democratic developments within the left in the twentieth century, nor the academics who co-opt alienation in an effort to make capitalism more humane and, not accidentally, more profitable, can lay legitimate claim to the concept of alienation as Marx – young or old – developed it in the course of his political evolution.

For the most part, the discussion about alienation has revolved around the debate given its widest currency by Daniel Bell in his essay, 'Two Roads from Marx', which appeared in *The End of Ideology* – itself the symptom of a disenchantment with radicalism – over the supposed contradiction between the views of the 'young' and the 'old' Marx, that is, between the Marx of the *Economic and Philosophic Manuscripts of 1844*, and the Marx of *Capital*.[3]

Necessarily, but at the same time unfortunately, the efforts of Bell's critics have been directed to establishing the by-now irrefutable point that the concept of 'alienation' and/or 'estrangement' is to be found in Marx's later work and that it indeed forms an essential element in his analysis of the nature of capitalist society.[4] This emphasis upon the essential continuity of Marx's thought, however, although generally correct, has focused exclusively on philosophical and theoretical aspects to the exclusion of a consideration of Marx's revolutionary political ideas. Not surprisingly, thus, both the academic and New Left writers have tended to ignore or at least not take seriously Marx's view of the role of the working class in the struggle for socialism. For these reasons, then, even the best of these critics have tended to obscure Marx's intellectual and political development, even to the point of denying that there are any real differences between the young and the old Marx.

However laudable and however correct this emphasis may be under the circumstances, it must be said that this somewhat apologetic attempt to assimilate the mature Marx to the young and not-yet-Marxist Marx of the *Manuscripts* not only does violence to the facts, but far more importantly does not adequately answer the real thrust of Bell and his co-thinkers: the proposition that the seeds of authoritarian degeneration in socialism – Stalinism – are to be found in Marx's mature writings. Merely to point to Marx's continuing humanism and his deep attachment to democracy leaves the argument on the weak plane of morality and good intentions which, even if they were Marx's, are hardly sufficient grounds for arguing against Bell's conclusions.

Simply put, this is unfortunate because it needlessly abandons the strong theoretical argument forged by Marx out of the original notion of alienation – an argument in which, in contrast to his utopian predecessors as well as to the 'young' Marx, a theoretical solution was found to link socialism with democracy.

Rather than merely expanding upon what others have done with varying degrees of success, I want to go back to Bell's original essay to show that the question it raises about Marx is a fundamental one that cannot be ignored or evaded merely by demonstrating that the *Grundrisse* contains explicit references to alienation or that the theoretical structure of *Capital* is incomprehensible without it. At the same time, I shall show that Marx neither abandoned the concept of alienation nor did he fail to add to it, bringing it down to earth from its Hegelian origins and sloughing off its mystical elements. To affirm the 'essential continuity' of Marx's thought, then, is not to deny that Marx developed beyond his early views.

Rather it is important to stress that too much attention has been paid to the use of the term and the question of its presence in the later Marx while ignoring the way in which Marx's ideas changed and, without abandoning the original impulse, broadened in their comprehension of the roots and solution to 'alienation' in modern capitalist society.

Apart from this very important theoretical value, the examination of Marx's views on the relationship between the overcoming of alienation and the achievement of a democratic collectivist social order serves another and no less important purpose. It provides a clear basis for understanding an essential theoretical and political difference between Marx's views and those of the large family of authoritarian socialisms which range from the Utopian predecessors of Marx, through the American-as-apple-pie anti-capitalist doctrines of an Edward Bellamy and down to the present-day expressions of 'technocratic' or 'managerialist' doctrines espoused by many of those who consider themselves socialists as well as by many nominal liberals who are discovering the future and liking what they see. (It is a special irony that the slightly younger Daniel Bell, who takes Marx to task for having allegedly fathered this trend within socialism, should have emerged in his maturity as a proponent, albeit an inconsistent one, of this new technocratic doctrine.)

To illuminate these differences, I propose in the closing sections of this chapter to describe and analyze a significant example of this latter sort of thinking – to show, as it were, what an alienated society in Marx's vision would look like and how it might be accounted for theoretically. In this connection I shall deal with the book by Clark Kerr and his associates, *Industrialism and Industrial Man*, as well as with the views of the sociologist Karl Mannheim who may well be described as the theoretician of the inevitability of, in Marx's terms, an alienated society run by a bureaucratic elite. These views, along with those of Herbert Marcuse, for example, represent the rebirth, albeit in conservative guises, of the very authoritarian utopianism which Marx rejected in order to develop and mature the concept of alienation without at the same time abandoning the root insights found in the *Manuscripts of 1844*.

'Two Roads From Marx': Another Look

In this well-known essay, Bell argues that the young Karl Marx who wrote in a humanist vein about the alienation of man in the posthumously published notes which have come to be known as the *Economic and Philosophic Manuscripts of 1844*, was submerged by the later Marx of *Capital*. Rather than one Marx, then, there are two Marxes: the first the humanist socialist and the other the cold economist whose only thought is of the destruction of capitalism. From this alleged bifurcation in Marx's development there led two roads: one toward some conception of restoring meaning to work, toward a socialism in which the idea of workers' control over industry becomes central, and the other toward the idea of socialism as nothing more than the negation of private property – a road which leads ultimately toward the totalitarian regime of Stalin.

Close attention to Bell's thesis is warranted here, not only because it is one which has been widely circulated, but also because Bell raises the question of the relationship of Marx's idea of alienation to workers' control in a more explicit form than is usual in sociological literature. Bell's thesis is fundamentally wrong. Yet the very wide range of his interests and the abundance of important questions which he poses require serious consideration. If, then, it is necessary to sharply contradict Bell, it is more because of his virtues rather than his mistakes.

Any discussion of socialism and socialist thought today must at some point concern itself with the rise, following the Russian Revolution, of a totalitarian collectivist social order that enslaves the masses of the population and imposes upon them the rule of a bureaucracy whose power is based upon modern technology. Although this new type of social order has come into being primarily in backward, predominantly peasant countries, there have been those who have raised the question of whether such an outcome might not be the likely or even inevitable result of socialist transformations in advanced, industrial nations. With this problem in mind it is crucial to ask to what extent did the thought of Marx, or of other socialist thinkers within the socialist movement, prepare the way for a socialism without democracy, for a socialism in which the workers, rather than being the ruling class, would instead be more exploited than they are under capitalism? It is this question that Bell, quite properly, makes the heart of his enquiry into Marx's idea of alienation.

Many self-described Marxists' inability to give a satisfactory answer to the question of whether or not, to use Michels' celebrated phrase, 'socialists may conquer, but socialism never' is, as Bell argues, the result of the fact that the socialist movement, including Marx, took the wrong road early in its origins 'away from alienation'. Thus for Marx in his maturity, and after him the socialist movement which followed his ideas, the triumph of socialism – and by this term Bell understands, as did Marx, democratic socialism – would be guaranteed simply by the abolition of private property. However, Bell contends, 'This argument which led to the rationalization of Russia as a worker's state – was only one road out of a great debate which had divided the radical followers of Hegel, the debate over the nature of alienation.'[5]

Bell correctly notes that Marx took the concept of alienation from Hegel and, locating it in work, gave 'social content' to it. For Hegel, alienation had been an inevitable part of the human condition; for Marx, a change in society would allow individuals to overcome alienation – to become whole once more. Yet, according to Bell 'in narrowing the concept, Marx ran two risks: of falsely identifying the source of alienation only in the private-property system; and of introducing a note of utopianism in the idea that once the private-property system was abolished, man would be immediately free'.[6]

And even then, in Marx's schema, Bell argues, man would not be immediately free, for before the arrival of the ideal society in which the slogan 'from each according to his ability, to each according to his needs' could become the guiding theme, humankind would first have to pass through a stage of 'raw communism'. 'Raw communism', or the transitional stage between capitalism and true communism, according to Bell, meant for Marx the negation of human personality, and would express 'envy and a desire to reduce all to a common level'.[7] In the thought of the later Marx, according to Bell, the period of 'raw' communism emerges as the 'dictatorship of the proletariat'. Freedom would come only after this stage had been successfully negotiated. It is this line of thought that leads Bell to his central conclusion about Marx:

> In his early philosophical writings Marx had seen, against Hegel, that alienation, or the loss of a sense of self-worth was rooted primarily in work rather than in the abstract development of consciousness. In the organization of work men become 'means' for the aggrandizement of others rather than 'ends' in themselves. As alienated labor there was a twofold loss: men lost control over the conditions of work, and lost the product of their labor. This dual conception is present somewhat in the later Marx: the loss of control of work was seen as *dehumanization*, occasioned by the division of labor and intensified by technology; the loss of product as *exploitation*, because a portion of man's labor (surplus value) was appropriated by the employer. But other than as literary references in *Capital* to the dehumanization of labor and the fragmentation of work, this first aspect of the problem was glossed over by Marx. In conflict with later sociologists, Marx felt that the solution to dehumanized work lay in the reduction of the hours of work, the automization of labor, and the development of leisure. What became central to *Capital* was the concrete social relationship created by private property, that of employer–employee, rather than processes generated by technology. Dehumanization was a creature of technology, exploitation of capitalism. In the key chapter of *Capital*, the section on the 'fetishisms of commodities', Marx sought to expose the process of exploitation: i.e., that while labor was formally free, in the complicated exchange process, surplus value was taken from the worker. The solution, therefore, was simple: abolish private property, and the system of exploitation would disappear. When critics asserted that socialism itself might become an exploitative society, the Marxist had a ready answer. The source of power was economic, and political office was only an administrative extension of economic power; once economic power was socialized, there could be no basis for man to exploit man. Q.E.D. Thus the goal and rationalization of socialism were fashioned.[8]

The 'other road' which Marx did not travel, according to Bell, leads to a search for the possibility of putting meaning back into work, and most importantly to the fundamental question of the possibility of democratic participation in the work process. It is a return to the original concerns of the young Marx, to the original discussion of alienation, which Bell pleads for:

> In the transmutation of the concept of alienation, a root insight was lost – that alienation is a consequence of the organization of work, and to end alienation, one must examine the work process itself. The time has come, perhaps, to move away from the transmogrified personifications, with their simplistic views of social behaviour and their simple-minded solutions for 'history'. If one is to deal meaningfully with the loss of self, of the meaning of responsibility in modern life, one must begin again with concrete problems, and among the first of these is the nature of the work process itself, the initial source of alienation.[9]

The charges which Bell makes against the older Marx are, if sustainable, quite damaging. For Marx, if Bell is correct, there must be a radical split between man the worker and man the thinker. Only in 'leisure' can he find an outlet for his creative impulses. Even if Marx believed the new society would be democratic and the workers no longer exploited, this belief could not be, if Bell is right, anything more than a hope, for in the most important area of life, which is work, people are denied not only creative satisfaction, but more importantly the power and control over the work process. It is in the light of this criticism that Bell calls for a return to the original idea of alienation, in order to provide a theoretical foundation for a theory of workers' control in industry. Only through democracy 'in the shop', side by side with democracy in political life, can the bureaucratic usurpation of the individual's powers be guarded against.[10]

One who shares Bell's values can only welcome his observations on workers' control as the foundation of a truly democratic society. Even if, as I shall show, Bell's view of Marx is very much mistaken, one can be grateful for the direct and clear manner in which he raises his criticisms, and even more for the clarity with which he links together the two issues of work and democracy with the idea of alienation. Perhaps even more important is Bell's assumption, the one which underlies this chapter, that socialism and democracy are two sides of the same coin: 'socialism' without democracy is, as we have seen in the Communist countries, a new kind of class society based on state property. It is, indeed, a society which corresponds to the vision of a 'new slavery' discussed below.

Contrary to Bell, however, it will be shown that Marx's transmutation of the idea of alienation to which Bell would have us return was an advance upon his earlier thought, particularly as he constructed there the foundation for doing precisely what Bell would like to see: a theoretical link between the overcoming of alienation in work and democracy in society. For Marx, the abolition of private property was not at all a sufficient condition for the establishment of socialism; rather – and it is possible to use Bell's own words here – the successful creation of democratic and socialist society requires the overcoming of alienation.

Marx: Alienation and Democracy

In a perceptive essay written a number of years ago, 'Socialism and the Problem of Bureaucracy',[11] Reinhard Bendix noted that among the many advocates in recent times of a planned society, including New Deal liberals, the socialists were the most apprehensive over the growing tendency toward bureaucratization and concentration of power. This worry, he rightly observes, was not the product of some new development within socialist theory; rather, 'fear of bureaucracy and dictatorial methods has been a new current theme of socialist thought', especially in the theories of the 'classical revolutionary socialists', Marx, Lenin and Luxemburg. Following Bendix's lead, I examine here Marx's ideas about the relation of socialism to a mass movement of the working class, and the social-philosophical views about social change which underlie them in order to see why Marx believed that socialism could and, indeed, *had to be*, democratic – that is, that self-government and the absence of a permanent bureaucratic state were inseparable from the aim of socialism.

Marx's repeated statement that 'the emancipation of the working class must be conquered by the working classes themselves' lies at the heart of the classical revolutionary socialist theory. It is largely what is meant by 'socialism from below'. In order to understand why this was such a central part of Marx's conception of socialism, it is necessary to refer to his theory of human nature and its relation to social change. As Sidney Hook has pointed out, very early in his political career Marx confronted the crude materialistic premises of contemporary utopian socialists, among whom he numbered Feuerbach, which held that human consciousness was the direct reflection of material circumstances.[12] The possession of consciousness of the part of some people, particularly the acceptance of the idea of socialism, could not then be explained by the utopians without the assumption that they were an elite of 'choice spirits' who by some mysterious means had risen above the ordinary run of humanity. Marx's third thesis on Feuerbach revealed his recognition of this logically inevitable conclusion, and at the same time counterposed his own 'materialism':

> The materialistic doctrine concerning the changing of circumstances and education forgets that circumstances are changed by men and that the educator must himself be educated. This doctrine has therefore to divide society into two parts, one of which is superior to society.
>
> The coincidence of the changing of circumstances and of human activity or self-changing can only be comprehended and rationally understood as revolutionary practice.[13]

The recalcitrance of human nature then could not be overcome, as the utopians against whom Marx was polemicizing held, by the creation of 'models' of socialism, or by an elite seizing power and establishing an 'educational dictatorship'. If the workers were not yet communists, and not, as Marx recognized, capable yet of ruling themselves, they would become so only as the result of their development as a class under capitalism and as the consequence of striving for the overthrow of capitalism. In *The German Ideology*, thus, Marx wrote:

> Both for the production on a mass scale of this communist consciousness, and for the success of the cause itself, the alteration of men on a mass scale is necessary, an alteration which can only take place in a practical movement, a revolution; this revolution is necessary, therefore, not only because the ruling class cannot be overthrown in any other way, but also because the class overthrowing it can only in a revolution succeed in ridding itself of the muck of ages and become fitted to found society anew.[14]

In the same vein, in his discussion of Max Stirner's individualistic anarchist views, Marx replied to Stirner's utopian contention that social change could not take place as long as human nature remained the same:

> Stirner believes that the communist proletarians, who are now revolutionizing society, putting the relations of production on a new basis – i.e., on the new men, on their new mode of life – remain 'the same as ever'. The untiring propaganda which these proletarians are making, the discussions which they carry on daily among themselves, prove sufficiently how little they want to remain 'the same as ever', and how little altogether they want men to remain 'the same as ever' ... they know too well that only under changed circumstances will they cease to be 'the same as ever', and therefore they are determined to change their circumstances at the first opportunity. In revolutionary activity, change of self coincides with the change of circumstances.[15]

For Marx, an organized, conscious socialist movement from below is a necessity for the creation of a socialist society, not only to capture political power, but as the means by which workers can transform themselves even as they struggle to transform existing class society to one characterized by democratic self-rule, including but not limited to, workers' control. From this idea too, sprang Marx's and Engels' lifelong antagonism to the 'plans' which the utopians drew up for the workers as well as other forms of 'socialism from above'. No doubt this was an overreaction on their part, as there is nothing intrinsically undemocratic in attempting to imagine what a socialist society might look like. But given the association of this tendency with the elitist assumptions of the utopian socialists, it is understandable that Marx overreacted. In Marx's comment on the Paris Commune, this idea of socialism as the product of the creative democratic upsurge from below by the workers, and his identification of 'utopians' with authoritarian prefabricated plans, are tied together in a well-known but still fresh passage:

> The working class did not expect miracles from the Commune. They have no ready-made utopias to introduce *par décret du peuple*. They know that in order to work out their own emancipation, and along with it that higher form

> to which present society is irresistibly tending by its own economical agencies, they will have to pass through long struggles, through a series of historic processes, transforming men and circumstances. They have no ideals to realize but to set free the elements of the new society with which the old collapsing bourgeois society is itself pregnant.[16]

The evolution of capitalism and the transformation of the workers into a class 'for itself' would, according to Marx, prepare the way for the coming socialist transformation. Not economic and technological transformation alone, but the development of the consciousness of the majority, the workers, was necessary for the transformation.

To summarize thus far: Marx found the answer to the utopian question of how a socialist society might be created, given the corruption of human nature under the adverse conditions of capitalist society, in the idea of the necessity of self-emancipation by the working class. In insisting upon self-emancipation as opposed to the various utopian notions of imposing socialism from above, Marx discarded the vulgar materialism of the utopians, and in its place put the proposition that as people actively alter their circumstances, they remake themselves. The construction of a socialist society, then, could only be the product of an organized, conscious mass movement. In order to understand what that society looked like to Marx, and to understand the sociological underpinnings of his theory, it is necessary to turn now to a consideration of Marx's ideas on the division of labour, bureaucracy and alienation.

Bureaucracy and Socialism

The question of bureaucracy and its relation to socialism in Marx's thought is an extremely complex one which is directly linked, theoretically, with Marx's concept of alienation. For Marx, Bendix points out, the possibility of eliminating bureaucracy and establishing democratic control and participation by the workers was dependent upon the possibility of abolition of the division of labour. Bendix writes:

> The problem of bureaucracy under socialism would be solved, because the coming revolution would reduce the necessity of coercion and by the same token diminish the division of labor. The oppression of the masses by the ruling class under capitalism had led to an inhuman division of labor. Once this oppression ceased to exist, there would be less need for a division of labor (especially between intellectual and manual work). Consequently a greater share in the planning of their work could be restored to the people. Marx believed that the masses would overthrow capitalist society because capitalists deprived them of all opportunities to the fullest. The desire of the masses to engage in creative work was to Marx a guarantee that the powers of a socialist government would not be abused.[17]

Bendix's conclusion is generally correct in its argument that the key to Marx's thought on bureaucracy and the possibility of democratic self-government is to be found in his ideas on the division of labour and upon what Bendix calls the desire for creative work. However, his formulation is sufficiently lacking in precision to make it necessary to consider this problem a little more closely.

Early in his development as a socialist, before he was a 'Marxist', properly speaking, and while he was strongly influenced by Hegelianism, Marx elaborated the concept of 'alienation' which was to play a critical role, sociologically transformed, in his overall view of socialism throughout his political-intellectual career. In *The Economic and Philosophic Manuscripts of 1844*,[18] capitalist society is criticized because by its very nature it condemns humanity to domination by the world of things. The system of commodity production means that the worker was him or herself a commodity. As a consequence, Marx writes

> … the object which labor produces – labor's product – confronts it as something alien, as a power independent of the producer … All the consequences are contained in the definition that the worker is related to the product of his labour as to an alien object. For on this premise it is clear that the more the worker spends himself, the more powerful the alien objective world becomes which he creates over – against himself – the poorer he himself – his inner world – becomes, the less belongs to him as his own. … The alienation of the worker in his product means not only that his labor becomes an object, an external existence, but that it exists outside him, independently, as something alien to him, and that it becomes a power on its own confronting him.[19]

At all points, Marx's analysis of the process of alienation is tied to the system of commodity production. The definition which Marx offers of communism, even in these early manuscripts, bears an organic relationship to his later conception of socialism. Real communism is, thus,

> … the positive transcendence of private property, as human self-estrangement, and therefore as the real appropriation of the human essence by and for man to himself as a social (i.e., human) being – a return become conscious and accomplished within the entire wealth of previous development. This communism as fully-developed naturalism, equals humanism … it is the *genuine* resolution of the conflict between man and nature and between man and man …[20]

It is not necessary here to trace the development of the idea of alienation in Marx's later thought in any greater detail. It is sufficient to note that Marx's central critique of capitalism rests upon the idea that it is a society in which people are mastered by the product of their own activity – capital. For example, in the analysis of the 'fetishism' of the commodity, in *Capital*, Marx writes, in terms reminiscent of the *Manuscripts*, that

> A commodity is a mysterious thing, simply because in it the social character of men's labor appears to them as an objective character stamped upon the product of that labor; because the relation of the producers to the sum total of their own labor is presented to them as a social relationship, existing not between themselves, but between the products of their labor.[21]

Capitalism is defined as a 'state of society, in which the process of production has mastery over man, instead of being controlled by him'. The essential character of socialism, therefore, is the conscious control by society over production, not 'society' as an abstraction but a community of 'freely-associated men'.[22] If one thing is clear at this point, it is that at no time, contrary to Bell, did Marx believe that the abolition of private property by itself would mean the end of exploitation.[23] Even in *Capital*, supposedly Marx's 'coldest' and least 'humanist' work, Marx makes it clear that the abolition of private property constituted only the necessary but not sufficient condition for the domination of the 'freely associated' producers over those forces which had hitherto constituted an 'alien' power over them.[24] This point and its relation to democracy will become clearer as we now turn to Marx's analysis of the division of labour.

As early as 1844, in the *Manuscripts*, Marx, who had by that time turned from the study of philosophy to political and economic questions, tied human alienation to the division of labour. As the section in the *Manuscripts* dealing with the division of labour makes clear, he had already associated the division of labour in modern society with 'estrangement'. The particular division of labour in capitalist society, its inner dynamic, is a function of the system of commodity production.[25]

Only in 1846 and 1847, however, in Marx's attack on Proudhon[26] and the joint work of Marx and Engels, *The German Ideology*, did he develop a clear theory, both in language and ideas, of the relationship between the future socialist society, work, the division of labour and the conditions necessary for the conscious domination of the working class over society – that is, for the establishment of democratic self-government which is the essence of Marx's socialism.[27]

The division of labour as such, Marx and Engels argue in *The German Ideology*, begins only with the division between manual and mental labour.[28] This stage in the division of labour

> implies the possibility, nay the fact, that intellectual and material activity – enjoyment and labor, production and consumption – devolve on different individuals, and that the only possibility of their not coming into contradiction lies in the negation in turn of the division of labor.[29]

With the development of big industry under capitalism, the division of labour proceeds to its highest point so that the individual becomes ever more subordinated in his work.[30] As a result of this process, 'Things have now come to such a pass that the individual must appropriate the existing totality of productive forces, not only to achieve self-prosperity, but, also, merely to safeguard their very existence.'[31]

Not 'creative dissatisfaction' alone then (cf. Bendix) but the need to protect their very existence, would force the workers toward the only solution which could serve their peculiar needs as a class: democratic collectivism – that is, socialism:

> In all expropriations up to now, a mass of individuals remained subservient to a single instrument of production; in the appropriation by the proletarians, a mass of instruments of production must be made subject to each individual, and property to all. Modern universal intercourse can be controlled by individuals, therefore, only when controlled by all.[32]

This passage very clearly reveals Marx's belief that the establishment of collective democratic control over the instruments of production by the workers was, under modern circumstances, the necessary condition for making the individual powerful. Any 'socialism' which denied to the individual his or her part in the collective control of society meant, conversely, that the individual would still be 'alienated'. For Marx, a socialism which was not democratic would not be 'socialism' at all, because only through democracy could the propertyless individual become master of their own social order. In short, Marx's views are a powerful critique of the identification of socialism with state ownership. No wonder, then, that the democratic oppositionists in Eastern Europe in the 1960s, faced by a 'socialist' ruling class which owned the state by virtue of its monopoly of political power, rediscovered the young Marx as the spokesman for a real socialism. It was hardly surprising that the Communist philosopher, Althusser, with his mechanistic Marxism, would insist upon the split between the young and the old Marx in order to justify the bureaucratic totalitarian regime as truly 'socialist' in the spirit of the mature Marx.

In *The German Ideology*, while the abolition of the division of labour was made the cornerstone of the new society, the concrete examination of the processes of modern industry which Marx later undertook for *Capital* is missing, and for this reason the discussion of the division of labour is only half-developed in the former book. Nevertheless, in keeping with the previously cited passages, Marx specifically drew attention to the conditions under which the division of labour could be abolished. It could only be done so collectively by the creation of a 'community', Marx wrote, in a passage which might be illuminating to those writers who claim to see Marx as the advocate of a society of individual atoms bound together in the iron hoops of an all-powerful state:

> The transformation through the division of labor of personal powers (relationships) into material powers cannot be dispelled by dismissing the general idea of it from one's mind, but only by the action of individuals in again subjecting these material powers to themselves and abolishing the division of labor. This is not possible without the community. Only in community with others has each individual the means of cultivating his gifts in all directions; only in the community therefore, is personal freedom possible. In the previous substitutes for the community, in the State, etc., personal freedom has existed

> only for the individuals who developed within the relations of the ruling class, and only in so far as they were individuals of that class. The illusory community, in which individuals have up till now combined, always took an independent existence in relation to them, and was at the same time, since it was the combination of one class over against another, not only a completely illusory community, but a new fetter as well. *In the real community individuals obtain their freedom in and through their association.*[33][Emphasis added.]

We shall have occasion to come back to this passage; it is sufficient to note here that it is the development of the individual and his powers, together with the creation of the kind of collectivist society, a real, not illusory, 'community', which would make possible that development and is a basic premise of Marx's idea of socialism.

It is in *Capital* that Marx's most mature thought is found, based on an analysis of the development and history of modern industry. In *Capital* the alienation of the worker – the subjection of the worker to the instruments of production, the process by which the product of the worker's labour becomes an alien power over him or her – is described in a wealth of detail. In especially vivid terms Marx revealed how the division of labour under capitalism

> converts the labour into a crippled monstrosity by forcing his detail dexterity at the expense of a world of productive capacity and instincts ... Not only is the detail work distributed to different individuals, but the individual himself is made the automatic motor of a fractional operation.[34]

It is through the division of labour, especially the division of manual from mental labour, which becomes more intense and extreme with the growth of capital. The worker is made more and more into a mere cog in a machine, less capable and with less opportunity to develop individual talents and intelligence:

> The knowledge, the judgment, and the will, which though in ever so small a degree, are practised by the independent peasant or handicraftsman, in the same way as the savage makes the whole art of war consist in the exercise of his personal cunning – these faculties are now required only for the workshop as a whole. Intelligence in production expands in one direction, because it vanishes in many others. What is lost by the detail labourers, is concentrated in the capital that employs them. It is a result of the division of labor in manufactures, that the labourer is brought face to face with the intellectual potencies of the material process of production, as the property of another, and as a ruling power ... It is completed in modern industry, which makes science a productive force distinct from labour and presses it into the service of capital.[35]

The key mechanism by which the individual is 'alienated', then, becomes for Marx of *Capital*, the division of labour, in particular the separation of intelligence and knowledge from manual labour. Stripped of the ability or capacity to use reason or intelligence by the organization of capitalist industry, the workers, if they are to emancipate themselves, and become truly free, self-determining or unalienated individuals, must find some way to overcome the effects of the division of labour. For Marx the answer to this dilemma lay in the conscious control over society as a whole by the associated producers. Only in this way would it be possible to end the division between control and work, between 'brain' and 'hand', between the managers and the managed. That is to say, for Marx, contrary to Bell, the collective ownership of the means of production and exchange was in itself only the necessary condition for socialism: the sufficient condition lay in the democratic control by the producers themselves not only of the workplace, but of society at large. And indeed it is the growing complexity and rapid change of capitalist production which itself requires overcoming the division between hand and brain. Marx argued that the nature of modern industry and technology necessitated the abolition of the division of labour because

> It becomes a question of life and death for society to adapt the mode of production to the normal function of this law. Modern industry, indeed, compels society, under penalty of death, to replace the detail-worker of today crippled by lifelong repetition of one and the same trivial operation, and thus reduced to a mere fragment of a man, by the fully developed individual, fit for a variety of labors, ready to face any change of production and to whom the different social functions he performs, are but so many modes of giving free scope to his own natural and acquired powers.[36]

It may be seen that this last point has now brought us around full circle in the discussion. If one side of Marx's conception of socialism as democracy was premised upon the necessity of the self-emancipation of the working classes, the other side was based no less firmly upon the idea that the necessary condition under modern circumstances for people to rule themselves, to 'win the battle of democracy', was the gradual abolition of the division of labour, especially that between mental and manual labour. It is this separation which makes some people 'brains', capable of comprehending the workings of society, possessed of a monopoly of culture and skill necessary for self-government as well as rule over others, and at the same time keeps the vast majority of 'hands' subordinated to the minority, socially and politically. The two sides are inextricably linked together for Marx: the situation of the workers as a class under capitalism gives them the cohesion necessary for successful collective action. While being forced as a class to act collectively, the individuals making up the class begin to learn in the course of their practical struggle the skills necessary for self-rule, transforming themselves as persons in the process, which in turn makes them fit to begin to construct a socialist society upon the winning of political power. The abolition of the division of labour which is central to the transition from the lower to the higher stages of socialism, makes possible the exercise of intelligence and reason not by one class or a minority, but by the vast majority of the people.

The ideal of individual reason as the basis for social action would become a reality, according to Marx, in a society in which 'the mastery of the product over the producer' had been abolished, and conscious social planning had replaced the anarchy of production under capitalism.[37] 'Then for the first time', Engels writes,

> ... man is marked off from the rest of the animal kingdom, and emerges from mere animal conditions of existence into really human nature. The whole sphere of the conditions of life which environ man, and which have hitherto ruled man, now comes under the domination and control of man, who for the first time becomes the real conscious lord of nature, because he has now become master of his own social organization. The laws of his own social action, hitherto standing face to face with man as laws of nature foreign to, and dominating him, will then be used with full understanding and so mastered by him. Man's own social organization, hitherto confronting him as a necessity imposed by nature and history, now becomes the result of his own free action. The extraneous objective forces that have hitherto governed history pass under the control of man himself. Only from that time will man himself make his own history – only from that time will the social causes set in movement by him have, in the main and in constantly growing measure, the results intended by him. It is the ascent of man from the kingdom of necessity to the kingdom of freedom.[38]

The solution to the 'alienation' of men thus for Marx can be seen to have rested upon the attainment of conscious collective control over society. That is to say, the end of alienation was to be found in the democratic control and participation by the people in all aspects of social life. Democratic control and participation require the fusion of intelligence and power in the overwhelming majority of individuals in society. This was both the goal as well as the means to the goal for Marx. Only in this way was socialism, or what Marx meant by socialism, possible.

Democratic Socialism and Authoritarian Collectivism

Without claiming for even a moment that the foregoing exposition or exegesis of Marx's views has not glossed over many vital points and avoided many complexities and difficulties, nevertheless I think that it is a correct presentation of the central elements of Marx's theory of socialism as it bears upon his belief in the necessary, not fortuitous, connection between socialism and democracy. Contrary to Bell, the idea of a 'socialism' without democracy was a theoretical impossibility for Marx. Socialism meant the rule of the vast majority of people or it meant nothing, and the only way in which they could as individuals determine their own fate, could have social power, Marx recognized, was through the possession of political power. Such political power could only be exercised through democracy. The abolition of private property was, as we have seen far from an end in itself for Marx, but only a means for ensuring real democracy. For people without property to rule society, in a society in which capital was increasingly socialized in the form of the joint-stock company or corporation, it was necessary to control the state which would collectively own the economy, and this was only possible through a democratic public life.

In short, statification of the economy without political democracy, the system which Communists and their co-thinkers have dubbed 'economic democracy', could not have been for Marx any kind of socialism at all, and certainly could have had nothing to do with democracy. It is in this sense that the equation of Marxism with Stalinism or Communism is a gross distortion of the truth. If in Marx's view the idea of socialism without democracy was a contradiction in terms, it was also a moral and ethical abomination. Human freedom, not 'planning'; individual reason, not 'efficiency'; self-rule, not domination by a permanent bureaucratic elite; democracy and not anti-capitalism, were the goals which for Marx were the essence of socialism.

Marx's belief in the possibility of human reason and democracy place him intellectually in the tradition of the Enlightenment, with its belief in universal reason and progress. For Marx, of course, as we have seen, 'reason' was not possible for the majority of human beings in a class society. Only in a classless society after the social antagonisms arising out of the capitalist mode of production had been overcome, and after the division of labour had been abolished could 'reason' fully rule.

The hallmark of all of the socialisms that I earlier labelled as partaking of the technocratic or managerialist tradition, is that they deny, implicitly or explicitly, the possibility of universal reason and hence of democratic self-rule. More specifically, it will be found that the division of labour within society between the 'brains' and the 'hands' is seen as a permanent and, indeed, ever widening, gap. At the same time the possibility of meaningful public life in which the citizen can participate directly and indirectly, making 'politics' in the classical sense a part of everyday life, is seen to be increasingly impossible and undesirable. Administration from above replaces active participation in government from below, and the gap between the managed and the managers, the same gap, essentially, between the hands and the brains, widens constantly. Such a vision – to be found in authoritarian utopias such as Bellamy's; in the bureaucratic socialism of the Fabians and in the politics of the supporters of totalitarian collectivism – is an affirmation that alienation is the desirable or, in any case, inevitable, outcome of the struggle of the human race's conquest of nature.

Karl Mannheim: Turning Marx Upside Down

To understand this point more clearly and to give us a vocabulary in which to place these politics, it will be useful at this point to consider some of the key ideas of Karl Mannheim concerning the liberal and Marxist views of rationality, set forth in *Man and Society in an Age of Reconstruction*.[39]

Mannheim argued that as modern society became more complex in its political and social organization, both industry and the state would necessarily be characterized by a bureaucratic form of organization. The division of labour in production and the division of labour in society at large would become more extreme. Knowledge itself would become more specialized, more compartmentalized, while ordinary people would become even more subordinated to the means of production. The ability of the ordinary individual to exercise the 'intelligent insight' into the workings of society necessary for making choices between alternative social policies and for participation in their implementation, even to the slightest degree, would become increasingly difficult. In place of the rationality of the individual, which Mannheim termed 'substantial rationality', there would of necessity arise a new and different kind of rationality – the rationality of the bureaucracy, which was of a purely technical kind, without 'interests', supposedly. Mannheim termed this kind of rationality, 'functional rationality'. The individual would live life increasingly within bureaucratic organizations, and being locked up in a specialized job, would lose the capacity for individual reason and the opportunity for it, becoming unable to see into the overall structure of relationships shaping his or her own life.

It was Mannheim's conclusion that if the net effect of functional rationalization was to deprive the individual of the capacity and opportunity for the exercise of reason – 'intelligent insight' – then it was only those who directed or organized society (bureaucrats, managers and perhaps intellectuals), who stand at the peaks of the vast bureaucratic structures, who would be able to possess and to use reason and hence to exercise power rationally. They and they alone would be able to see the 'major structural connections': the *Gestalt* of modern society.

Democracy, self-government and the function of citizenship, the possibility of which for both the liberal and the Marxist tradition rested upon the belief in the possibility of the individual's exercise of intelligence, would become, Mannheim was to conclude, increasingly impossible except in a new, radically different sense. For Mannheim, the problem for 'democrats' was to find some way to make the new elite of knowledge (if indeed this elite itself could be found) responsible to the people in order to prevent tyranny, and yet to shield the elite at the same time to prevent the irrational masses from attempting to intervene directly in the public life.

Clearly, any notion of democratic socialism, not to speak of the ideal society of democratic liberalism, if Mannheim were correct, would be a practical and theoretical contradiction: a utopia. The understanding, the knowledge, the capacity for judgement necessary to any conceivable system in which workers might participate or control their work, or rule over society, would be impossible. The rule of the 'masses' would then necessarily mean the eruption of the mob and of mass irrationality and could only be succeeded by a totalitarian 'mass' society: the product of democracy itself, or at least of mass, popular and participatory democracy – as if there were any other kind. But, of course, for Mannheim, as for Schumpeter, there was a different kind of democracy: 'elite democracy', the self-contradictory character of which cannot concern us at this point.

It may be seen from this exposition of Mannheim's deeply conservative thought, that his conception of a functionally rationalized society is an attempt to translate Marx's idea of alienation and its sociological underpinning, the division of labour, into structural terms and to specify the political meaning of such an order if and when it came into existence. Mannheim's theory of the nature of modern industrial society and its evolution is, essentially, Marx turned upside down: individual reason is usurped by the bureaucratic organization of society and only those occupying the strategic positions in the bureaucratic command posts can possibly be able to understand what is going on – if indeed even *they* can. Conscious democratic control by the masses of people – the overcoming of alienation for Marx – becomes progressively more remote as an ultimate goal, and more attenuated as a realistic ideal in the present.

It is not my purpose in presenting Mannheim's view here to discuss its theoretical merits. His argument is, to say the very least, an important one that cannot be dismissed out of hand. Certainly its impact as well as that of similar theories, has been enormous as far as sociology and present-day political and social thought are concerned. Its value for our purposes here is of a different kind. Mannheim's specification of 'alienation' in terms of functional and substantial rationalization provides us with the conceptual framework for analyzing the authoritarian collectivist ideologies noted above.

Work, Democracy, and the 'New Slavery'

To understand just what a totally alienated society in Marx's sense would look like, it will be useful to examine here *Industrialism and Industrial Man* by former University of California president, Clark Kerr, and a number of fellow industrial relations experts.[40] George Friedmann has accurately called the various attempts to extrapolate the future of society from the automation of industry, 'technicians' utopias'. Kerr's portrait of the coming society can with similar accuracy be called the utopia of the managerial revolution which is a result of the ongoing bureaucratic collectivization of capitalist society. In its pages, the functional rationalization of society is drawn to its logical conclusion.[41]

The development of industrial society points to what Kerr and his co-authors term 'pluralistic industrialism'.[42] The society of the future will be free of class and political conflict. The protests of the working classes, the authors believe, were the product of an early stage of industrialization.[43] In the new industrial society, the workers have 'proved themselves much more adjustable to the impacts of industrialization on their technical and social skills, and much more agreeable to the imposition of the web of rules than was once suspected. *The led are more easily led.*'[44] The labour organizations themselves are, and will increasingly be, 'a part of the established system. This explains, in part, the increasingly constant threat to them from shop steward movements.'[45] In the society of pluralistic industrialism ideology comes to an end, and 'the new realism' takes its place.[46] There are few 'real ideological alternatives' in the new society, in any case.[47] Those conflicts that do exist are over details, not over questions of broad social strategy,[48] and these conflicts are settled not by 'prophets', 'idealists' or 'demagogues', but by the negotiator.[49] As ideology comes to an end, so does political life as we know it. But that presents little problem, for 'the great political causes of old may become little more than technical issues; and oratory may give way to committee work'.[50] Consensus reigns.

The managers in the new society, the authors predict, will play an increasingly important role, for

> industrial society must be administered; and the administrators become increasingly benevolent and increasingly skilled. They learn to respond where response is required; to anticipate the inevitable. The benevolent political bureaucracy and the benevolent economic oligarchy are matched with the tolerant mass.[51]

In the 'managerial evolution', it is the managers who are to be 'basically responsible for the web of rules within the plant and industry which relate them to the managed', although they will share this responsibility with the state and the organized workers.[52] The 'web of rules' is a 'universal' phenomenon to be found in all industrial organizations, regardless of the kind of society:

> Basically this web of rules must spell out the authority of the managers. Economic enterprise is always basically authoritarian under the necessity of getting things done, and the limits to this authority must be specified. The distribution of power comes to be as important as the distribution of income, and much more unequal.[53]

People everywhere, the authors write, want both 'progress and participation'.[54] Industrial man will, 'in the end' press for both. 'Progress means a higher standard of education, better health, more consumer goods and services', while 'participation means choice of jobs, choice of consumer goods, a chance to influence the web of rules, even a chance to influence those who guide society itself'.[55] If Kerr and his fellow authors nowhere in their book discuss democracy, they at least cannot be accused of inconsistency. 'Politically', the authors tell us (after, we must note, having predicted the decline of parliamentary life and the bureaucratization of political parties), the individual 'can be given some influence'. For in the future, they say, unconsciously imitating the passive future syntax so well developed in Anne Morrow Lindbergh's apologia for totalitarianism, *The Wave of the Future*,

> ... society has achieved consensus and it is perhaps less necessary for Big Brother to exercise political control. Nor in this Brave New World need genetic and chemical means be employed to control revolt. There will not be any revolt,

anyway, except little bureaucratic revolts that can be handled piecemeal. An educated population will want political choice and can be given it.[56]

I have jumped very quickly over the authors' main points to indicate the framework for their ideas on the future of work. The individual will, on the one hand, it is predicted, be the 'organization man' and, on the other hand, will find a new kind of freedom in 'the new Bohemianism':[57]

> In his working life he will be subject to great conformity imposed not only by the enterprise manager but also by the state and by his own occupational association. For most people, any true scope for the independent spirit on the job will be missing. However, the skilled worker, while under some rules, does get some kind of control over his job, some chance to organize it, as he sees fit, some possession of it. Within the narrow limits of this kind of 'job control' the worker will have some freedom. But the productive process tends to regiment. People must perform as expected or it breaks down. This is now and will be increasingly accepted as an immutable fact. The state, the manager, the occupational association are all disciplinary agencies.[58]

The conformity of the individual in his productive life will, however, the authors claim, be compensated by the freedom in leisure, by the 'new Bohemianism':

> This will be the hunting ground of the independent spirit: Along with the bureaucratic conservatism of economic and political life may well go a New Bohemianism in the other aspect of life and partly as a reaction to the confining nature of the productive side of society. There may well come a new search for individuality and a new meaning to liberty. The economic system may be highly ordered and the political system barren ideologically, but the social and recreational and cultural aspects of life diverse and changing.

It is this duality in pluralistic industrialism, the authors insist,

> that makes it forever a split personality looking in two directions at the same time. The new slavery and the new freedom go hand in hand ... If pluralistic industrialism can be said to have a spilt personality, then the individual in this society will lead a split life too; he will be a pluralistic individual with more than one pattern of behaviour and one dominant allegiance.[59]

This then, according to the authors of *Industrialism and Industrial Man*, is the probable direction in which all industrialized societies will inevitably and inexorably evolve, presumably impelled along their course by the inner logic of industrial organization itself. The interest which the book has for us, however, is not its theory – it is, unfortunately, more an ideological than a theoretical exercise – but rather the clear and stark portrait that it draws of a society in which individuals are 'free' and yet completely without power, in which intelligence and control are all concentrated in the hands of the managers who run society.

In Mannheim's terms, the society they draw is one in which functional rationality has totally replaced the individual citizen's exercise of reason. The managers, who are an external category, alone can understand and hence direct society. The primary function of the authors' assumption that conflict will vanish is to prove that there is no need for substantial rationality on the part of individuals. If there is no need for the individual, at least not a critical need (the authors hedge from time to time on this), to defend their interests in society, then there is no reason why they should participate, intelligently or otherwise, in the making of social decisions. Social decisions themselves become a matter of technique, for there are to be none of the divisions in society which give rise to politics and conflict. Thus, experts or administrators can decide all important questions without in any way violating the 'freedom' of the individual.

The absence of a free public life is paralleled by complete regimentation of the individual in the industrial sphere, particularly in work. Therefore, it is not accidental that nowhere in Kerr's work – which claims, after all, to be an analysis of the major trends in modern society – is there a discussion of democracy, except for a reference to 'guided democracy'. This omission is not an inconsistency however, for clearly whatever the personal feelings of the authors, under the conditions they describe, democracy becomes irrelevant. Perhaps we ought to be grateful that, hard-headed realists that they are, they do not bother to confuse the issue by talking about 'elite democracy'.

In work the individual is to be a slave, and in society a completely privatized and powerless person. All that is left is the 'new freedom'. Freedom for what? Those who stand at the top of society, the authors insist, make the decisions, and that is the way it must be in 'industrial society'. The average citizen cannot (need not, according to the authors) participate in the direction of the general community or social matters. That is left to the managers. In work the imperatives of technology dictate that there can be little or no control or participation in the work process, and even the individual's own organizations, as we have seen, are primarily instruments of discipline over their members. The function of those at the bottom, the 'managed', the great majority, is to take orders from those on top; except in their own restricted realms, they need not think, use their intelligence, about larger matters. That will be taken care of by the managers whose job it is to think and command. There remains only the 'new Bohemianism', that is, the pursuit of those ends which can have no possible relationship to the power structure. Thus, to put the matter in its correct light, we would have to say that for the authors of this book, the new society will mean slavery for the individual when it comes to questions of power, and freedom only where it doesn't matter.

It is just such a society, or rather a vision of society – call it managerial or technocratic – which, as I have shown, constitutes the very essence of alienation for Marx and against which his ideas, theoretical as well as moral, are directed. It is undoubtedly true, as Daniel Bell has claimed, that there are two roads to the future. But it is also undoubtedly true that only one of the roads stems from

Marx's thought while the other originates in different, sometimes quite respectable, quarters. The latter's respectable origins, however, cannot conceal its virtual identity with authoritarian and anti-democratic ideologies, ones that bring with them the threat of a new barbarism which, indeed, Marx warned could happen should the socialist project be defeated and alienation, in the sense we have explained, not be overcome and replaced by a fully democratic society, economically and politically. 'Modern industry compels society ... under penalty of death' to strive for this outcome.

We have shown how, for Marx, the idea of alienation as it was 'transmuted' in the course of his intellectual and political development, became inextricably linked to the possibility of democracy. Marx, who took over from classical liberal political theory the ideal of individual reason, sought in his analysis of modern production to find a theoretical and practical foundation for the reunification of reason and power in humanity.

Given this analysis, it is possible to see how Marx's idea of alienation is a powerful analytical tool for understanding all modern class societies, including totalitarian Communist societies in which there is no private property. It is true that Marx did not himself visualize the possibility of a society in which the means of production would be owned by the state with the state in turn 'owned' by a bureaucracy through its total monopoly of political power. Nevertheless, in such a class society where the workers lack the democratic rights by which they can defend themselves in a capitalist society, it is entirely consistent with Marx's use of the term to speak of such a social order as alienated, despite the fact that there is no capitalist class and all property is owned by the state. Not merely abolition of private property, as Daniel Bell would have it, but the possession of political power – democracy – is the necessary condition for an un-alienated, socialist, society for Marx.

CHAPTER 10

The Authoritarian Socialism of H.G. Wells[1]

The books of H.G. Wells are not widely known today, certainly not among the under-30 generation and perhaps not even the under-50s. And yet for 50 years, from 1895 to 1945, Wells wrote dozens of widely-read books, fiction and non-fiction, as well as innumerable articles in the popular press on an astonishing range of subjects. From the start of his writing career in the 1890s, Wells attracted notice for his visions of new forms of social and political organisation which today would be called 'post-capitalist'. *Anticipations* (1901) and *A Modern Utopia* (1905) were among the most important of these, culminating in his last, *The Shape of Things to Come* (1933), later made into a portentous film starring Raymond Massey (1938).

Michael Coren has written *The Invisible Man*,[2] which differs from the earlier biographies by Norman and Jeanne MacKenzie and Anthony West in its more detailed account of Wells' sexual life and emphasis upon the anti-democratic, authoritarian nature of Wells' social and political views.

About the former, Coren shows that Wells was a particularly loathsome character who systematically humiliated his wife and most of the women with whom he came in contact. If there were ever evidence for the otherwise dubious idea that the 'personal is the political', Wells provides it. The tyrant in the home who clearly hated women dreamed of dictatorship in the coming society. Coren does not explore this link but provides more than enough evidence to sustain it.

The latter is by far the more important and interesting aspect of this biography, at least as a starting point for rethinking the history of the socialist movement in light of its present crisis.

Wells was invited to join the exclusive circles of the Fabian Society but his relationship with its leading lights, Beatrice and Sidney Webb and Bernard Shaw, was a stormy one. He accused the Webbs of being advocates of a 'bureacratic collectivism' and although the charge was true, his ideas were no more democratic than theirs. His own version of socialism, drawing upon his great intellectual inspiration, Plato's *Republic*, leaned upon an elite of 'Samurai' who would create a new, scientific social order over the heads of the unfit masses.

As Coren demonstrates, Wells was a vicious anti-Semite and racist with deep-seated contempt for ordinary people. Wells had a lifelong belief in eugenics as a way to breed a master race which would be fit to live in the scientifically designed societies which Wells described in his science fantasy novels. He did not hesitate to draw the logical genocidal conclusions about the desirability of wiping out the unfit masses and lower races to make way for the new order. When the horrible reality of the gas ovens was revealed, Wells, by then an old man, was at best equivocal about the Nazi genocide.

Unfortunately, Coren seems to have little knowledge of the intellectual history of the socialist movement and of the ways in which anti-democratic and authoritarian socialist currents such as those represented by Wells, Edward Bellamy, the Webbs and Bernard Shaw merged into the intellectual pro-Stalinism of the 1930s and, in the case of Shaw, admiration for Mussolini and Hitler.

Of course, this is only one side of the story: the labour and socialist movements have also been the great engine for democracy and democratic ideas. Without their renewal we shall certainly descend in the twenty-first century into the kind of barbaric nightmare advocated by Wells.

And yet, as Coren's book reminds us, these two antithetical currents existed under one roof and, even at times, within the minds of individual socialists, throughout most of the history of the socialist movement.

All of this ought to make socialists, at least some socialists, squirm. And so they should, particularly since the identification, on the part of many on the left, of socialism with anti-capitalist dictatorial regimes lasted literally until the day the Berlin Wall came down and then some. Coren is not equipped to deal with these issues, either theoretically or as an intellectual historian, but he does supply a lot of the raw material for their examination.

In the midst of a deepening crisis of capitalist society, the willingness to look unblinkingly at the way in which the kind of 'socialism' advocated by Wells and his lineal descendants helped to discredit the idea of socialism as a democratic movement is more imperative than ever. As imperative, that is, as is the need for a democratic socialist alternative to the social and economic crisis of capitalism which looms before us. We need to understand that one need not exchange Wells' horrible *Modern Utopia* for a vacuous modernizer's utopia. Need not and must not because given the tendencies of really existing global capitalism, it would only lead back to a Wellsian-like version of the future.

CHAPTER 11

Right Face: Sociology Under Attack[1]

Sociology in the United States has a history dating back to post-Civil War social reform movements for whom 'social science' contained the answer to *laissez-faire* capitalism. Lester Ward's anti-Social Darwinist writings continued the tradition of social reform, inspiring both liberals (in the modern sense) and socialists to see sociology as an ally of social change and a source of criticism of capitalism.

In the 1920s and 1930s the most influential sociology department was at the University of Chicago. Its focus was The City and 'social disorganization', not surprisingly, because its main practitioners were recent arrivals from the small towns and farms of the Midwest, and they carried on the tradition as critics, reformers – and trouble-makers. One of the most famous cases of academic freedom in American universities before World War I centered on Chicago sociologist, E.A. Ross, for daring to criticize the local captains of industry.

In the pre-World War II period, Chicago was only rivalled by the rural and agricultural sociologists of the University of North Carolina. Once again, the radical impulse, even a kind of anti-capitalism, rooted in Southern populism, behind their work was clear. Studies of social conditions, including the racial dimension of Southern poverty, were its stock-in-trade and they produced a brilliant series of monographs documenting the social and economic ills of the South.

In the late 1930s yet another current flowed into American sociology from abroad, replenishing the native strain of radicalism, as a group of brilliant European social researchers, many of them rooted in socialism and Marxism, fled from Nazism. They brought 'theory', as in the case of the disciples of Max Horkheimer, but at the same time also brought a high level of sophisticated empirical research, as in the pioneering work of Mitzi Jahoda and Paul Lazarsfield, one-time leaders of the Austrian Revolutionary Socialists.

The radical roots of American sociology were also nourished by a rebirth of the American left in the 1930s. Robert Lynd set a radical agenda for sociology in his influential book, *Knowledge for What?* and most of the leading names associated with American sociology in the period between 1940 and 1970, passed through and were deeply influenced by their radical experience, often in small but intellectually influential independent socialist groups opposed both to communism and capitalism.

As Cold War consensus, reinforced by McCarthyite repression, began to bite in the 1950s, and American intellectuals joined up to support the West in the Cold War, so American sociology became more conformist. It proclaimed itself 'value free' and soured on democracy which was seen as the source of 'mass society'. Much of the New Left contempt for democracy was learned in the classrooms of the former liberals turned conservative who (objectively, of course) scorned ideas of democracy. Only in the work of Seymour Martin Lipset was there a continuing exploration of the conditions under which democratic participation was possible, most notably in *Union Democracy*.

The main critic of the drift to the right of American sociology was C. Wright Mills, whose trenchant books on the 'new middle class' and then *The Power Elite*, were a reassertion of an older tradition of native American radicalism, one owing less to Marx than to Veblen and Texas-style populist radicalism, although Mills for many years considered himself an independent anti-Stalinist socialist, contributing several of his best essays during the evil days of McCarthyism to *Anvil and Student Partisan*, a student socialist magazine of which I was then an editor.

Irving Louis Horowitz, author of the sensationally titled *Decomposition of Sociology* (New York and London: Oxford University Press, 1993) brings to his task the credentials of a one-time disciple of Mills. Editor in the 1960s of *The New Sociology*, an important collection of critical and left-leaning essays honouring Mills' memory, and, as Mills' literary executor, editor of his collected essays, Horowitz also wrote a substantial intellectual and personal biography of Mills in 1983, subtitled, significantly enough, given the politics of the present work, 'an American Utopian'. His once-hero deserved this label (the ultimate put-down among academic philistines of the right) because Mills believed that 'social theory must contain a moral edge' and, in time, 'as his work became more strident, losing sight of the distinction between analytical research and journalistic blandishment, the turn toward the utopian became ever more manifest in his writings'.

Some 30 years after *The New Sociology*, a book he professes to still value, the older Horowitz has written what he believes to be a stinging indictment of the left in American sociology for its politicization of sociology and its consequent 'decomposition', by which Horowitz seems to mean its breakdown into numerous specializations as well as its loss of a defining theoretical core.

I think it is fair to say that the present book represents the culmination of Horowitz's progressive disenchantment with the left which he now sees as a combination of fascism and Stalinism. From *enfant terrible* of the left to its scourge is not an unfamiliar trajectory.

Perhaps the oddest thing about this book is its stridency and, to use Horowitz's own words, the degree to which it loses sight of the distinction between analytical research or, in this case, the need to make a strong, intellectually grounded case, and raw, unsubstantiated invective. If one were to invent an acronym to summarize the style of this unfortunate book, it would be CAR: Computer-Assisted Rant. Unfortunate, first, because Horowitz is a capable sociologist, and, second — from the point of view of a partisan of the democratic left — there is, I regret to say, a case to be made, although not the one Horowitz presents. This is a rant-at-length, some 280 pages, of which an ordinary reader, whether sympathetic or critical of Horowitz's Complaint, must quickly tire.

I say there is a case to be made although not the exaggerated one over which conservatives hyperventilate. A case, for example, about the way in which aspects of American academic life, particularly in English literature departments, have been turned into an arena for academics, some of whom, but by no means all, describe themselves as radical critics of existing society. It is a current whose views are embodied in the speech codes and the very real phenomenon of 'political correctness' and combined with a contempt for the ideas or practice of free speech. It stands for indoctrination rather than education, thereby exposing the authoritarian and anti-democratic roots of its mission. There is also a case to be made, it must be emphasized, about the 'political correctness' of the right and its shabby history of hostility to academic freedom, reaching back to the days of McCarthyism and extending to the denial of tenure to radicals in the 1970s and 1980s. It is a bit rich now to read Sidney Hook's statement that university academics in the 1950s were a bulwark against McCarthyism, this from the author of *Heresy Yes – Conspiracy No!*, the book which provided the main rationale for the liberal collapse into the McCarthyite camp. As a student activist in the 1950s, at the 'little red schoolhouse' as UCLA was then dubbed, I observed every liberal academic (with two notable exceptions) slither under the nearest rock when it came to supporting the right of Communists to teach or the right of students to freely organize on the campus.

Horowitz, understandably enough, given his current political sympathies, ignores political correctness on the right, but curiously enough, he gives few examples of this point of view from the self-described (largely self-deluded) 'left' and the serious abuses it has led to, although many are to be found in the records of the conservative National Association of Scholars with whose newsletter he is associated as the publisher of Transaction Books.

Instead he relies on a few out-of-date and random quotes from some overheated academics to make his case, while overlooking contrary evidence. For example, the main public conference for left-wing academics, the annual Socialist Scholars Conference at the City University of New York, attended by over 2000 academics, many of them sociologists, and now in its eleventh year, is masterminded by a professor of sociology, Bogdan Denitch, who is also a key figure in the Democratic Socialists of America (DSA) and a respected figure in the councils of the Socialist International. The conference has only the slightest tinge of this kind of pseudo-radical 'politically correct' post-modernist talk. Its star participants have included such consistent defenders of democracy and high intellectual and academic standards as Irving Howe, founding editor of *Dissent*, Michael Harrington, Barbara Ehrenreich, William Julius Wilson, Frances Fox Piven and

Cornell West. Horowitz takes no notice of the Socialist Scholars Conference, although I am certain he is aware of its existence, nor of the DSA among whose 10,000 members there are many, many academic sociologists. It is understandable because it would immediately undermine the caricature of the left and, indeed, of sociology, he has created.

Nor, for that matter is decomposition *à la Horowitz* particularly visible at the annual conferences of the American Sociological Association. The 1993 ASA meeting in seedy and decomposing Miami Beach (something a cultural analyst of the modern school could make something of, reinforced by the knowledge that the 1994 ASA meeting will be in Los Angeles) was a tribute to S.M. Lipset, president several times over of both the ASA and the American Political Science Association. Its theme was democratization and in a series of brilliant panels and papers, topped off by a paper by Lipset, the importance of democracy and the collapse of authoritarian and totalitarian regimes and ideologies was discussed, analyzed, peered at, anything but disparaged. And before an audience of 700 to 800 sociologists, William Julius Wilson made a powerful case for a radical program of social change to benefit both African-Americans and whites alike. Hardly a sign of the fatal malady Horowitz attributes to sociology.

This brings me to the second aspect of Horowitz's case, the one he fails to seriously argue and for which he substitutes what Trotsky called the 'amalgam' technique of lumping together different and even opposing strands. This is the charge, one utterly bungled by Horowitz, about the 'fascist left'. Horowitz complains that the academic left is quick to condemn American capitalism but is (or was) slow or utterly resistant to attack totalitarian regimes and practices. There is some, perhaps much, truth in this: apologetics for Third World 'socialist' dictators like Castro and contempt for democracy were and still are common enough. But so is support, far more of it, for democracy and human rights as the 1993 ASA conference and the Socialist Scholars Conference demonstrate. On the other hand, the American political establishment has never hesitated to support dictators or failed to keep silent about human rights abuses whenever it was convenient, an inconvenient fact which Horowitz fails to mention in the course of his rant about the 'anti-American' left. In any case, such authoritarian views on the left are in reality the mirror-image of establishment views. Indeed, read present-day apologetics for the Chinese dictators or for 'Asian exceptionalism' and the denial of human and worker rights by pillars of American corporate capitalism or the spokesmen for the IMF or the American Enterprise Institute and you will think you are back to the days of listening to academic Stalinist/Third-Worldist fellow-travellers: 'Economic development first, comrades [gentlemen], and then we can let the masses [swine] have a carefully limited dose of freedom. In the meantime development requires authority and discipline ... etc.' (This occasions the thought, which has occurred to me more than once as I've listened to grey-suited advocates of hard-line structural adjustment, that at least some of the refugees from the 1960s New Left might possibly be found in the IMF rather than in departments of sociology, as Horowitz suggests.) Equating criticism of the American establishment with 'anti-Americanism' may go down well in Peoria with the Rotarians or right-wing academics, but it is simply another example of concocting a political amalgam. True enough, in the US as in Britain, anti-Americanism exists on the left, and there as here it constitutes the socialism of political fools; but to roll it up into one big ball as Horowitz does is false and intellectually irresponsible.

Such an equation is all the more curious in Horowitz's case since he seems to have forgotten that in his former incarnation he wrote with great passion about the US government's attempts to subvert democracy in Latin America using establishment social scientists. But that was many years ago and memory fades.

In addition to the subversion of sociology's once supposedly scientific and value-free tradition by the left, Horowitz presents another argument for the conclusion that sociology has decomposed (although I must say that he never seems to be able to make up his mind whether it has actually decomposed or whether it will arise, Lazarus-like, from its grave). This argument is twofold and in both cases it is simply absurd. First, there is the proliferation of special fields within sociology and the rise of new social science disciplines and a corresponding decline of the core discipline. Things are a bit sad, I admit, when a publisher's ad for a 'highly respected' American textbook which recently crossed my desk boasts that it avoids 'falling into the common pitfall of presenting sociology as though it were hopelessly divided by competing perspectives'. Grist for Horowitz's mill! But when was it ever any different? Not at Berkeley in the 1960s when we had the choice of, I think, 16 'fields' to take for our Ph.D. examinations. What was 'sociology' then? Hardly surprising that in time some of these special fields became full-fledged departments. Intellectual reasons apart, anyone who understands the sociology of academic life and professional careerism ought to understand why this happened.

As for theoretical unity, it was equally non-existent. Reinhard Bendix, the great Weberian scholar, held Talcott Parsons in contempt, referring to him in conversation with his post-graduate students in disparaging terms, while Kingsley Davis arose in a rage from the audience, in the middle of the Berkeley 'core theory' course, to say he realized from a colleague's lectures that the functionalist theory he had hitherto espoused was sheer nonsense. Normally, however, the peace was kept by the usual methods of compromise, tolerance and small-talk. Anything more, certainly an attempt to find a 'core' sociology, would have ended up (as the experience of some departments demonstrated) in a civil war between factions reminiscent of the conflict between the Peoples' Liberation Front of Judea and the Judean Front for Peoples Liberation in Monty Python's *Life of Brian*.

The *pièce de résistance* in Horowitz's argument is, however, statistical and proves, if nothing else, that young Horowitz missed out on this part of his training as a sociologist – perhaps he was passing out leaflets instead. This is the news that regular individual membership in the American Sociological Association in 1980 was 12,868. But 'by the end of 1992' – wait for this clincher! – 'the membership roll listed 12,300'. Thus is demonstrated a 'pattern of long-term stagnation' and 'decline' in American sociology. I suppose that in a way, statistical ignorance aside, this kind of argument is proof of the tenacious intellectual grip of the old American adage, one that every small-town Booster believes as an article of faith: 'If you're so smart why aren't you rich?' or, in this case, why hasn't sociology grown and grown, doubling or even trebling its numbers every decade, until it swallows the whole of academic social science?

After nonsense of this sort, we are left to wonder what or, indeed, *who* has decomposed?

CHAPTER 12

Culture of Complaint: The Fraying of America: A Review[1]

Robert Hughes is lucky to be the art critic for *Time* magazine. Lucky because if he were an American academic, especially an untenured one, he might be in deep trouble with his colleagues or his students. He has written an angry, devastating attack on the newest wave of conformity in American intellectual life which, given the absorption of intellectuals in the sterile halls of the academy in the United States, mostly means an attack on the academic practitioners of political correctness and what passes for multiculturalism. His book, which is passionate, polemical and eminently readable, would be dismissed as mere journalism and, worse yet, as yet another white middle-class male diatribe in support of conservative conformity of the Allen Bloom or Dinesh D'Souza variety.

It isn't. Hughes writes from the standpoint of the democratic left and the values of universalism and of a common but diverse human culture. He thrashes the conservatives as thoroughly as he does the self-described 'academic left', but understandably concentrates most of his fire on the latter.

The conservatives have their own brand of political correctness to peddle: their's is the defense of Western civilization (no less) as embalmed in the immutable 'canon' of great classical thinkers and writers taught to generations of American students. Hughes values this tradition, citing his own education in Australia, but recognizes its limits and the need for the inclusion of other traditions, especially as the world grows smaller and more interdependent. He recognizes too the need for standards of intellectual and esthetic judgement and even, when it comes to history, that objectivity and truth cannot be absorbed in relativistic post-modern theories about the arbitrariness of language.

At the same time, unlike the conservatives, Hughes appreciates history which includes the excluded and voiceless – 'history from below' in the tradition of Edward Thompson – and castigates the older politically correct conservative teaching of American history which left out women and blacks and workers and the multitude of ethnically diverse cultures, including non-European ones, which went into the making of modern American society. He affirms the need for changes in the educational curriculum as new immigrants, especially Hispanics and Asians, and new cultural influences in a borderless world challenge the sterile view of 'Western Civilization' (itself a mosaic of cultural traditions) held by the conservatives.

Second, and worse yet, Hughes rumbles the academics' game: all of the talk about post-modernism, post-structuralism, Foucault, Derrida, etc., is in large part just the newest professional hustle. He quotes critic Louis Menand's savage but entirely accurate view that 'most of the academic world is a vast sea of conformity, and every time a new wave of theory and methodology rolls through, all the fish try to swim in its direction'. Right now the fish are swimming one way: promotion, financial reward, professional recognition all depend upon it. Just as 20 years ago professional political science in America was overcome by the need to demonstrate its 'scientific' credentials and the professional journals were soon filled with unreadable and meaningless mathematical formulas designed to advance careers rather than knowledge, so too the humanities have retreated into a secret language which only small circles within small circles can understand. Hughes writes

> ... most contact between academe and the general intelligent reader seems to have withered, because overspecialization and the *deformations professionelles* of academic careerism have killed it off. Within the lit and humanities departments of the modern American university the angle of specialization – of topics, of ways of thinking, and above all of language – has become so narrow, so constipated by the minutiae of theory, so pinched by the pressure to find previously unworked thesis subjects, that it can't extend into a broader frame.

Over and over again, Hughes punctures the claim of the new academic left to radicalism:

> In the late 80s, while American academics were emptily theorizing that language and the thinking subject were dead, the longing for freedom and humanistic culture was demolishing the very pillars of European tyranny. Of course, if the Chinese students had read their Foucault they would have known that repression is inscribed in all language, their own included, and so they could have saved themselves the trouble of facing the tanks in Tiananmen Square ... The world changes more deeply, widely, thrillingly than at any moment since 1917, perhaps since 1848, and the American academic left keeps fretting about how phallocentricity is inscribed in Dickens' portrayal of Little Nell.

'The writer who drops in on this world', Hughes adds, in his delightfully rude way, 'is bound to feel like Gulliver visiting the Royal Academy at Lagado, with its solemn "projectors" laboring to extract sunbeams from cucumbers, build houses from the roof down and restore the nutritive power of human shit, all convinced of the value of their work.'

Third (and this would certainly cook Hughes' academic goose), he locates the 'culture of complaint' in the sterile, brain-dead politics of post-Cold War America where no party and certainly not the latest incumbent of the White

House offers an alternative, shared vision and a practical program to address the problems of poverty, unemployment, racism and social decay afflicting American society. Like their conservative critics, Hughes says, the academic left 'posing as revolutionary' use 'academic complaint as a way of evading engagement in the real world'. The politics of identity and difference, of race, ethnicity, gender, sexual orientation, together with the slogan of 'multiculturalism' reflect and to a degree reinforce the balkanization of American politics, replacing any sense of 'common citizenship' which will 'draw all Americans back into the political process'. Against the 'ghastly background' of the 'dismembered corpse' of Yugoslavia, Hughes writes, 'we now have our own conservatives promising a "culture war", while ignorant radicals orate about "separatism". They cannot know what demons they are frivolously invoking. If they did, they would fall silent in shame.'

And then there is the cult of political correctness: the campus speech codes and the old-fashioned name-calling in place of discussion and analysis. If only this were a myth concocted by the conservatives! But it isn't and Hughes serves up enough examples to demonstrate it. Anyone familiar with American academic life today knows how chilling the atmosphere can be. Nothing like the McCarthy era, but bad enough to make many academics think twice about what they teach, not because they've been persuaded but because they're afraid of being labelled 'racist' or 'sexist'. Read civil libertarian journalist Nat Hentoff's account of Connecticut College's attempt to ban Carmen Paglia's *Sexual Personae* from its reading list to get an idea of the kind of thought-police atmosphere involved. Not that Hughes fails to recognize that there's a real problem of racism, homophobia and old-fashioned sexism on the campus and the larger society. He argues that education and open discussion and genuine social change brought about by a transformed politics provides the only serious answer to these problems. The idea that policing words, controlling the expression of prejudices against racial and other minorities and women, or of banning the discussion of certain ideas will somehow eradicate the underlying hostility demonstrates, for Hughes, how out of touch with reality is the academic left. And how corrupted too, one must add, by the many versions of authoritarian ideologies which masquerade as 'socialism'.

It would be tempting to make fun of some of the more bizarre politically correct terminology if it were not for the well-articulated – 'theorized' would be the correct word – hostility to free speech which much of the new academic left displays. According to Fred Siegel, an editor of the socialist magazine *Dissent*, itself a stronghold of old-left sanity against the new academic left, when the guru of the Politically Correct Tendency, Professor Stanley Fish, was asked during a seminar whether the First Amendment was something more than an expression of power, Fish sneered: 'Free speech? Yeah, tell me another one.' Behind this contempt for free speech is the authoritarian yearning, so well-analyzed by Orwell, of an intellectual elite for the exercise of dictatorial power, a sentiment stated with startling frankness by Fish. Asked, according to Siegel, where his kind of academic leftism is leading, Fish responded that he wants students and faculty 'to do what I tell them to do'. Moreover: 'I want to be able to walk into any first-rate faculty anywhere and dominate it, shape it to my will. I'm fascinated by my own will.' Familiar stuff and pretty ugly at that.

Hughes' last chapter is devoted to a discussion of 'art and the therapeutic fallacy' in which, once again, he demonstrates, in the course of a discussion of the homoerotic photography of Robert Mapplethorpe and the controversy over federal funding of art which it raised, that the conservatives and their radical critics have a common view, one rooted in America's Puritan past: good art is art which is good for you – morally uplifting, edifying, instructional, containing the right social or political message, and (on the pseudo-left) portraying the victims of society. The argument about Puritanism is right out of H.L. Mencken, of course, but here it seems to me Mencken did a better job of flaying the Babbitts and 'booboisie' and ridiculing the comstockery of the day. What Mencken would have done to the advocates of censorship like Catherine MacKinnon or Andrea Dworkin and the thuggery of Senator Jesse Helms (as he did to William Jennings Bryan during the Scopes trial) or the Will-to-Power fantasies of Professor Fish can only be imagined, but it certainly would have been funny; I suspect that being laughed out of town might after all be the best cure for the culture of complaint. Even without the humour, however, Robert Hughes' relentless polemic has struck the new philistines a mighty blow and made a fine contribution to the cause of a genuinely democratic culture and to the creation of a new politics of intellectual engagement in an America which sorely needs both.

PART IV

After the Cold War

CHAPTER 13

Civil Society, Democracy and the Cold War

In The United States and the End of the Cold War,[1] *John Lewis Gaddis tells a revealing story about a meeting at a Washington foreign policy institute in 1985. After several hours of discussion about relations between the United States and the Soviet Union, 'I very tentatively raised my hand and asked whether we should not be looking ahead to the possibility that the Cold War might someday end: should we not give at least some thought to how we like it to do so, and to what might then replace it? An embarrassed silence ensured, broken finally by this observations from a highly-respected senior diplomat: "Oh, it hadn't occurred to us that it ever would end."'*

This chapter is based on a paper presented at the American Sociological Association meeting in 1988, in which I also assumed that the Cold War was coming to an end – a year before official circles were willing to admit it. Anyone who travelled to Eastern Europe in those years and had contact with the democratic opposition knew that the system was slowly crumbling – and all the more so (shades of de Tocqueville's The Coming of the French Revolution*!) when members of the Communist establishment began to indicate their disenchantment with it. I argue here that there was an alternative to the arms race and the Cold War – a 'third camp' which supported neither Washington nor Moscow – and which pointed to the kind of democratic socialist alternative which was implicit in the Hungarian revolution of 1956, Czechoslovakia in 1968 and, of course, Solidarity during the decade of the 1980s. This was not to be – popular disillusionment with anything 'social' because of experience with the totalitarian 'socialist' regimes and the weakness of the democratic opposition plus the policy of the Western powers who feared, as I point out, just such a development, led to the collapse of the existing regimes and a rush to the market – 'shock therapy'.*

We are now, in the late 1990s, seeing the fruits of these policies: the return of Communist parties, growing authoritarianism and the emergence of a new Russian imperialism. Overly optimistic as I certainly was in 1988, the paper points to a 'road not taken', one foreclosed by the reactionary and blinkered policies of the Cold Warriors. The larger conclusion about the need for a democratic foreign policy remains as valid in the post-Cold War period as before.

In 1988 as in 1848, to quote the famous opening line of the *Communist Manifesto*, 'a spectre is haunting Europe'. Of course it is not the spectre of communism but of the internal collapse of totalitarian collectivism and the rise of a new democratic movement from below which is haunting the Communist parties of Eastern Europe and the Soviet Union.

But the spectre of radical democratic change in the East is, ironically, also haunting the Cold Warriors in the West who denounce the 'evil empire' and offer the world salvation in the doctrine appropriately labeled 'MAD'.

For the ordinary people of the world, however, there is at last hope of a peaceful world free of the threat of nuclear annihilation.

Gorbachev's reforms from above, the measures of 'liberalization', real and welcome as they are, are an attempt to head off the radical democratization of Soviet society which this movement promises and which alone can solve the massive economic crisis to which decades of one-party, totalitarian rule have led. However, reforms from above feed the appetite for changes from below which go beyond the limits which the old order can allow. In time, this new democratic movement will result either in the democratic transformation of the existing social order – a social order which is inseparable from the monopoly of political power held by the Communist parties – or, in a desperate attempt to save the power of the ruling class, a reactionary but ultimately futile attempt to reinstitute total control. The latter would probably be based on the military and, in the case of the Soviet Union, might draw upon a nationalist movement such as Pamyat.

The best protection against the reversal of the progressive aspects of Gorbachev's reforms and the possibility of a resurgent 'conservative' force is the growth of independent democratic centers of power in Soviet society. Fortunately, the democratic forces in Eastern Europe and the Soviet Union are growing in strength as the economic and social crisis of the entire system goes from bad to worse. Even the more conservative leaders who resist change recognize that reform is essential to the survival of their rule and that repression would be difficult and economically disastrous. In the very nature of such things, however, a democratic outcome is not guaranteed and thus one of the concerns of this paper is to focus on the way in which the peace movement and, more broadly, the genuinely democratic forces in Western Europe and the United States, can assist this nascent democratic movement in the East.

Indeed, as I shall argue, the possibilities for a new politics in the West – a politics of radical democracy – are bound up with and mutually dependent upon the success of a genuinely democratic movement in Eastern Europe and the Soviet Union.

I stress the idea of a genuinely democratic new politics in the West as against the Reagans and Thatchers and their fellow Cold War leaders who use the language of democracy and freedom to conceal their conservative and anti-democratic aims. Their concern to retain the status quo in Europe makes them hostile to a democratic movement from below in the East out of fear that it will infect the

West. 1968 in Paris is a symbol of what is possible when the ideological structures created by the Cold War begin to crack. Solidarity in Poland, for all of the Cold Warriors' hypocritical words of praise, was a source of great worry. Someone like Thatcher who has based much of her political career on stripping British trade unions of their democratic rights and whose passion for authoritarian government makes Reagan look like the wettest of the wets by comparison, only saw in Solidarity a stick to beat the Soviets with – and then with great caution.

If the winds of radical political and social change continue to gather real force in the East, they will prove to be far more dangerous to the ruling groups in the West than any highly improbable Soviet invasion. It would mean the rebirth of a democratic left at last free of the curse of the equation of socialism with Stalinism and able to confront the difficult task of creating a democratic and humane society in the West which could help to lay the economic and social foundations for a truly peaceful world. Only such a new movement can begin to address the massive question of Third World poverty and the arms race there which grows more dangerous every passing day.

In short, the developments which the present conservative leaders of the West fear give us hope.

Across Frontiers: Détente From Below

This fear of a democratic wave from Eastern Europe is hardly new nor is it a secret. It first came to the surface after the Hungarian uprising of 1956 and was made explicit in the Sonnenfeldt doctrine. Today the idea that the Soviets themselves may wish to get rid of Eastern Europe through some sort of Finlandization 'horrifies' the Western leadership, or so we are told by Irving Kristol, a leading American neo-conservative thinker. Kristol angrily admits that because of their 'addiction to the status quo with which they are basically comfortable', the governments of Western Europe 'privately pray that the peoples of Eastern Europe will remain passive and quiescent – indefinitely'. But, of course, as Kristol correctly observes, they will not be quiescent and passive indefinitely, nor, for that matter, will the peoples of the Soviet Union. The result, Kristol points out, is a crisis for the Western alliance. The division of Europe at Yalta is coming to an end and it worries the guardians of the status quo.[2]

But what is a worry for the old order is welcomed by the new independent movement for peace and democracy which has sprung up on both sides of the divide. This movement, of which Edward Thompson and Mary Kaldor, leaders of European Nuclear Disarmament (END), are the most eloquent spokespeople, welcomes the dissolution of the blocs and the possibilities for social transformation, East and West, which are opened up. And above all, for the end of the Cold War and the threat of nuclear war with which the old order is bound up:

> Peace is more than the absence of war. A lasting peace can only be obtained by overcoming the various political, economic and social causes of aggression and violence in international relations as well as in the internal affairs of states. A comprehensive democratization of states and societies would create conditions favorable to this aim. Such democratization includes the existence of a critical public which has the capacity to exercise effective control over all aspects of military and security policy ... The economic systems in East and West urgently need democratization. Social needs such as housing or work in safe and human conditions have to become more important in defining economic priorities. In the West a primary task is to ensure that people are no longer marginalized by massive unemployment. In the East, decentralization of the economy is an essential task in order to make the economy more efficient and responsive to the needs of the people ...
>
> The Europe we envisage would consist of people and nations that are willing to live together as good neighbours. A Europe where all peoples have the possibility to organize their mutual relations as well as their internal political, economic and cultural affairs in a democratic and self-determined way ...
>
> The Europe we envisage will gain strength from its internal democracy and should be able to play an important role in international affairs. In particular, Europe needs to find ways to transform North–South relations and become a pace-setter for political equality and economic justice in dealing with the Third World. Such a Europe would oppose any form of military interventionism, like, for example, the present US actions in Central America or the Soviet invasion of Afghanistan.[3]

These are the views of the new democratic peace movement on both sides of an artificially divided Europe. Needless to say, they are anathema to the Cold Warriors, East and West, including the 'peace movement' in the West which opposes only one side of the arms race. The Europe the democratic peace movement advocates is a Europe in which the old leaders, the old structures of authority, and the very social order which has bred the cold war, would cease to be.

Little wonder then that there exists a mutual admiration society between the Hungarian Prime Minister and Mrs Thatcher or at Mrs Thatcher's own instinctive recognition of Gorbachev as a man 'I can do business with' (a phrase which echoes another British Prime Minister, upon whom Thatcher is said to model herself, as he carved up the world with Stalin during World War II and thereby helped to lay the foundations of the Cold War). The objects of Mrs Thatcher's admiration both seek change from above and fear, very much as Mrs Thatcher does, genuine democratic movements on either side of Europe which could subvert the stability of their rule. Independent trade unions, the essential building block in democratic civil society, have no place in their 'socialism', just as they have no place in Mrs Thatcher's capitalism. The Sonnenfeldt doctrine is a shared one: détente from above, carefully managed without disruption of the very social orders which have given birth to and sustained the Cold War is the core of their policy.

To which the new movement for peace with freedom counterposes its own idea of détente from below.

In short, what is going on is the beginning of a political and social struggle for the future of Europe and, in the long run, the United States. Three views are competing, three camps with differing goals. *Thatcher's goal*: a well-armed but not-too-united capitalist Europe under the barbaric slogan of 'the free market' together, perhaps, with the gradual dissolution of Eastern Europe into a kind of colonial periphery subject to the rules of the IMF, while the Soviet Union under Gorbachev or his successors evolves into a modified, more 'liberal' state collectivist society. *Gorbachev's goal*: to save the life of the bureaucratic ruling class in the Soviet Union through a set of reforms the limits of which are drawn at the organization of a genuinely independent political party (or parties) which would undermine the monopoly of political power which is the lifeblood of the ruling class. *The goal of the democratic peace movements, East and West*: a peaceful united Europe whose foundations will have been laid by a revitalized movement for the democratic reorganization of society.

The future of this new democratic movement, which is only now coming into being in Europe and which ultimately must spread to the United States if it is to be successful, is intimately bound up with the development of the movement for democracy in Eastern Europe and the Soviet Union.

For this reason, the phrase from the *Manifesto* ought to be taken literally as involving all of Europe – and the United States as well.

The End of the Ice Age

What has begun in Eastern Europe is the beginning of the end of the political ice age which started with the consolidation of the Stalinist counter-revolution in Russia. The thaw has already produced enormous cracks in the frozen politics of the post-war confrontation between the Communist rulers of the Soviet Union and the capitalist West: the age which we were told had seen 'the end of ideology', by which its author meant the end of democratic socialism, has itself come to an end.

It is the end of a long historical era and the beginning of a new one.

First the Russian Revolution, then Stalinism and the consequent rise of fascism and the outbreak of World War II, and then the Cold War with its threat of nuclear annihilation: this is the history of our era. This era has now been brought to a close by the developments in Eastern Europe and the Soviet Union.

As the ice melts, an extraordinary profusion of new ideas and movements thought to have been made extinct by the terroristic rule of totalitarian communism, but in reality only dormant, now spring to life. Of course, we have had previews of this in 1953, 1956, 1968, and 1980–81. But these first movements appeared only on the edges of the empire and the reality or threat of armed intervention was sufficient to arrest their development, or at least to slow them down and leave them in a state of suspended animation.

The ice age has not been limited to the East. The ideologists who hailed the end of ideology were pointing fatalistically to a profound decay of democracy and democratic values – not just socialism – in the West. I would not want for one moment to understate the importance of the persistence of basic individual freedoms, of civil liberties, of the right of opposition free from police thuggery and the oppression of the one-party state, in the West (although not in the entirety of the so-called 'free world'). These are precious to everyone who values democracy and human dignity. But in the West many have forgotten – or chosen to forget – and many of the democratic opposition in the East do not understand – that these freedoms were secured by popular movements and that their continued existence, particularly with the Cold War and the growth of the Security State, has become precarious. They have been undermined by the demands of 'secrecy' in the face of The Enemy and the inherent drive of modern capitalism toward increasing statification and authoritarian controls. Irangate and the growth of the CIA in the US and the sham of Parliamentary democracy, together with laws and practices eroding civil liberties (such as the notorious *Spycatcher* case in Britain) are just a few examples from among many of the way in which democratic institutions and values have been attacked in even the most democratic of the capitalist countries.

In the world of Ronald Reagan and Margaret Thatcher, the choice is between the 'freedom' of capitalism or the totalitarian collectivism of the East. In the real world, the one that is coming into being, the choice is between a bureaucratic corporatist order and democratic collectivism. The former may take a devolved and liberalized form as in Gorbachev's scheme for a reformed communism, or it may take a Thatcherite form, where democratic institutions are steadily undermined to be replaced by a mythical 'freedom' of the market, on the one hand, and the growth of an all-powerful authoritarian state on the other. 'Democratic collectivism', radical democratic control from below over all political and economic life, combined with a maximization of individual freedom and choice, is only, in my view, another word for democratic socialism, although given the authoritarian stain on the word 'socialism' (from many sources) I can understand why it creates a negative reaction in the East and in the West.[4] It is this latter alternative (whatever term is used), which the End of Ideology ideologists pronounced utopian (and substituted their own technocratic views for) which developments in Eastern Europe and the Soviet Union have made possible again after decades of being frozen by the ice of Stalinism and the Cold War.

Civil Society

This alternative of radical democracy, or rather the striving toward this alternative, is at the core of the phrase, 'civil society'.[5] Civil society is less a coherent concept than a bundle of ideas and the statement of a yearning for a free and dignified human life without the all-embracing control of the state and statism.

Its origins in current debate are to be found in the East but it has found fertile soil in the West as well – evidence of the recognition of the institutional developments which are common to the existing rival social systems. In one version, 'civil society' takes the market as its starting point as the guarantor of individual freedom and a necessary complement to democracy. In its extreme form, the market is the *substitute* for democratic institutions. This is the underlying point of view of the Thatcherite new right.[6] In another, the one which I would adopt here and which I think describes the most consistently democratic vision, 'civil society' means the creation of a genuinely self-governing, democratic society in which the state is the servant of society and economic power is democratically controlled as well. In short, economic and political democracy are joined together.

There are many other concepts of civil society and the debate over them goes off in many directions. The very confusion, untidy as it may be for theorists, is testimony, I believe, to the complexity of the problems which are being grappled with and an expression of the explosive creativity in political thought which is now going on in Eastern Europe. It is, above all, evidence of a great movement from below which cannot be captured by sterile ideologues who claim to know *the* path forward: in short it is a movement which is in its very essence democratic. Rosa Luxemburg's well-known injunction that 'what we possess ... is nothing but a few main signposts ... socialism by its very nature cannot be decreed or introduced by *ukase*' remains as fresh and relevant as the day it was written and a reminder of why Gorbachev's and his apologists' (both East and West) version of socialism by permission of the single, ruling party – socialism from above vs. socialism from below – is a contradiction in terms.[7] No wonder East German police tear banners bearing Luxemburg's words from the hands of young demonstrators.

If one needed further evidence of the democratic power of the idea of 'civil society' there is its use by the ruling circles in Eastern Europe and the Soviet Union who are attempting to find legitimacy for the liberalization (but not democratization) of their rule. This appropriation of 'civil society' by the rulers demonstrates not only the pressure which they are under (and how ideologically demoralized they are as well) but why the present situation in Eastern Europe deserves to be called 'pre-revolutionary'. Still, there is also a warning here: 'civil society' without democracy can lend itself to cooptation: to be meaningful and truly radical it must mean a free public life and the ability of individuals to associate together for the purpose of exercising power over the decisions, small and large, which affect their lives.

The Iron Cage

We are, then, in the middle of a political earthquake which is beginning to shake the foundations of the world which came into being after the Russian Revolution of 1917 and which in the last 40 years has brought the world close to nuclear annihilation.

For the last 40 years of the Cold War, and even before it, with the rise of Stalinism in Russia and the domination of the left in the West by the ideas and movements of Stalinism, those who have feared the outbreak of war and wished for peace have felt themselves to be locked into a cage in which there were only two choices, choices which mirrored the division of the world between the totalitarian collectivism of the Soviet superpower and the imperialist world of American capitalism.

The existence of a third way, or a 'third camp' which gave its allegiance neither to Moscow nor Washington, was derided by the hard-headed thinkers of American liberalism and European social democracy. One had to 'choose freedom' and disillusioned former Communists and liberals, many of whom had apologized for or covered up Stalin's crimes, announced their support for the West and the 'free world' – which included (and still does) not a few of the most gruesome dictatorships to be found on the face of the earth. But these were anti-Communist dictatorships and the religion of the free world and of American liberals as well as European social democracy became 'anti-communism' with democracy running a very poor second. Cold War liberalism took center stage.

Only a few isolated figures, such as C. Wright Mills or Supreme Court Justice William O. Douglas, one of the last of the old-fashioned democratic liberals in the US, continued to call for a democratic foreign policy.[8] Jeanne Kirkpatrick's theoretical distinction between authoritarian and totalitarian regimes was only a frank admission of what the policy meant (as if the victims could distinguish between a totalitarian torturer and an authoritarian one). It is hardly surprising that the undeniable fact of the appearance of an opposition in the Soviet Union, and real if insufficient reforms from the top, has sent the hard-line Cold Warriors into an intellectual tailspin. 'Totalitarianism' in the theoretical framework of the Cold Warrior is, by definition, a seamless web of oppression in which all social movement, all class and national conflict, ceases, and it can therefore only be changed by pressure from without, chiefly by the acceleration of the arms race. This version of 'totalitarianism' was one of the foundation stones of the Cold War ideology: it could not be sustained as a serious theory after 1953 and certainly not after 1956 or 1968: but truth is hardly an important matter for ideologues and so the ideology rolled on in the face of reality, continuing to underpin the rationale for a perpetual Cold War and an unending arms race in the West.

Enemies of One's Enemies

The majority of the peace movement and, in the case of Vietnam, the anti-war movement too were locked in the iron cage of either/or. Even if they rejected the Cold Warrior's view of the 'evil empire' (Reagan's vulgar but accurate summary of the key idea in the Cold Warrior's politics) then it was still a matter of choosing one side or the other or, at best, pleading with both to slow down the arms race or even to disarm. Some advocates of peace simply chose the other side, either openly, as in the case of the apologists of the World Peace Council, whose unquestioning defense of everything the Soviets ever did, including Khrushchev's criminal stationing of missiles in Cuba, earned them a well-deserved contempt; or tacitly, by their refusal ever to criticize or question the Eastern bloc and certainly never to raise any questions about human rights or about the right of Soviet or East European citizens to challenge their own governments' preparations for war. These were opponents of the Cold War who were in reality only the supporters of the other side in the Cold War.

In the case of the anti-war movement in the US during the Vietnam war, opposition to the genocidal American intervention led many to political support for the Vietcong and an admiration for Ho Chi Minh's own murderous style of 'socialism'. It was, when not thought out, a matter of 'our enemy's enemy is our friend' and, when more developed, a matter of absorbing wholly the totalitarian politics of the North Vietnamese regime, as in the case of an entire wing of the anti-war movement and the New Left of the 1960s and 1970s.

This idea of allowing your enemy to dictate the content of your political views is a mode of thought not unknown in Eastern Europe among oppositionists who admire Reagan and oppose the Western peace movement because of their hatred of their own rulers. As the Helsinki statement illustrates, however, it is a point of view which is diminishing because of the efforts of groups like END, the Network for East–West Dialogue, and the Campaign for Peace and Democracy, East and West. Leaders of the democratic opposition have, to the dismay of American Cold Warriors, expressed their opposition to the crimes of one of America's favourite dictators, General Pinochet, as well as to the South African apartheid regime for whose welfare those great democrats, Reagan and Thatcher, have been so solicitous.[9]

During the depths of the Cold War, in the 1950s, a few independent voices, some 'third camp socialists' such as Michael Harrington and a handful of radical pacifists like A.J. Muste and Bayard Rustin challenged these assumptions of the Cold War:

> The two great power-states, Russia and the United States [are] engaged in a fantastic race to develop weapons of mass destruction [and] exist essentially in order to wage the power struggle against each other … In Russia to an extreme degree, in the United States increasingly, the liberties of the people are sacrificed to the exigencies of the garrison state. For these power-states to overcome or liquidate the power struggle, and to devote themselves to the achievement of world peace, would require and reflect a revolutionary change in attitudes and in the socio-economic systems of these countries. All 'peace' activities which do not proceed on this assumption are based on an illusion and, no matter how much those who take part in them may wish otherwise, will serve as a screen behind which war preparations go on … To offer genuine hope to mankind, the social and political movements which make

> up the Third Camp must be opposed to the social orders of *both* war camps, and hence to the military and diplomatic cold war which they are waging … [The Third Camp] must be animated by a positive principle, the goal of a new, free, human, and democratic order which is superior in all ways to what the two war camps have to offer, and which, therefore, the peoples in Stalinist and capitalist countries will recognize as the goal in which they also will find freedom and peace.[10]

This was in 1953. In 1988, we find in the new independent peace movements in Eastern Europe and in the Soviet Union this same idea: freedom *and* peace, the two inseparably linked.

But in 1953 the doors of the cage were well-locked. The idea of a third camp was ridiculed as utopian or denounced as subversive. McCarthyism, unleashed by Harry Truman's loyalty-security plan and the witch hunt of the Communist Party and its sympathizers epitomized in the Smith Act prosecutions which Truman initiated, silenced all but a few opponents of the Cold War. More important than fear, however, was the total acquiescence of the liberals to the logic of the Cold War and the arms race and the belief that totalitarianism could only be confronted by an endless arms race.

Politics had no role in a situation in which national revolt was impossible and totalitarianism had created a 'mass society' of atomized individuals unable and, worse yet, as in Orwell's *1984*, not even capable of knowing themselves to be unfree. Among academic intellectuals only C. Wright Mills spoke out strongly in *The Power Elite* (1956) and *The Causes of World War Three* (1958) against the 'crackpot realism' and complicity of American liberal intellectuals with the drive to nuclear annihilation.

In 1953 the East German workers' revolt gave the lie to the idea that Stalinist regimes were invincible and that the working class had ceased to be a force in modern society or, more preposterously, that the Stalinist regimes had succeeded in brainwashing their population through the methods of totalitarian control. If it was possible to ignore East Germany, then the Hungarian uprising demolished these ideas once and for all.

'Totalitarianism' as a theory died quietly although the Cold War ideology lived on. Then came Czechoslovakia in 1968, and Poland in 1970–71 and again in 1980–81.

What all of these events had in common was the almost spontaneous and nearly unanimous rebirth of democratic ideas: workers' councils, independent trade unions, parties, freedom of speech and association, religion, culture, etc. In short, the re-emergence of society – civil society – from the all-encompassing embrace of the totalitarian state. No cynical lectures here about the 'impossibility of democracy' in the manner of Robert Michels.

And what they also had in common was the fact that these uprisings of democracy and national independence were all crushed by Russian tanks or the fear of Russian intervention.

What East Germany, Hungary, Czechoslovakia and Poland all demonstrated was that the Soviet empire was held together by force and that the Soviet presence in Eastern Europe was necessary above all to keep hold of its empire. It demonstrated that the massed divisions of the Warsaw Pact contained troops whose reliability was doubtful. And it demonstrated that what the Russians feared above all was the appearance on their borders of genuinely democratic movements – movements which could strike a sympathetic chord among their own people. Hence the ruthless crushing of the revolts.

For the Western Cold Warriors, the Hungarian revolt was the end of any notion of 'liberation' and tacit recognition that it was to the advantage of the West to recognize that Eastern Europe was in the Soviet sphere of influence. In short, the division of Europe at Yalta was a permanent fact of life.

From the standpoint of those who continued to hope for a continuation of the movement which had started in East Germany, what the revolts demonstrated was that until the center of the empire was affected by the same economic rot which had sparked them, and until there was the possibility of a beginning of dissent and pressure in the Soviet Union, there would be a stalemate in Eastern Europe. Solidarity found itself poised on the edge of power but was frozen by the fear of Russian intervention: instead there was a military *coup* led by Poles which forestalled the possibility of direct Soviet intervention but which has been unable even after seven years to bring society to its knees. 'Civil society' remains alive in the huge crevices of this military-bureaucratic collectivist society and only the glue of the fear of Soviet military intervention keeps it together in an uneasy, sometimes murderous compromise.

Civil Society and Democracy

But, as the case of Poland demonstrates, as did Hungary after 1956, and even, to a more limited extent, Czechoslovakia and East Germany, military force and repression could not stamp out the assertion of civil society. As the utter economic failure of the bureaucratic command economies grew ever more evident, as the regimes crumbled from within, there appeared a public opinion, much less than entirely free, more often than not having to express itself in *samizdat* books and periodicals, but also a growing force which not even the more repressive regimes could ignore, particularly when it found the protection of the only independent institution which survived, the Church.

Public opinion, first of all, was concerned about human rights and about the denial of democracy in these 'people's democracies'. And a public opinion concerned about both NATO and the Warsaw Pact: about the need for the removal of Russian missiles and troops from Eastern Europe as well as Western troops and missiles. This development of a politics of opposition to both war camps was greatly helped by the new peace movement which emerged in

Europe organized around European Nuclear Disarmament in response to a call by the indefatigable campaigner and historian, Edward Thompson.

But public opinion, to be a genuine public opinion, has to be *organized* opinion. This requires, depends on, freedom of association, freedom of speech, and above all, the freedom to organize opposition political parties. True democracy cannot be confined to one party by the fiat of the party which rules the state, even if it 'permits' factions.[11]

If one speaks about a 'return to Soviets' it is important to remember that when the Soviets first made their appearance, in 1905, and then again in 1917, the representatives were members of parties. The banning of opposition parties during the Civil War and the banning of factions within the Bolshevik party (which followed as night follows day from the first) spelled the end of the Soviets. It was the beginning of the end of the revolution as a democratic movement and the birth of the Stalinist state. The state then became the property of the single, totalitarian party and gave birth to the new class which today rules in the Soviet Union.

The Soviet Communist Party and its sister Communist parties in Eastern Europe or Cuba or Ethiopia or China cannot rule without a monopoly of political power because the class which it represents could not continue to dominate the society and the economy. This is why although the single party may be forced to allow more freedom of speech, even for independent associations to form, it cannot allow the appearance of a rival party. A rival party, a genuinely independent party, not one like those which have survived to this day in the 'people's democracies', is the death warrant of the ruling class in Soviet-type societies. This is old-fashioned Marxism applied to a new situation, one which Marx hardly foresaw, but in no way inconsistent with his theoretical views about the state bureaucracy as a class. One can only speak of socialism if the people have democratic institutions: ordinary people can only 'own' their state collectively and this requires democracy. The new class of bureaucrats or party/state chieftains, and their supporting strata which rests upon state property, can only 'own' the state and extract the economic surplus for its class needs (which include the military machine) by denying effective democracy to the people. Democracy without the right to organize an opposition party (or parties) is sham democracy: elections and multiple candidates do not change this basic fact of modern political life.[12]

Freedom of association, including the right to freely form parties, is essential: without it individuals, however 'free' they may be to utter opinions or answer the questions of pollsters, are essentially powerless to change the societies in which they live. Contrary to Michels, the real 'iron law of oligarchy' is the iron law of *non-organization*: in the absence of the effective right to organize collectively from below, oligarchical elites rule from above.[13]

The right to organize a political party in opposition to the Communist Party must be denied because the Communist Party's function is to enforce the class power of those who rule in Soviet-type societies. This is the line which the rulers must draw and have drawn. This is the limit of reform: cross it and you go beyond liberalization towards genuine democracy.

Peace and Democracy in Eastern Europe

What would democracy in Eastern Europe and the Soviet Union mean for the cause of peace? It would mean first of all the right of the people of Eastern Europe and the Soviet Union to national independence and to question their own war machine, in the way that we question ours. The new independent peace movement has already done that. It would mean the right of young people to stand up at a public forum and question the representatives of the regime about *their* war policies (their 'brinkmanship' as, for example, in the Cuban Missile crisis) and to brand the leadership for the criminality of their actions. And this too has happened – in the Soviet Union.[14] It would mean the right to openly organize opposition to the war in Afghanistan and, in the aftermath of withdrawal, to hold accountable those who initiated it. It would mean the right to organize independently of the state-run 'peace movement' and to meet and seek out the Western peace movement, to be able to travel freely without the shackles of the police state, to have the right of conscientious objection to militarism and the race to war on the part of the leadership of the Warsaw Pact. And this too has happened in parts of the Soviet system.

But above all, it would mean the right to organize a 'peace party' to offer an alternative to the militarists and Cold Warriors who run these societies. In short, to create a public opinion there, as we can do here, which can challenge the Cold War *from below* by the organization of popular opposition to the arms race of their own government. In this way the central tenet of the Western Cold Warriors can be labelled for the lie that it is: that the Cold War is a matter of weapons not politics because 'they' have no public opinion to which 'we' can speak. There is, of course, in my view, no single 'they' on the other side, and just as importantly there is no single 'we' in the West. Those of us who live in the West who believe in a society based on genuine democracy and freedom on this side have *everything* in common with our friends in the new democratic opposition in Eastern Europe and the Soviet Union, just as we have nothing in common with the Reagans and Thatchers, Mitterands and Kohls, here, and the Gorbachevs and Groszs, Honekers and Jakes, there.

In 1949, as the icy blasts of the Cold War seemed to freeze the choice for democrats, liberal or socialist, into two camps, Arthur Schlesinger, Jr, wrote in *The Vital Center* that

> … it is idle … to delude ourselves into thinking that totalitarianism and democracy can live together happily ever after. Until Russian public opinion can control its rulers, and not be controlled by them, we are not dealing with a nation in any intelligible sense; we are dealing with a group of men whose

> objective is the retention of power and who sacrifice anything to that objective. The problem of world peace, in other words, is to get some element of popular control into the Soviet system.[15]

Schlesinger's comment was a perceptive one. It was a tragedy, however, that he and his fellow liberals identified democracy with capitalism and Cold War social democracy and failed to see that there was a third way which could help to open up a space in the Eastern bloc, in which public opinion could begin to emerge even against the terrors of the totalitarian state. Yet, even after East Germany and Hungary, liberalism remained locked in the political cage it had constructed. It remained wedded to the 'crackpot realist' view of the world which underpinned the arms race and kept the world on the edge of destruction for decades, through the Bay of Pigs, the Cuban missile crisis, and directly to the crimes of the Vietnam war.

Intellectuals can choose to be either the servants of power or its critics. Schlesinger and his fellow liberals chose to be servants of the Cold War establishment. Edward Thompson and C. Wright Mills chose to be critics and to lend their intellectual skills to undermining the insane premises of the Cold War and to helping to build a political opposition which would combine reason and power. 'We ought,' Mills wrote,

> to act as political intellectuals ... We must realize ourselves as an independent and oppositional group. Each of us, in brief, ought to act as if he were a political party. We must act on the assumption that we are called upon to state issues, to judge men and events, to formulate policies on all major public issues.

Our objective, Mills argued, ought to be to 'break the political monopoly of the current powers that are set toward World War III' and that task 'required that their monopoly of ideas be broken'. It is this monopoly of ideas about the causes of war and peace which the new movement and the new ideas about civil society and democracy have begun to undermine. Mills' statement of the moral responsibility of intellectuals and social scientists is as relevant as it was 30 years ago:

> The epoch in which we stand is pivotal; the tradition of classic social analysis is clear. We must respond to events; we must define orienting policies. Should we fail to do so we stand in default of our intellectual and public duties; we abdicate such role as reason may have in human affairs. And this we should be unwilling to do.[16]

The threat of a third world war has not vanished, only lessened. But we are now at the end of the period in which the two war camps seemed to be impermeable. The ice age of the Cold War has ended with the emergence of civil society and a new democratic movement in Eastern Europe. In the West we need a new way of seeing things too and a new politics which links peace and democracy, and seeks allies in the peoples rather than the rulers of Eastern Europe and the Soviet Union. This is détente from below: a reaching out across the frontiers whose walls are erected to prevent citizens from finding their common humanity.

There are signs, even in America, that such a new politics is emerging, one that is free of the bondage of the Cold War. Not in the mainstream, not yet at any rate, but at the fringe, which is where all genuine change from below starts. A new politics will lead to a new democratic foreign policy in place of the Cold War. One that starts with the reality of an emerging public opinion in Eastern Europe – civil society arising out of the decay and collapse of totalitarianism – and proclaims its support for democratic movements everywhere: on both sides of a divided Europe, in South Africa just as surely as in the Soviet Union, in Chile just as firmly as in East Germany.

In the context of the danger of nuclear warfare, a new democratic foreign policy means unilateral initiatives such as the withdrawal of American troops from Europe, the dismantling of NATO and masssive cuts in the American defense budget. To the extent that the process of democratization in Eastern Europe and the Soviet Union remains incomplete, such a political unilateralism could open up breaches among the member states of the Warsaw Pact and even within the Communist parties themselves. At the same time such a new policy could help to create the political space for the democratic movement for peace in the East to make its own demands on its leaders for a unilateral end to the occupation of Soviet troops along with nuclear and conventional weapons and an end to the huge arms expenditures which exacerbate the economic crisis of their societies.

This is the prospect today for peace, real peace, not the 'peace of the graveyard' in a permanently divided Europe to which the East European opposition rightly objects. It is a peace which goes hand-in-hand with freedom and democracy, East and West, North and South. It is the possibility of realizing this goal, the only secure foundation for a peaceful world order, which the rebirth of civil society in the East and its reinvigoration in the West offers a new generation which can look beyond the Cold War and break down the barriers which the last generation has built.

CHAPTER 14

Transnationalism From Below: International Labour into the Twenty-first Century

Transnational corporations (TNCs) control a third of the world's private-sector productive assets according to the UNCTAD *World Investment Report* for 1993. In a restructured global economy, at present afflicted by a world-wide recession, wages and conditions of work in all developed countries are subject to massive downward pressures and long-term unemployment grows while capital seeks out ever cheaper or more 'flexible' labour to exploit in societies where an independent labour movement is weak or non-existent and human rights are denied.

The implications of the GATT agreement which has resulted in the setting up of the World Trade Organization (WTO) and of the North American Free Trade Agreement (NAFTA) must be examined in this context, as must the responses of the labour movements in Canada, Mexico, and the US. This chapter surveys the role and policies of the organizations of international labour in responding to transnational corporations and international institutions such as the International Labour Organisation (ILO), the International Monetary Fund (IMF), the World Bank, etc., which play a critical role in shaping the global economic system.

Just as the structure of national labour unions has been determined by the shape and structure of business in the single nation-state so too the organizations and policies of international labour have to adapt and change in response to the post-Cold War global economic system and the power of transnational corporations. The experiences, policies and politics of the European labour movement within the European Union are directly relevant to the formulation of a response by the North American labour movement to NAFTA. Transnational trade union collaboration and the seeds of transnational collective bargaining can be seen in the experiences of the European labour movement while the Maastricht Treaty's 'social chapter' provides a model which is worth close examination by the North American labour movement. It is in this context that we shall examine the question of cross-border collaboration of European trade unions in response to the restructuring of the European automobile industry. This collaboration involves unions within the industry as a whole as well as in particular companies:

provisions for employee representation within companies as part of 'social Europe' may provide the entering wedge for transnational collective bargaining, a goal long sought but never truly achieved.

In a larger, global framework, on the eve of the twenty-first century, the historic role of the labour movement in the nineteenth and twentieth centuries in fighting for democracy and social and economic justice, always internationalist to a degree, becomes one of assuring peace, democratic institutions, universal human rights and environmentally sound sustainable economic development on a global scale.

Trade unions are a vital part of any democratic society and play a critical role in providing economic and social protection for their members and, in the wider social and economic order, are a powerful force for the extension of those protections to society as a whole.

This wider social and political role is as much a part of the role of the labour movement as is collective bargaining or representation of workers to a particular employer or group of employers. Just as the labour movement in Canada and the United States is confronted with the low-wage economy of Mexico, so too the European labour movement has had to confront directly, following the end of the Cold War, the need to help establish independent trade unions in Central/Eastern Europe and to provide social protections which will raise living standards and mitigate the effect of the ill-advised policy of 'shock therapy'. In this context I shall examine the role of trade unions in the economic and political transformation of Central/Eastern Europe and their contribution to the alleviation of social and economic problems as part of a broader strategy to prevent 'social dumping' in Central/Eastern Europe and to protect economic and social gains of Western European workers.

Of particular interest are the links of the Central/Eastern European trade unions with European and international labour movement structures: the European Trade Union Confederation (ETUC), the International Confederation of Free Trade Unions (ICFTU), the 15 or so International Trade Secretariats (ITSs) and their European affiliates, and 'industrial councils' (EICs), representing metal workers, food workers, chemical workers, etc.

In having these organizational connections, the trade unions are unique as democratic membership organizations whose international ties mirror the structure of European and international business as well as the European Union, both in its present form and its potential one incorporating Central/Eastern Europe, however problematic that may still be. They are also unique in that their policies and actions, including solidarity campaigns, are, to a degree, formulated in a transnational context both out of necessity as well as ideological conviction.

Also to be considered is the place and role of the International Labour Organisation (ILO) in setting standards for social protection and providing a model of tripartite cooperation on these issues. Of course, this can only be a sketch of a very complex set of issues and institutions, but it is clear that the European labour movement is evolving willy-nilly toward a strategy of *transnationalism from below* to counter the organization of global, transnational capital. In this respect it is similar to the tactics of the independent European peace and democracy movement of the 1980s – one which was far more important than was ever given credit by the ideologues of the Cold War in Europe or America – and also bears many similarities to the mode of operation of the environmental movement. Or, to put it otherwise, we see in the international and European labour movement (East and West) the seeds of an alternative democratic or labour transnational political economy: an alternative to the unaccountable, undemocratic, increasingly authoritarian and anti-social political economy of transnational capital. Whether these seeds will take hold depends on many, mostly unforeseeable, factors, not least of which, however, is the political dimension, primarily the role of the European labour and social democratic parties and the European Socialist Party which provides a European umbrella for the former.

International Framework

The dilemmas posed by NAFTA and the World Trade Organization to the Canadian, Mexican and US labour movements are no different in principle than those confronting the European labour movement. The issues of national collective bargaining, employee representation and social policy in individual Western European countries or in Central/Eastern European societies cannot be addressed without consideration of the larger European, international, indeed, global, economic context which shapes the changes now taking place in this area. Nor, for that matter, can these issues be discussed in isolation from political and philosophical considerations about the role of the state and, in particular, the question of democracy: there is no way to take a neutral view of social policy, even if, of course, objective analysis of the conditions and techniques for achieving given ends is also required.

To be more specific, thinking clearly, theoretically as well as empirically, about these issues requires that it be done in the context of the following considerations:

(1) The current recession in Western Europe and much of the industrialized world and the restructuring of production which decreases rather than increases employment, leading to a long-term crisis of mass unemployment in the developed countries as well as the developing countries (See the *ILO Labour Report*, 1994).

(2) The intellectual and ideological assault under the slogan of the 'free market' by institutions such as the IMF and neo-liberal politicians and ideologues on the welfare state and social protection, and the demand in Western Europe as elsewhere for 'structural readjustment' through cuts in state expenditure, particularly targeted at social expenditure, and 'flexible' labour markets and

the deregulation of controls over conditions of health and safety, hours of work, protection for women, etc., are fundamental challenges to the trade union movement. 'Flexibility' and 'deregulation' are code words for, among other things, an assault on social protection and welfare provisions as well as on trade unions which are rightly perceived as at very least impediments to change and, especially when they exercise power politically and through collective bargaining or through strikes and demonstrations, opposed to the freedom of the market. If the labour movement cannot find an alternative economic and social program, beyond the post-World War II social democratic arrangments which are now demonstrably collapsing, even in Germany, where the peaceful co-existence of capital and labour was only until recently hailed as the evidence of the continuing viability of social democratic policy, then the prophets and advocates of a 'post-trade union' world will have been proven right. That it will also inevitably be a post-democratic world is not a matter which concerns them as it does us.

(3) The debate about placing human rights/worker rights clauses and environmental clauses in international trade agreements such as GATT and NAFTA.

(4) The crisis of democratic institutions and ideas reflected in the rise of neo-fascist and right-wing movements and political leaders as well as the construction of models from the right which started with Pinochet's Chile and continues with the latest version of authoritarian roads to development (one which has many, many similarities to old-fashioned Stalinism) put forward by the oligarchs of Singapore, Malaysia and China whose appeal to certain of the leaders and parties in Central/Eastern Europe is well known.

(5) The transnational nature of labour markets and the corresponding mobility of capital which allows it to move across borders in search of more favourable conditions in the form of low wages and minimal social protections. What began with industrial workers is now hitting skilled technicians, white-collar workers, and middle managers.

In all of these matters we are speaking of, of course, (to borrow a locution popular in the 1980s when speaking of the bureacratic state collectivist social order which collapsed in Central/Eastern Europe) the world of really existing capitalism – a world which corresponds as little to the ideological fantasies of neo-liberal ideologues as did the supposed 'socialism' of the Communists.

Central/Eastern Europe: Downward Pressure on Wages and Social Conditions

The greatest challenge which the European labour movement faces today is the integration of Central/East European (henceforth C/EE) economies into the

European Union to prevent 'social dumping', that is, both wage reductions and the absence of adequately funded social provision. The dilemma arises out of the fact that the 'Visegrad' countries (Hungary, Slovakia, the Czech Republic and Poland) who are at the front of the line in applications for membership in the EU have per capita incomes which are 30 per cent lower than Western Europe as a whole. The current threshold for structural funds or subsidies is 75 per cent and even if the Visegrad countries were to grow at 6 per cent a year from now on (and EU countries 2 per cent) it would require 20 years to reach this level. To provide structural funds at the present level would increase EU spending by 63.6 billion ECU annually. We have already seen the devastating economic effect of German reunification on the former West Germany: the cost has been high for the living standard of West German workers and the levels of unemployment (compounded by the world recession) in the country as a whole and in the former East Germany, the latter in particular, are extremely high.

When, in a few years, or even sooner, students of these issues look back at this period of transition in C/EE countries, the adoption of the policy of 'shock therapy' will be viewed with incredulity and regret for the lost opportunity to create a genuinely democratic third way. In Russia it has proven to be nothing less than a catastrophe, both economically and politically. The Russian case is particularly serious because it remains a major power capable of reconstructing, as it already has in the 'near abroad', Russian military power and of flexing its military muscles in other areas not so near.

It is worth noting in passing, in order to counter assertions that the present state of affairs was unavoidable, that any serious consideration of what has happened in Central/Eastern Europe would take us back to the history of the Cold War and the way in which year by year the options for internal political and social-economic development were foreclosed, not least of all by the policies of the former Soviet Union, but also by the unremitting military pressure of the West with its fear of a radical democratic transformation which would rebound into Western Europe. This can be seen in the reaction to the Hungarian revolution in 1956 and the upheavals of 1968 and, too, in connection with the rise of Solidarity, which it was feared might help to reinvigorate the democratic labour movement in Western Europe. To be sure, Solidarity was praised even by the purest of neo-liberal politicians, Mrs Thatcher; her elevation to heroic status in C/EE was indicative of the depths of justifiable popular hatred against the Communist status quo. It is worth remembering, however, that even as she praised Solidarity, Mrs Thatcher was helping to raze the British welfare state and cripple the democratic labour movement, preparing the way for the decaying society and low-wage economy which now exists. She was able to praise Solidarity in the same breath, significantly enough, as she discovered in Lee Kuan Yew's Singapore a veritable capitalist paradise, a model for the development of society she wished to see extended to other parts of the world.[1]

Trade Unions and Civil Society

In the course of the emergence of the opposition to Communist rule in C/EE during the 1980s, the concept of 'civil society' came to the fore. More a bundle of ideas and impulses rather than a coherent theory it had (and still has) one unifying thread: the idea that society, not the state, is central to human freedom and well-being, that the state must serve society rather than the other way around. 'Society' itself in this case requires a plurality of organizations and social movements organized independently of the state: parties and trade unions, pressure groups of all kinds such as those speaking for the interests of women and the protection of the environment.

It is at this point, however, that there appears a deep and irreconcilable division in the idea of civil society: one side advocates the freedom of property and domination by the market as, in its most extreme formulation, a substitute for democracy,[2] while the other, although accepting a role for the market, makes democracy and participation the key to social and economic progress that can benefit the majority of the population. The idea that the market can exist without the state or that modern capitalism does not require a vast centralized state, one in which democracy may be reduced to the merest formality, is one of those myths propagated by the neo-liberal ideologists. Thatcher's legacy to Britain of an authoritarian centralized state provides more than enough evidence for the refutation of this myth.

Within civil society, apart from political parties, the labour movement, organized into trade unions and associated parties, is the keystone of a democratic society in which the objective of social policy is to achieve social justice and economic equity rather than the mere alleviation of poverty. John Kenneth Galbraith, American liberal economist, has frequently written that the best cure for poverty is putting money into the pockets of the poor. Gainful employment, full employment, at a level of economic reward far above the minimum used to designate the poverty level, is the best means to assure this goal, together with a high level of social provision for education, health, old age and the other services which only the state can provide. In short, democracy requires social as well as political citizenship.

The labour movement is a redistributive force: for its members in its narrowest form, but in its broader role for the whole of society. It is inherently hostile to the free market in labour, which is the meaning of the neo-liberal call for 'flexible' labour relations, and to freedom of movement of capital in search of ever cheaper labour to exploit.

The attainment of these objectives as well as individual freedom depends upon effective organization from below – this is the root meaning of pluralism and (in its democratic non-neo-liberal version) of civil society. As the history, past and present, of the labour movement everywhere demonstrates, the labour movement plays a critical role in securing these goals. One recent example is the contribution to the transition to democracy of the South African trade union federation, COSATU, which organizes 50 per cent of the South African work-force. It ought not to be necessary to say this, but given the zeal of some to rewrite history, especially in Central/Eastern Europe, without the role of the democratic labour movement (here I include the democratic socialist movement as well), there would be no modern democratic welfare state and the standard of living of ordinary people in societies would have been far lower than it is. Only in exceptional circumstances, where a tiny oligarchy (for example, Kuwait, Saudi Arabia, Malaysia, Singapore) has sought to buy social peace, does there exist a simulacrum of a welfare state, ones without personal liberties and freedom of expression and by no means inclusive of the entire population, without an independent democratic labour movement. Even in these cases, apart from the degradation of the spirit which comes with a lack of political and intellectual freedom, the wealth which is available is by no means shared with any degree of equity and, in the long run, as must certainly happen in, for example, Saudi Arabia, the corruption which festers in such a closed system results in economic ruin.

The irreconcilabilty and the importance of these two ideas of civil society, between the pure free market and the social goals of a democratic society, is demonstrated by the deep hostility, for example, of the International Monetary Fund and the World Bank to democratic institutions and practices and, in particular to the regulation of the labour market and powerful collective bargaining laws for which organized labour stands, in their programs of structural adjustment. So extreme has this been that it has generated criticism from within other international agencies, most notably the UNDP and the ILO.[3] In the most recent edition of the *World Economic Outlook* (1994), the IMF has once again reiterated, perhaps in the strongest language yet, its policy in Europe and elsewhere, of weakening labour market regulations and its support for more flexible labour markets on the US model. This is coded language which means, if the American model of 'flexibility' introduced by the Reagan administration or the draconic New Zealand example also cited by the IMF mean anything at all, an assault on the welfare state and organized labour movement not dissimilar to that launched against the British labour movement in the 1980s – under a Tory policy which brought ILO censure for violation of basic rights agreed to by Britain as a signatory to ILO. These agencies of supra-national capitalism are, then, the vehicles for transnational corporations and their neo-liberal agenda for the world's working people and as such the deadly enemies of the democratic labour movement.

How central this issue is to the new world economic order which is conceptually at the heart of the Clinton transnational corporate policy may be seen in the recent controversies concerned with labour or workers' rights in connection with the ratification of the North American Free Trade Agreement (NAFTA) and the final ratification of the Uruguay Round of the General Agreement on

Tariffs and Trade (GATT). It may also be seen in the deepening controversy over the granting to China of 'most favoured nation' (MFN) trade status by the US government, a policy from which Clinton has, with his usual grace, now abandoned in response to the pressure from American business. In the recent speech to the Inter-American Development Bank[4] Lawrence Summers, Undersecretary of the US Treasury, suggests that the Bank ought to act to restructure 'labor laws to ensure stronger, more independent labor unions and protect workers' rights, including minimum standards for health and safety'. This has drawn a sharp rebuke from the *Financial Times* which in a leader (18 April 1994) finds that 'ominously, the new American emphasis on social ideals has parallels with its stance on labour and environmental standards in trade negotiations'.

The response to the *Financial Times* (21 April 1994) from Luis Anderson, General Secretary of ORIT, the Latin American regional organization of the ICFTU – significant in itself for the focus in this essay on the important role of the international labour organizations – deserves to be quoted for the way in which it highlights the positive link between strong trade unions and the objectives of social policy in contrast to the agenda of the neo-liberals:

> There is a close link, between reducing income inequality and encouraging trade unions, since only strong trade unions will be able to raise incomes for the low paid and so reduce income inequality ... Mr Summers is, therefore, quite right to argue for the strengthening of trade unions as the basis for social progress in this region ... The experience of countries which have proceeded to privatise their health and education systems, which your editorial appears to advocate, has been a serious decline in the quality and availability of services and the introduction of user fees.

According to the ILO, privatization of health and education has had negligible effects on efficiency but has caused a substantial worsening of available indicators of the health and education standards of the poor, hardly the way to address social problems. It ought to be added that Summers' welcome verbal departure from the Reagan/Bush approach is almost entirely the result of the political pressure which the American labour movement, the AFL–CIO, is able to place upon the Clinton administration. Its translation into policy is, of course, another matter: the back-down over the linkage of MFN to labour rights in China by the Clinton administration is evidence that it is not a serious policy. It is interesting to speculate about how a similar statement about labour rights would go down in, say, Arkansas, or for that matter in the rest of the United States. But, of course, that is just the point about how the rhetoric of labour rights can be turned around and used against those who use it for their own reasons, which is why even the purely formal insertion of social and labour rights clauses in the recent GATT agreement is fought against with such tenacity by opponents of the labour movement.

In the theory of 'comparative advantage', which in one form or another underlies the neo-liberal approach to such questions, free trade and workers' rights are incompatible. Writing of the US initiative to add workers' rights to the GATT agenda, the *Far Eastern Economic Review* quotes Noordin Sopiee, Malaysian chairman of the Pacific Economic Cooperation Council: 'They call it social dumping. We are dumping because our workers will accept lower wages and work longer hours and sweat and toil, whereas theirs won't.' The *FEER* comment on this reveals starkly – as if Mr Sopiee's Asian version of Victorian sweat-shop values were not stark enough – the underlying thinking of the free-market approach:

> Yes, there are abuses of workers in Asia, though we note that workers choose many alleged abuses such as salaries that may be low by Western standards. The claim that Asia's success is built on the exploitation of the worker gets the equation backwards. Asia is succeeding precisely because market opportunities make life better for those willing to work hard. Even in America and Europe, the children did not leave the factories because of legislation. They stopped working when their parents became wealthy enough to feed their families on their own. How outrageous it would be if a West whose workers already enjoy the fruits of affluence uses its economic muscle to make it more difficult for workers elsewhere to make the same progress.[5]

One can only comment that it is precisely this outrageous course of interference with the natural working of the free market which the international labour movement proposes to undertake now, as it has in the past, along with political parties and social movements whose conservatism – as in the case of the Christian Democracy – now seems positively left-wing when viewed from the standpoint of the neo-liberal global economic agenda. It ought to be mentioned at this point that the realization of the neo-liberal agenda in its Asian guise has little use for democracy and the exercise of human rights which might allow workers to 'choose' differently through the organization of trade unions and independent political parties. Thus, once again, is the indissoluble link between democracy and social policy which aims at a more equitable distribution of wealth and resources and the availability of social protections as well as environmental ones underscored.

'Comparative advantage' means cheap labour; while crocodile tears are shed over the Third World's inability to lift itself out of poverty, the reality is that it is the interests of transnational corporations and the world capitalist economy which are determinative as well as the ability of the local ruling groups to enrich themselves. What is true of the so-called Third World is no less true of Central/Eastern Europe.

In the coming months and years, especially as the new order brought into being by the GATT agreement and the formation of the World Trade Organization is completed, it is safe to say the issue of worker and human rights will become even more central to the debate over economic policy and it will require all of those who are concerned with social policy to understand that the question of social protection and workers'/human rights are two sides of the same coin.

Central/Eastern Europe: Challenge to Democratic Transnationalization

These considerations bring us back to Central/Eastern Europe and to the contextual considerations listed above. For Western Europe and for transnational capital, the C/EE countries now provide a new market as well as providing cheap labour in the context of a deregulated, hence profitable, labour market in which social protections have been seriously eroded. For the high wages and protected conditions of Germany there is now the alternative of C/EE (not to mention Britain) where workers may be paid, in a deregulated labour market stripped of antiquated protections provided by wages councils, as little as 89 pence an hour. General Motors, for example, pays workers in its Hungarian assembly and engine manufacturing plant 13 per cent of what it would pay in Germany. The downward pressure on wages and social provision throughout Europe as well as in the United States is exacerbated by the deepest recession since the 1930s and resulting levels of unemployment higher than any since then: unemployment which is not cyclical but structural. For C/EE, however, as for Western Europe and the US there awaits the threat of competition from yet lower wages and conditions of employment in China.[6]

Even without this threat and putting aside for the moment the looming prospect of the same type of permanent mass unemployment now seen in Western Europe, where unemployment will persist despite and, to a certain degree, because of, economic recovery based on investment in high productivity, there has been as the result of shock-therapy reform a massive rise in poverty and unemployment in Central/Eastern Europe. This is well-documented by the important study conducted by UNICEF in 1993 (*Public Policy and Social Conditions*). How and, indeed, whether, these consequences will be reversed, remains to be seen. But it is clear that unemployment and deteriorating social conditions will continue to be at the very center of the politics of social and economic policy for a very long time. Whether the outcome will favour redistributive policies will depend, to no small extent, on the role of the labour movement in C/EE and its Western European counterparts.

The demand for workers' rights is denounced by free traders as concealed 'protectionism', an undermining of the sacred theory of comparative advantage under which the benefits will trickle down, in time, to the population. And so it is: it is hard to see what is wrong with protecting living standards of working people in this way even if, in the longer run, it may be ineffective given the freedom with which capital moves. But in the context of an expanded European Union with, as the labour movement advocates, a floor placed under conditions of work, equalization of social protection and (if cross-border single or multiemployer collective bargaining becomes a reality) of wages provides at very least an impediment if not a final answer to the downward pressure on wages and conditions. Until, that is, it becomes feasible to move production to China or other parts of Asia where the 'Asian Way' protects low wages and social benefits are minimal.

The neo-liberals are right, then, from their standpoint, to denigrate social clauses and worker rights. Unions are inherently a challenge to the neo-liberal free market: they aim to restrict the labour market through collective action, both directly (collective bargaining, strikes, etc.) and indirectly through legislation which restricts the freedom of capital on issues of wages, working conditions, hiring, firing, child labour, women, health, safety, pensions, etc. In the course of these actions, in order to gain allies and to the degree that the unions are or see themselves as part of a social movement to redistribute wealth, they seek allies and form political coalitions (within one or more parties) to generalize their program.

In the so-called 'reform' programs of Central/Eastern Europe, unions play at best an ambiguous role, resisted by the new ruling groups, who are more often than not drawn from the old *nomenklatura* which used totalitarian one-party power to control workers (one vehicle for which was the old state trade unions) in order to maintain their control over the economic surplus, such as it was, generated by economic activity.

European and International Labour Organizations

With these considerations in mind, I want now to turn to the role of the international labour organizations which, in the European context, also mean the national federations and individual unions affiliated to these bodies.

The international labour organizations are, surprisingly enough, relatively unknown although some of them have been in existence for nearly a hundred years. The key organizations which are players in Europe, East and West, as well as globally are described below.

International Confederation of Free Trade Unions (ICFTU)

Originally founded as an alternative to the Communist-controlled World Federation of Trade Unions (now defunct in fact if not in name) the ICFTU emerged at the end of the Cold War as the dominant umbrella organization. Its affiliates are national trade union centers or federations of individual unions such as the TUC (UK), AFL–CIO (US), etc., with regional organizations in Latin America, Asia and Africa. Membership of the affiliates represents a total of some 80 million individuals. In most of the countries of C/EE there are now national affiliates of the ICFTU. A global congress is held every two or three years: the last was in Caracas. The ICFTU has been active since the collapse of the Communist regimes in C/EE and the Soviet Union in giving assistance and aid to the emerging independent trade union movement. It has worked closely with the East European operation of the AFL–CIO international department which, however, maintains an independent organizational structure in Eastern Europe, having recently opened an office in Prague. The AFL–CIO was notable for the enormous amount of direct material aid which it gave to Solidarity from the late 1970s onward. There is also a far smaller but not unimportant Christian trade union international body, the World Labour Confederation, with whom merger talks have been held from time to time over the last several years.

The European Trade Union Congress (ETUC)

The ETUC is similar in its basis of membership to the ICFTU: it is composed of national centers or federations in each of the member countries of the European Union. It plays a role similar to the ICFTU in mobilizing support for independent trade unions in the C/EE countries, often, of course, in collaboration with the ICFTU and the ITSs as well as, most importantly, the national federations affiliated to it who may, similarly to the AFL–CIO, have a presence in C/EE countries independently. This is especially true of the German trade union federation which, in turn, works closely with the Friedrich Ebert Foundation, the state-funded educational organization of the Social Democratic Party.

International Trade Secretariats (ITSs)

ITSs represent unions in particular industrial or professional areas: public service employees (increasingly in the private sector), metal workers (automobile and steel), food and hotel workers, journalists, teachers, clerical and retail workers, chemical and energy workers, etc. There are fifteen or so in all, though mergers are now pending between some of them. Individual unions in a given country may be affiliated to one or more ITSs depending on the composition of its membership. Many of the ITSs have regional organizations and, in particular, European organizations (European Industrial Councils or EICs) which correspond to the membership of the European Community. Their European character makes them eligible for financial support from the EU, just as the ETUC and its national affiliates are. The EU also funds European-wide industrial meetings of unions and, where there is agreement with employers in a given industry, EU funding is available for union participation in these meetings . The role of the ITSs in C/EE countries varies: most have affiliates in each country but several of them, notably the metal workers (IMF), chemical and energy workers (ICEF), the food workers (IUF), and the clerical and retail workers (FIET) are far more active than the others.

Other European support programs

In addition to the American and European-based unions and national centers which are active in C/EE, there are also Scandinavian unions and national centers which give considerable material support and provide educational and training programs for unions, especially those in the Baltic countries. With the entry of Sweden and Austria into the EU a strong push will be given to the European social dimension.

Funding for educational activity by these organizations, either singly or in partnership, in the C/EE countries comes from a variety of sources: national federations and individual unions as well as from some of the more affluent ITSs, particularly the metal workers and the chemical workers. A new and important source of funding is the PHARE Democracy Programme under which, for example, the 'Citizenship and Democracy' program jointly sponsored by the ICEF, IUF and the Michael Harrington Centre and the national affiliates of the ITSs is funded in three countries: Slovakia, Hungary and Romania. The PHARE Democracy Programme is now beginning its second round and the third will follow in September, 1995. The PHARE program's objective is to strengthen democratic practices through education and, to use the jargon of the international agencies, through 'capacity building', that is, enabling the institutions and organizations which are the recipients of the funds to carry on their activities once external funding has ceased. In short, its purpose is to strengthen the institutions and culture making up civil society, of which trade unions are counted a significant part. The British equivalent of the PHARE Democracy Programme may be said to be the Westminster Foundation which gives support, part of which is funnelled through the two major British political parties, to parties and trade unions, women's groups, etc., throughout C/EE (although its reach is far broader: roughly to the members of the Commonwealth and other regions of concern to the British government).

The International Labour Organization (ILO)

The ILO is the oldest of existing UN organizations dating back to the post-World War I period when it was part of the League of Nations. Its structure is tripartite: employers, unions and the state are all represented in its councils and its activities are aimed at strengthening a 'social partnership' between these actors. ILO Conventions setting standards for labour relations and social protections, particularly health and safety, pensions, etc., have been ratified in whole or in part by most of the new C/EE states. The ILO is particularly important for injecting a social dimension into structural adjustment programs. It is worth noting here that the end of the Cold War and the agenda for structural adjustment has seen a serious attack on the past policies of support for social protection and labour rights by the employers' organizations within the ILO. It should further be noted, in support of the point about the way in which human/worker's rights is coming to be at the center of the debate over the nature of the new world economic order, that the ILO Director General, Mr Hansenne, was, *de facto*, excluded from the 1993 United Nations Human Rights Summit in Vienna although, of course, it is itself a United Nations agency.

At the present time the ILO works in C/EE through the Central/East Europe Team (CEET) whose offices are in Budapest. CEET provides policy advice to government agencies as well as to workers' and employers' organizations on labour market issues and social policy.

The European Parliament

When considering the various organized forms of international trade unionism, particularly in Europe, the role of the elected European Parliament must be kept in mind. One of the promises of Maastricht is for a strengthening of the democratic role of the European Parliament, as a check on the European Commission. In the European Parliament, social-democratic representatives constitute the largest single block and there exists too a European Socialist Party to which all of the relevant parties are affiliated. Unlike the US, but not Canada, then, there exist parties to which the labour movement is directly or indirectly linked which support the policy of a social Europe (as do the Christian Democrats) to which the parties of the right, new and old, are increasingly hostile. Caught by surprise, at least in the case of the Tories, by the emergence of a supra-national Europe, one pointing to a Federal Europe with a democratically elected parliament, and aware now of the radical implications of such a Europe, right-wing parties now speak of a return to the idea of Europe as a free-trade association of independent states. Transnational capital will remain transnational, of course: hence their dilemma, forced to choose between nationalism or a Europe in which, to their discomfort, the trade unions and the left can play a powerful role. Increasingly strident appeals to nationalist and chauvinist sentiments by the 'respectable' right are on the rise to undermine the developing sense of a common European citizenship – a sense which goes far beyond the traditional left or labour movement, of course, but which must be the basis of a labour program if it is to be able to confront transnational employers. Once again, then, as in the period before World War I, labour and its parties represent a powerful force for internationalism or, more properly, given the political framework which points in the long run to a federal Europe of nations and regions, to democratic transnationalism – a transnationalism from below which the labour movement is ideally, indeed, solely, able to provide the social and political basis for in alliance with greens and the other new social movement.

Transnational Labour: 'Together in Europe' – Together in North America?

'Together in Europe' is the title of a recent FIET (clerical and retail workers) report (1994) on its program to bring together around a common European program the labour movement in Western and Central/Eastern Europe. These aims are shared by the other ITSs and the ETUC. It is, as it was when Portugal,

Spain and Greece were admitted to the EC, an attempt to place a social and economic floor on conditions in C/EE countries through an extension of the striving for a European Union Social Chapter, which is a central aspect of the labour movement's policy in Europe – and the target of the British Conservative Party, which has 'opted out' of this element in the Maastricht Treaty.

The involvement of the West European trade unions and the international bodies listed above has been primarily one of giving direct assistance to their affiliates in C/EE. For the most part, as a recent ETUC report notes, they have been systematically excluded from participation in the main PHARE program, from the 'Group of 24' (G–24) which is the umbrella group providing a framework for the coordination of bilateral assistance to C/EE. The G–24 consists basically of the same members as the OECD: the EC countries, the EFTA countries, Australia, Canada, New Zealand, the USA and Turkey. 'Relevant international organizations' are invited to attend the meetings of the G–24, but these are limited to the OECD and international financial institutions such as the World Bank, IMF, the European Investment Bank and the EBRD. NGOs such as the ETUC are excluded from the G–24. By way of underscoring the point made earlier about the fundamental hostility of neo-liberal-oriented structural reform to any institution, not just trade unions which seek to further social policies and labour rights, it should be noted that the ILO is excluded from the G–24 except on the expert level.

The trade unions in C/EE, as the ETUC notes, 'are faced with a very difficult situation':

> First of all they have to prove their credibility either as reformed successors of the former communist trade unions or as newly established trade unions, which may lack experience. They also find themselves in a rather paradoxical situation, supporting the restructuring process on the one hand while on the other hand defending workers' rights and the jobs jeopardised by that very process. A further problem is the generally negative attitude of the post-Communist governments towards trade unions, the social dialogue and social aspects in general – a reaction to the failure of the former 'socialist system'. Many of these neo-liberal governments believe in market forces and have no wish for interference from the trade unions ... In all of these circumstances the danger of social explosion and the need to develop a social policy and industrial relations, to establish a social safety net and to restructure the labour market through an active employment policy is more than evident.[7]

Because the independent trade union movement is in many respects, with the exception of Solidarity, in its infancy, and because the economic changes introduced by the new governments of the C/EE have been so drastic, it would be hard to describe much less to analyze the various aspects of social policy with which they have been commonly concerned. The vacuum created by the stripping of the old state unions' role as dispensers of welfare and other benefits which accompanied the collapse of the old order has been filled, when it has been filled at all, by the state, although such social provision has been seriously diminished. There is, however, still a fair degree of social provision in individual countries which is the result of collective bargaining between unions and employers, particularly the state sector which is still predominant in all the C/EE countries despite the exaggerated claims of the proponents of privatization.

Trade union pressure in securing improvements in wages and social protection, particularly in the area of pensions, has been important in all the C/EE countries. The continuing role of Solidarity in Poland is probably the best-known and important example of this: the recent strikes which resulted in the abolition of wage controls in certain industries demonstrate that even after a long period of decline and relative quiescence the tradition created by Solidarity in the period of Communist government remains a powerful one.

By C/EE standards, the roots of Solidarity are very old ones, almost two decades, and, in all accuracy, even longer because of ties to the old, pre-war labour movement in Poland. This makes the case of Romania all the more important because of the relative newness of the independent trade unions, although, it must be said, the successful internal reform of the old state trade union apparatus has played an important part in the emergence of a strong, relatively unified, labour movement. Romania is a country where the institutions of civil society and a democratic political culture were savagely repressed by the Ceausescu regime, particularly in its systematic assault on living standards and on women. Out of a historical background which even in contrast to the other repressive regimes of C/EE was especially brutal, Romania's rebirth, while not exactly spontaneous, and the emergence of a strong, democratic labour movement concerned with social policy as well as democracy are further evidence of the natural place of the labour movement in economic reconstruction.

Since 1993, the main Romanian trade union confederation, CNSLR-FRATIA, along with Alfa-Cartel and other smaller federations, have been holding a series of mass demonstrations and strikes in pursuit of its demand for a serious program of privatization and restructuring of state industry, investment in public works and infrastructure projects to fight unemployment, social protections for the elderly and poor, an increase of the minimum wage to 60 per cent of the average wage and the repeal of repressive anti-union legislation passed by the incumbent party.

The demand for privatization by the Romanian trade unions illustrates graphically how the social and economic programs in C/EE countries must be understood not simply as a response to pressure from the institutions of Western capitalism, but also as a popularly supported reaction to the dead-hand of the former bureaucratic state collectivist order in which the state owned everything and was, in turn, in the absence of political democracy, 'owned' by the elite which exercised a monopoly of political power.[8] When we speak of societies in 'transition' it is important to have a clear answer to both parts of the question, 'from what to what?' and at the same time to avoid, in response to the second part a determinist or fatalist (some would say, triumphalist) answer as if what has or will happen is the unfolding of a Hegelian world-historic process as in Fukuyama's tract, *The End of History*.

For the Romanian trade unions, privatization is less a serious economic program than a device to break the back of the still-powerful *nomenklatura*, for whom state industry is the source of continuing wealth and privilege.[9] Even though they use the slogan 'social market economy', the labour leaders have not yet squarely faced the contradictions between defending the living standards of their members and what will be required if they are forced to follow out the road mapped for them by the IMF and other advocates in Romania of privatization shock-therapy style. Their dilemma is summed up in a recent North Atlantic Assembly document:

> The enormous challenge facing the current [Romanian] government will be to balance the pain of restructuring on a population that has already undergone tremendous hardship and, at the same time, reduce state and inter-industry credits. Sadly, achieving these two goals simultaneously will be highly unlikely.

Of particular significance for the argument presented here is the blunt warning of the Assembly report that 'the gathering strength of Romania's unions could prove to be a new and important obstacle to any attempt of the government to begin severely reducing credits and increasing privatisation of state-run companies'.[10]

It is possible that the threat of an enforced austerity – an austerity which is hard to imagine given the awfulness of present conditions, unless it were backed up by an openly authoritarian regime which would restrict or, as in Pinochet's Chile (the most frequently cited model among the neo-Stalinist free marketeers), suppress the trade union movement altogether – will force the Romanian trade union leadership to think seriously about the much maligned 'third way' in which social and economic reconstruction goes hand-in-hand with the construction of an equitable and democratic society. The evidence, if the recent Polish and Hungarian election results are a guide (a very imperfect one, to be sure), is that the tide is turning in this direction. If so, its success will require a renewed effort by the labour movement and social democratic parties to bring about a European-wide economic and social policy.

This observation brings us back to the main concern of the ETUC and the various ITSs for, in the first instance, a European social policy, although increasingly this in turn requires an international if not global policy, the outlines of which are just beginning to emerge around the issue of human and workers'/labour rights. The correct emphasis on globalization as a trend should not obscure the fact that much transnational economic activity is regional, as Charles Oman, director of research at the OECD Development Centre, has cogently argued.[11] This is not an uncontroversial point of view, but it is fair to say that continuing to view Europe, an enlarged and inclusive Europe to be sure, as a viable regional economic entity is in the short and medium term a justifiable basis for the type of program put forward by the ETUC and European social-democratic parties.

There are other and perhaps far more important aspects of international labour policy which may have a profound effect on the labour movement in C/EE, particularly if the European Union is enlarged to include some of them:

(1) the long-dreamed-of but yet to be realized idea of cross-border collective bargaining with common employers;
(2) the related possibility of solidarity campaigns supporting workers in both the same industry or company as well as other workers subjected to government and/or employer pressure, and
(3) the creation of transnational works councils as now, however imperfectly, provided for by European law, which may be extended to the new members of the European Union.

The importance of these features of international trade unionism, underscoring the point about its unique characteristics as a movement that necessarily is driven to transcend the boundaries of the nation-state, cannot be overstated even if, at this stage, it is as much an idea as a reality. Yet the fact that the European Union now finances such cross-border meetings among employees and union members ought to be noted for what it promises in the way of future links between Western and C/EE labour movements. Solidarity campaigns – practical and moral support for workers in other countries – are not to be dismissed lightly, particularly when they involve a common employer or industry and open up the possibility of pursuing not only public relations campaigns but, more tangibly, boycotts and even sympathy strikes. (There is no European law, as far as I know, against secondary boycotts.)

In the long term (and the long term nowadays seems to be getting shorter and shorter), powerful global transnational forces will tend increasingly to overwhelm regional entities even as they have eroded the nation-state. In this respect, the arguments of British Tory anti-European Union politicians about the importance of other markets, particularly in Asia, ought not to be dismissed lightly. One can at least imagine the consequence of this, if all other things were equal, as the Singapore-ization of Britain and Europe rather than the reverse, as the advocates of the theory of political liberalization through free markets like to argue.

If so, the twenty-first century may come to resemble one of a number of dystopias in which a relatively small labour force sitting on top of an ill-paid underclass of under- or unemployed workers, provides the labour for a tiny economic and political oligarchy. This is surely not the end for which social policy is intended which is why I have insisted that democracy and human rights and positive non-marketable values of social justice and economic equity are an integral part of social policy. Fortunately, all other things are not equal and there is no 'wave of the future'; just as in Europe, the labour movement in Asia and Africa has girded itself to resist this trend.

In this context, the program for an inclusive European Union is one in which the social dimension is a powerful element, of which the program of the ETUC and the various ITSs can be seen as a first, important step, toward a global policy, one which will (or ought to) profoundly shape the debate about the future of employment, collective bargaining and social policy in Europe, West and East.

The European Car Industry: Social Europe vs. Free Trade Europe

There can be little doubt that the world-wide recession which has affected car production has had a serious impact on European producers and workers. According to the 'Second Tongue Report' to the Committee on Economic and Monetary Affairs and Industrial Policy of the European Parliament (September 1993), there have been, between 1987 and 1992, approximately 90,000 job losses per year in the European industry. In 1993, total European car sales were down by 17 per cent, the highest percentage decline since World War II. This is the equivalent of a sales reduction of 2.3 million vehicles. By 1996, there is likely to be 6.5 million units of excess capacity in Europe. By 1994, the German car industry will have reduced jobs by 300,000 from its late 1980s peak. Ford of Europe, now in the throes of a global reorganization to position itself as a genuinely global producer, cut 10,000 jobs through restructuring in 1992. Mercedes Benz made 40,000 job losses by the beginning of 1993. Continental AG, the tyre manufacturer, will cut 3 to 4 per cent of its 50,974 jobs in 1994 after having already made a 20 per cent cut in employment in 1991–93 and by 1996 it will transfer 25 per cent of its car-tire production to lower wage countries, particularly Portugal and the Czech Republic.[12] The list goes on and on. Moreover, in Central/Eastern Europe where almost all of the car producers have become subsidiaries of large Western corporations, the market has also slumped with the rise in unemployment and slowing economies. In some cases, notably Volkswagen's investment in Skoda, plans for a modernization loan and further investment have been shelved.

These developments and the wider recession, plus the pressure from the low-wage economies of Central/Eastern Europe, have put into question the future of 'social Europe', that is, the web of policies for social security, employment, etc., which were designed to place a floor on the economic conditions of working men and women in Europe, equalizing conditions between the poorer countries and regions of Europe.[13] At the extreme are the 'Euro-sceptics' of the British Conservative Party who wish to see the European Union revert to a free-trade association with Britain free to continue to opt out, as it has, of the Maastricht Treaty's social provisions. The point of opting-out is clear and explicit: to maintain and even deepen the low-wage British economy – now rivalling Portugal and perhaps, in time, the economies of Central/Eastern Europe – and, more subtly, to shore up the deeply undemocratic and corrupt British state over which the Tories have presided since 1979. Mrs Thatcher, who used to warn that the Labour Party would bring Eastern Europe to Britain, may have been right, except that it is her policies and those of her successors which points in that direction rather than those of the Labour Party and the trade unions. Surely it is ironic confirmation of this point that the major democratic reform movement in Britain, Charter 88, took its inspiration from the Czech opposition group Charter 77, and had the blessing of then dissident and frequent inhabitant of Czech jails, Vaclav Havel, who has since moved on to a rather more official position.

From the trade union standpoint, the feature of European social policy which stands out is the proposal for worker representation in transnational (that is, European as well as those based outside Europe with multinational European production) companies which employ over 1000 workers. UNICE, the European employers organization, and the European Trade Union Confederation (ETUC) have been negotiating for some time about the terms and conditions of setting up the formal machinery through which employers must consult with their employees over business issues which affect them. Even British employers, despite the Tory government's opt-out from the social protocol of the Maastricht Treaty, will be forced to accede to the establishment of some form of works councils precisely because of their transnational nature: British companies are by far the largest trans-European producers. Some 330 British companies employing 6.1 million people throughout Europe will be mandated to set up such works councils. Even non-union employers such as IBM and McDonald's will be affected. Whatever the practical effect of such arrangments, the symbolic impact would undoubtedly be very great. Among car manufacturers, chosen from a list of the largest international companies in the EU, four would be required to set up the machinery for worker consultation: Daimler Benz, Fiat, Volkswagen and Peugeot. All of these, of course, are already subject to national-based systems of employee representation, the best known of which is the German. It should be stressed here that employees rather than unions will be represented, a fact which has led many if not most British unions to resist, at least initially, because of their fear of how such a consultative set-up could be manipulated by employers against union collective bargaining. As they have come to realize that a cohesive trade union presence can lead to trade union domination of such consultative bodies, the resistance has waned.

As mentioned earlier, there already exist EU funds for cross-border meetings of unions with their counterparts within a single industry or with a common employer such as Ford Motor Company or Eastman Kodak. Meetings and agreements with employers take several forms, ranging from providing information about the state of the business to a degree of consultation about business decisions. Among the automotive companies which have participated either informally or formally in consultation and information sharing meetings are Volvo, Volkswagen, Renault, Toyota and Ford. Such meetings may involve joint exchange visits of managers and employee representatives from a multinational's operations in more than one country: Ford and Goodyear do this. In addition to these, there are the 'World Councils' or 'Company Councils' which are international meetings of work-place union representatives and union officials within a given transnational company. However, because of the nature of the single European Market and the high degree of political and economic cohesion between the participating countries, such international meetings have tended to recede in importance when compared to the European Industrial Council meetings.

One other important factor, more potential than realized, is the mobility of labour across Europe: the possession of a common European Passport and the corresponding ability of the national of one country to work (and vote, if resident) in any of the member-states means that a common European citizenship is emerging, although very slowly because of cultural and language barriers. It also means that members of a British union may be working in the same industry, perhaps for the same employer, in, for example, Germany, while retaining their British union membership as well as that of the relevant union in the country of residence.

National unions are not, on the whole, given the mixed industrial character of their members (especially true for the so-called 'general' unions), affiliated to just one ITS or its European equivalent. Manufacturing, Science and Finance (MSF), one of the most progressive unions, is affiliated to six European trade union organizations: metal workers, chemical and energy workers, commercial and clerical workers, food workers, transport workers and pharmacists. A similar list could be drawn up for other unions and thus the contact and collaboration between unions in the same country as well as transnationally is reinforced. One could take the list of legislative demands for Europe, drawn up as long ago as 1988 by MSF, as representative of the views of most of the big British unions and their European national and transnational counterparts:

(1) Establishment of Industrial Sector Joint Committees as a matter of right. Such committees have already been established but their creation can still be blocked by employers. These committees bring together trade unionists, the European Commission, and representatives of the principal companies operating within clearly defined industrial sectors [e.g., auto] in the Community in order to consult on matters of mutual concern and interest.

(2) Language training should be made available for all trade union nominees serving on joint committees with appropriate release time with pay and reimbursement of all travel costs.

(3) Trade unions to be given the right of six-monthly joint consultation meetings with the management of individual firms operating in more than one Community country. (See above.) This would include a statutory right to discuss all issues relating to the enterprise. MSF has a number of such voluntary agreements as do the the unions and International Metalworkers' Federation (IMF) and its EIC operating in the automobile industry. Out of such arrangements should emerge framework legislation to allow for 'best

practice' on industrial democracy to be activitated by trade unions at company level.

(4) Protection of employee interests in mergers and takeovers as well as a consideration of the public interest. This would include a statutory right to consultation for unions and special provisions to cover takeovers involving companies based outside the EU, for example, Nestlé's takeover of Rowntree in Britain.

(5) Removal of national legislative obstacles to trade union solidarity action so that all trade unionists in the Community have common rights. Thus British workers cannot take sympathetic action on behalf of other British workers or even of French workers, while French workers can support British workers.

(6) Require all companies to set up jointly with trade unions vocational education and training committees. This would be backed up by Community readaptation funding to assist with restructuring and retraining to avoid technological and other redundancy.

(7) Trade unions to adopt collective bargaining objectives aimed at moving toward an upward harmonization of terms and conditions within the Community including a minimum wage, a 35-hour normal basic working week and the right of all workers to an occupational pension scheme.

(8) Health and safety standards to be set at the highest level with trade unions guaranteed involvement in their implementation and monitoring.

(9) To deter multinational companies from relocating production and investment to countries where either free-trade unionism is restricted or where the government refuses to agree comparable standards, the Community ought to support the ETUC demand for a 'social clause' in GATT covering minimum requirements on health and safety, union rights and environmental protection.[14]

Undergirding the hopes of the European trade unions is the concept of 'social partnership' between unions and employers. Launched by Jacques Delors, it provides, at least in theory, a framework for collaboration between employers and unions, including the proposals for European works councils. Given the resistance and final defeat by the employers of the Vredling proposals over five years ago and the worsened industrial relations scene at the present time, not to mention the escape valve provided by Central/Eastern Europe and, more broadly, the globalization of production, one would be right to be sceptical about the future of 'social partnership'. In very large part, the struggle over a successor to Delors was connected to the issue of the social dimension of EU policy: its resolution in the direction of the right-wing policies of the British government and their new-found allies, for example, in the Italian government of Mr

Berlusconi, is not impossible. If so, it would be a major setback for the labour movement.

At the same time, the elections for the European Parliament which took place in June 1994, will provide a measure of the political support for a progressive, democratic Europe.

Conclusion: NAFTA and the European Union

Comparisons are imperfect, but it is fair to say that NAFTA as a free-trade area is not dissimilar to the original form of the European Community over 40 years ago. NAFTA is now a fact and the predictions about its consequence from both supporters and opponents will be tested in the not-too-distant future. For those who opposed it, however, it is not necessary, nor would it be wise, given the dire nature of their warnings, to wait until their fears are confirmed to begin to press for basic changes in the terms of the agreement. What I have suggested in this chapter, in focusing on labour's role and the social dimension in the European Union, is the need to think about changes which move beyond the free-trade model to social and political change.

The sheer weight of the US and the conservative nature of its dominant political formations argue strongly against any idea of political union in the near or even middle distance while the authoritarian nature of the present Mexican regime reinforces this conclusion. And yet, just as the labour movement in Europe is a force for transnational democratization from below within the EU, so too the labour movements in Canada, Mexico and the US have at least the potential, the subversive potential it must be said, of slipping underneath the formal structures of NAFTA and of opening up the field to change, challenging transnational capital and its supra-national agencies such as the IMF with a radical democratic program for social and economic change.

Desirable changes in a direction which would benefit ordinary working people in all three countries would involve a social-economic as well as a political dimension, perhaps starting with the idea of an Assembly of the Peoples of North America. There is also much to be learned from the EU program for a 'social Europe', particularly the demand for an upward harmonization of conditions. These ideas, suitably modified, might be borrowed along with the idea of structural funds to begin to equalize conditions, especially for Mexico, but for the poorer regions and peoples of the US and Canada as well, to offset the costs of economic dislocation and change. These funds, let it be said, would be paid for by the transnational corporations and financial institutions rather than by the taxes of working people.

Political change – which, in the case of working people, is not separable from economic and social changes – can take as its fulcrum the demand for human and workers' rights and democracy. It ought not to be thought that Mexico's authoritarian government with its frequent violation of democratic norms and human rights is the sole target of such demands. On the contrary, these demands are fully applicable to the United States with its anti-labour laws and practices. Moreover, the terrible poverty and squalor in both urban and rural parts of the US are no less the legitimate subject of concern for the reform of NAFTA.

Here, however, we come to the black hole in US politics, the invisible force which determines and distorts any agenda for progressive change: the absence of oppositonal politics and an oppositional political party of the left. Because it is invisible, just as a black hole is, it does not mean that it does not exert an enormous influence on US political and economic policy and, therefore, indirectly on any program for progressive change within North America as a whole. What the ruling American establishment can do (or not do) depends on whether the vacuum on the party political left continues. We have already seen how a billionaire populist demagogue can take advantage of this vacuum: far, far worse could be waiting in the wings – indeed its shape may be seen clearly enough in the form of Patrick Buchanan.

It may well be that one of the most important contradictory effects of NAFTA will be not only to bring together the labour movements of the three partner countries, but to awaken the American labour movement to the necessity of creating its own party. Such a change is needed, of course, in Mexico as well. Recent events there point to the breakdown of the previous monopoly of the ruling party: what will fill it will depend, in part, on the development of sympathetic forces in Canada and the US: stronger trade unions, first of all, but because real change requires politics and politics requires equal partners, imbued with the ideas of social and economic justice for all beyond the boundaries of the present nation-states, working class political parties are essential as well.

Certainly the forces of economic globalization and the realization of the agenda of transnational capitalism which have culminated in the GATT agreement and the pending formation of the World Trade Organization were at work in the massive pressure from key sectors of US, Mexican and Canadian capital for its passage. In finding in Bill Clinton one of its most vociferous champions, the fundamentally conservative and anti-working class nature of the Democratic Party was revealed, the opposition of a majority of elected Democratic representatives notwithstanding. The pressure from below, from rank-and-file voters, in opposition to NAFTA, was a demonstration of a fundamental cleavage between the Democratic Party's traditional supporters, particularly the labour movement, and those who have accepted their support over the years in exchange for only the most minimal legislative program of benefit to labour or working people in the United States.

To conclude, it is appropriate to quote the Mexican poet, Octavio Paz, whose sentiments eloquently express the underlying theme of this chapter:

> No matter what the future holds, one thing seems certain to me: the institution of the market economy, in its heyday now, will change. It is not eternal; no human creation is. I do not know whether it will be modified by human

> wisdom or destroyed by its excesses and contradictions. In the latter case, it could drag democratic institutions down with it – a possibility that makes me tremble with fear, since we would then enter a dark age, as has happened more than once in history. Whatever happens, it is clear that the immense, stupid and suicidal waste of natural resources must come to an immediate end if the human species wishes to survive on this earth. The cause of the colossal squandering of riches – or our present and future life – is the circular process of the market … No civilization of the past was ever ruled by such a blind, mechanical, destructive reality. (*The Other Voice*)

In the rush away from totalitarianism in the early 1990s, such views came to be seen as old-fashioned although they could be applied with as much justification, with appropriate modifications, to the bureacratic collectivist social order which imploded five years ago. The excesses and contradictions are now becoming apparent, nowhere more so than in the unnecessary impoverishment and diminution of life in Europe as well as Canada, Mexico and the United States, not to forget the developing nations of Latin America and Africa. What is now old-fashioned is coming, slowly to be sure, to be recognized as the basis of a true reconstruction of society and economy, a concern which must focus of economic and social justice. It is the only alternative to a descent into a new barbarism whose outlines can be seen in the disintegration of the former Yugoslavia and in the rise of nationalist and fascist currents which provide an answer other than the one presented here to the crisis which confronts us all.[15]

Note on Sources

For this essay I have drawn on interviews with trade unionists involved in the ICEF/IUF/Harrington Centre project. I am especially indebted to Peter Schmitt, Central/East European coordinator of the ICEF, David Clement, co-director of Labour and Society International, and to Denis MacShane, MP, until recently the communications director of the International Federation of Metal Workers (IMF – the other one, that is). Denis generously allowed me to read chapters from the manuscript for his forthcoming book on the international labour movement. Documents published by the various ITSs were also very helpful, particularly those produced by the IUF, FIET and ICEF as were the publications of the European Trade Union Institute. The ICFTU monthly newspaper, *Free Labour World*, is an invaluable source of information. Also of considerable assistance have been the *Working Papers* and issues of the newsletter published by the 'Transitions to Democracy' network in Belgrade, of which the Harrington Centre is a founding member.

CHAPTER 15

The End of 'The American Dream': The Crisis in American Politics

'The American Dream': it sounds like an advertising slogan but until recently it seemed real enough to many middle and working-class Americans. Get a good education, work hard, own your own home, expect an ever-rising standard of living, be reasonably secure in a well-paying job with fringe benefits, including employer-paid health insurance. And above all know that your kids will be able to aspire to the same and more: a moving Stairway to Heaven, always with a happy Hollywood ending.

When I was growing up in America, being 'middle class' meant being a doctor or a lawyer, or like my father, a small businessman. However, because it was the 1930s, and my father was not a typical small businessman – the kind of true-blue Republican portrayed in the Lynds' *Middletown* – he, having been a socialist in his youth, now, like a lot of other small businessmen sympathized with the rising labour movement. After all, social security (on which my mother was later to live following his death) also included self-employed people like him, and he knew, as many middle-class Americans knew, that it had been gained because of the pressure of a growing, militant labour movement. He boasted that he had been the first wholesale produce broker in Phoenix to recognize the newly organized over-the-road Teamsters union, to the disapproval of his fellow brokers.

Ten years later, after World War II, 'middle class' gradually began to take on its present meaning. First, as the old, entrepreneurial middle class visibly declined, it meant the new employees of large corporations and government and even the no longer self-employed professional engineers and lawyers. Doctors were an exception, and the conservative ideology of free enterprise represented in the AMA continued for many years as a reflection of this fact. In 1951, in *White Collar*, C. Wright Mills wrote about the 'new middle class' (and in Britain, David Lockwood, about the 'blackcoated worker') while a brilliant journalist, W.F. Whyte, discovered the 'organization man' who was the 'man in the grey-flannel suit' in one of the most popular post-World War II novels. Arthur Miller's *Death of a Salesman*, both in its theatre and film versions, gripped large audiences of anxious middle-class people who, having grown up in the Great Depression, feared a return to the bad old days and realized that American society was changing in ways no one fully comprehended.

'Working class' still meant working class – although many, perhaps most, American workers preferred to *call* themselves middle class. But working for a living and admiring those who did, including those who worked with their hands or at least didn't scorn getting grease on them as engineers or supervisors, was also a powerful tendency. Walter Chrysler had called his autobiography, *the Story of a Workingman*. What was missing in America was a socialist or labour party: testimony to the relative absence of class conflict and growing affluence after the war. Still, Richard Centers' panel study of class consciousness in America which happened to coincide with the triumph of the Labour Party in 1945, showed a statistically large leap in the number of Americans who identified themselves as working class.

By the 1970s, after two decades of prosperity brought about by expansion and the permanent war economy, and with the prodding of sociologists determined to prove that there were no real classes in America, only the middle class (the contradiction still eludes them), 'middle class' gradually took a turn toward being defined in terms of income rather than occupation or position in the production system. To make this consistent new definitions were being given to occupations even at the same time as, it is true, the older industrial working class went into decline and an even newer group of service and professional employees as well as government employees began to grow exponentially.

But the illusion that the old, entrepreneurial middle class was still, somehow, intact persisted. Even industrial workers, chained to the production line dreamed, as Harvey Swados showed in his wonderful little novel of the early 1960s, *On The Line*, the American dream of escaping their drudgery and finding independence from their corporate employers by starting a small business.

Finally, to fit the dominant conservative ideology the working class was made to vanish – conceptually, that is – and everyone, with the exception of the very, very rich and the very, very poor who had dropped out of the class system entirely, became 'middle class' to the point that in 1995 the editors of *Parade* magazine see nothing absurd in telling its readers that the definition of middle class is a two-person household under age 65 with a total annual income between $9,977 and $66,794![1]

It would be closer to the truth, of course, to say that most of the American middle class, the 'old' independent self-employed middle class, that is, had become members of a new working class, employees, dependent upon corporations or government for their livelihoods. The revolution – perhaps it would be more accurate to call it a counter-revolution – in American health care which is now going on is rapidly transforming medical doctors, the last great hold-out of the independent professional class, into a class of professionals entirely subservient to the giant insurance companies and corporate HMOs which have taken over American medicine in just the last few years. 'Managed care', says one professional medical manager writing on 'medicine's industrial revolution' means the end of '2,500 years of clinical hegemony'.[2] When one adds in the tiny number of independent farmers left in American agriculture, most of whom are directly or indirectly dependent on huge transnational agribusiness corporations, the inescapable conclusion ought to be that the 'middle class', in the sense that the term was used as late at the 1940s, has vanished for ever in America. In the next ten years, one can reasonably expect medical doctors, to be organized into unions along with the rest of the medical professions. And if or when the few remaining small farmers revolt before they disappear for ever, they will probably be assisted in their attempts to organize, as they have been throughout the past 20 years, by organized labour.

However, the dominant ideology and fear of class and social conflict being what they are in the United States today – as the Republicans confirm when they charge their enemies with the sin of threatening to wage class war even as they wage the most intense ruling-class war in many years on the American people – everyone in the US is still 'middle class', even though the meaning of the term has been changed beyond recognition. Thus, President Clinton sees fit to tell trade unionists assembled at the 1995 Alameda, California, Labor Day picnic, how important it is to defend the interests of the endangered 'middle class' which is embodied in the trade union movement. Change just two words, and the President's speech would be a clarion call to class war (something he is not inclined to do, to say the least). But that is something that is to be avoided at all costs in American politics, at least for the time being, for fear of what it will unleash given the deep discontent and insecurity among Americans today.

Throughout these ideological shifts and a growing reality gap, the American Dream persisted and was given material support by the Cold War defense economy, although after the Vietnam war even members of the establishment began to see that the growing deficit born of the arms race was beginning to undermine American capitalism. But, in the first 20 years after the end of World War II, upward mobility through higher education supported by the GI Bill was probably one of the most effective means for children of the Depression generation to enter the ranks of corporate employees and independent professionals. Few of them dreamed any longer about owning their own small businesses. My brother, graduate of Caltech, became, in 1949, the first ever in our family to work for a large corporation: a government-spawned defense firm in which he was hired as an 'engineer' – which only a few years before had meant a self-employed or at least individualistically rugged professional – as in 'civil engineer'. True, Thorstein Veblen, radical critic of American capitalism and father of modern technocratic politics, had written of antagonism between the 'engineers and the price system' way back in the 1920s, but it was only in the post-World War II years that the engineer lost his (and it was certainly *his*) aura as an independent professional who now worked for a large firm of engineers, and shared an office with many other engineers and a nearly indistinguishable (except by their clothing) mass of draftsmen.

Prosperity, largely born of the permanent war economy: the American Dream. Work hard, move upward, own your own home. But the shine was off it in cultural terms long before it actually began to happen in the 1970s. William Whyte's enormously popular *The Organization Man* is at best ambivalent about the fate of the new managerial strata: independence has been lost and whether what will take its place is good or bad is left as a question mark. *The Lonely Crowd*, that brilliant book of social reportage, is more affirmative and upbeat, but its 'autonomous' man (always men) are still pretty lonely and rather unconvincing.

And then there is that enduring symbol of the false and empty nature of the American Dream: Willy Loman who, dreadful fate, works for a company, but half believes that he works for himself, like some modern-day former manager turned contract consultant. For the post-1945 generation still dreaming of independence, this was the great fear and the reality of their fathers, their brothers and themselves, exacerbated by the 1949 pre-Korean War and pre-defense economic recession. Willy owns his own home: but it is falling down around his ears as he ages and his income declines.

Owning your own home: possibly this was the most tangible symbol of the success of the American Dream after World War II, or even in the depressed 1930s when low-cost FHA-insured and government-subsidized loans were made available by the New Deal – two per cent interest and the right to 'homestead' the family house against repossession. Not today: many in the generation of the 1980s and 1990s have no hope of accumulating enough capital to own their homes.

The American Dream flourished in the period from 1945 to 1973. Prosperity gradually emerged. Willy Loman seemed a bit dated and John Kenneth Galbraith celebrated *The Affluent Society* whose title helped to create a myth which wasn't punctured until the early 1960s when Mike Harrington 'discovered' *The Other America*: the poor, mostly the working poor, but also what later came to be known as the 'underclass'.

In the 1970s the upward movement came to an end along with the last spasm of social and economic reform, Lyndon Johnson's Great Society.

Terms like 'middle class' don't travel particularly well between different societies. This was brought home to me many years ago, around 1971 or 1972, when I was asked to show a visiting Russian expert on automobile production to see the Fremont, California General Motors plant which was then the most advanced example of just-in-time production. He was accompanied by a hefty blonde woman who I assumed to be his KGB watcher, since most visiting Russians then came accompanied by watchers. As we toured the plant, with its smoothly functioning line, Igor became visibly depressed. When we finally left the plant he barked at me: 'Take me to see where the workers live.' I took him to the Fremont working-class suburb where the California sun shone on gleaming ranch-style houses, large well-trimmed lawns on which there were parked new cars and boats. Igor turned to me in a rage; 'Not working-class! Is middle-class!' (Today,

I am told, Fremont is shabby and depressed. The realities of capitalism came home to roost ten years after Igor's visit.)

Stung, feeling that I had been accused of being an agent of feel-good *Reader's Digest* capitalist progaganda, I protested in vain that this was a typical unionized workers' neighbourhood – not unlike those he might have seen Detroit, including its black working class. But Igor kept shaking his head in disbelief. 'OK, pal', I said, finally getting fed up, 'I'll show you "middle-class"' and I drove the 20 miles back to Berkeley, detouring on the way to show Igor the public housing estate in downtown Oakland which looked from the outside like luxury housing for the Russian middle *nomenklatura*, possibly Igor's level. By this time, even the KGB woman was beginning to look decidedly downcast. Up to the Berkeley Hills where the professionals and professors live in lovely bungalows overlooking the bay. 'This', I said in my best *Reader's Digest* manner, 'is middle-class.' His face fell, and I thought he and his companion, who became engaged in a heated conversation in Russian, might be considering suicide or, more likely yet, defecting. I drove them back to their hotel as they fell into a deeper and deeper state of silent depression.

Wallace Peterson's book, *Silent Depression: The Fate of the American Dream*[3] is the latest and one of the best of many books, stretching back to the mid-1980s, to demonstrate that the American Dream, whatever its post-World War II reality may have been, is in serious trouble, perhaps even finished for good.

I don't know whether he intended the title to be a play on words but there is evidence enough in this excellent book of the devastating psychological consequences of the economic developments which are summarized in it. As an economic term 'depression' certainly hasn't yet re-entered popular discourse even though most middle Americans are well aware that their circumstances and their expectations for their children have changed for the worse. When I asked for a copy of Peterson's book in the New York Upper West Side branch of Barnes and Noble, the young clerk directed me, not entirely inappropriately, to the psychology section. If Peterson is right, and I think he is, it's possible that the next Woody Allen movie, ever a barometer of middle-class *angst*, will be 'Down and Out on the Upper West Side'. If so, I am willing to give odds that it will be a smash hit at the box office.

'Depression', of course, is a technical word in the lexicon of professional economists. It's one that none of them would apply to the slow, two-decade-long downward slide of the American middle classes and the growth of a class of the permanently impoverished as described in *Silent Depression*. Peterson is the exception: an academic economist who argues convincingly that the US has been in an economic depression of a different kind for the last 20 years, one in which a 1930s-type crash has been avoided by government programs which have prevented, for example, the loss of individual savings in the disastrous Savings and Loan collapse of the 1980s, but which still deserves to be called a depression.

In chapter after chapter, dealing with unemployment, housing, the strains on the disintegrating American family, and much, much more, in a mixture of clearly presented statistics and illuminating anecdotal evidence, Peterson constructs a powerful argument. His case is simple enough: for two decades four-fifths of American families have experienced falling or stagnant real incomes. 'The paradox of the silent depression', Peterson argues, 'is that hard economic times have hit a majority of American families during years when the conventional measures of recession or depression ... do not tell us that the economy is depressed'. 'Conventional' means the definitions of economists who, captured by their categories, lack the common sense or humanity to ask what is happening to real human beings. Anxiety, insecurity, depression and fear of falling may not be economic categories but they are certainly the consequence of a massive economic upheaval which underpins much if not most of the volatility in American politics, as Bill Clinton knew in his 1992 election campaign.

The base period from which Peterson begins are the boom years from 1947 to 1973. Real weekly earnings grew at an annual rate of 1.9 per cent which meant real economic gains for growing numbers of Americans: 'The generation that survived the Depression and fought in World War II became accustomed to regular, substantial, and uninterrupted improvements in their material standard of life.'

After 1973, the figures tell a different story. In real dollars, the weekly earnings of individual workers dropped from a post-World War II peak of $308.03 to $279.56 during the 1982 recession and during the expansion of the Reagan–Bush years, real wages sank even further, to $260.37 in 1991: 'Thus, as the 1990s began, the buying power of the earnings of a typical worker was 15.5 percent below what it had been eighteen years earlier.'

The same trend, Peterson demonstrates, applies to median family income. Much of the apparent rise in the purchasing power and rising standard of living during these same years was due to the enormous expansion of the two-income family and the entry of large numbers of married women into the labour force. The rate of growth continued but it slowed down to a trickle. In contrast to the period between 1947 and 1973 when the rate of growth, if sustained, would have led to the median family income doubling every 25 years, or approximately every generation, the present rate means that it would now take nearly 400 years for the real income of a family to double. In an attempt to partially compensate for this, as a new US Labor Department report which lends support to Peterson's case demonstrates, married couples have resorted to multiple jobs. Seven million Americans or 6 per cent of the labour force, most of them married and nearly as many women as men, hold a total of 15 million jobs. This is in addition to a massive amount of overwork, often unpaid, in a primary job. But even with such desperate measures there is no chance at all that the old economic expectations can be met. The psychic cost is enormous and the consequences for the break-up of the family, alcoholism, drug-taking, stress, delinquency, etc., can be correlated directly with these developments. So much for fatuous and empty moralistic slogans about the restoration of community and family values without basic economic and social changes.

In short, Arthur Miller's Willie Loman is back. The stairway moving endlessly upward, smiling nuclear family and all, has reversed direction for most Americans. It has become at best a terrible treadmill and for most an irreversible slide.

'Dumpies' not yuppies are the norm. Peterson demonstrates that million of working people have to run faster just to try to stay even or to prevent themselves from slowly being carried out of the middle class, while their less fortunate friends and neighbours, not to mention their children, take pay-cuts or suddenly lose their jobs and find themselves, if they are lucky, in a job paying half or less than their former job. If unlucky, they end up homeless and in the netherworld of the underclass. Peterson is surely right to say that it's something that every American knows, even if they don't know what to do about it. It's a widely shared experience: the phone call on a quiet Sunday afternoon from a son who has suddenly been told that his pay has been cut from $6.00 to $5.34 per hour. Where will the school clothes for the kids come from? Fact, not fiction. No wonder there are a lot of angry working Americans out there and why there is now clear evidence, surprising as it may be to those who have pronounced them dead, that American unions are once again beginning to grow.

Most Americans, four-fifths of them, are going down. But for the fortunate upper fifth it's not bad at all. Hardly surprisingly, the share and the absolute wealth of the upper 20 per cent continues to grow and grow, as Peterson demonstrates, while the middle class descends and the size and poverty of the lowest fifth of the population increases. Theories of the 'underclass' serve a useful if obvious ideological function. Growing inequality is just another blow at the American dream, not that it ever was really an economically egalitarian society, only that everyone seemed to move up at the same rate and poverty shrank – for a while.

A declining middle class; a growing and desperately poor underclass, disproportionately black; a rich, contented and powerful over-class: social and political dynamite, a situation begging for solutions. The evidence itself is no longer seriously disputed, as it once was by the Pooh-Bahs of the official economics establishment, and it is all the more powerful because it is a long overdue concession by the right and the centre to the left, where the case was first made in the early 1980s by Barry Bluestone, Barbara Ehrenreich and Michael Harrington, among others. 'Silent depression' is a good and accurate way to describe it.

In the concluding sections of his book, Peterson sketches out a program for resurrecting the American Dream which can fairly be described as a revival of the New Deal in the changed circumstances of the late twentieth century. It is valuable and worth discussing but not particularly convincing.

First, it doesn't begin to take into account the global and regional economic forces which have affected the economies of all of the developed countries or the powerful downward pressures generated by NAFTA. Second, one of its major premises, the 'skills mismatch' thesis, which is the basis of the Clinton-Reich economic program, is seriously flawed, as a recent study by economist David R. Howell shows.[4]

Last but not least, the organized political forces on the left which are necessary for such a task do not yet exist in the US, although the possibility is now greater than it has been in many, many years. Peterson doesn't grasp this, relying instead, at the time the book was written, on the doubtful hope of solutions from the newly elected Bill Clinton. The American economy as a whole may be on the upswing again but there is no reason to think that the downward pressures which are at the heart of the silent depression will be reversed. The failing Clinton presidency is far more than the failure of an individual. A reorganization and realignment of American politics of a kind and depth that hasn't been seen for at least 60 years will have to take place to address structural problems of the magnitude Peterson describes. *Silent Depression* demonstrates that the volatile material for such an electoral upheaval is clearly present but what its outcome will be is another matter.

How relevant is all of this to Britain? Comparisons are dangerous and there is nothing equivalent to the illusory American Dream. Yet, on the evidence the answer is: very relevant. Certainly the middle classes in Britain have expanded and dreamed modestly of an ever-better future for themselves and their children. It's a dream that seems to have come to an end, for reasons not unconnected to the American case. Downsizing of corporations, financial institutions and government means that middle managers, white collar employees and even university lecturers, no longer have a secure employment future, while the strangling of the welfare state, especially the National Health Service, which provided a safety net Americans could only envy, makes British politics ripe for change. All of this is hardly a secret either to the Tories or Labour. But reading Peterson's contribution may be a way to see the very near future and to discover that it's pretty damned awful. Luckily, it's not inevitable.

Notes

Chapter 1: Direct Democracy and Progressive Political Reform

1. The literature on the history of the direct primary and the initiative and referendum is very extensive. The basic material on direct legislation may be found in Charles Beard and Birl E. Shultz, *Documents on the State-Wide Initiative, Referendum, and Recall* (New York, 1912). Two studies of particular states are important: V.O. Key, Jr and Winston Crouch, *The Initiative and Referendum in California* (Berkeley, 1939) and James D. Barnett, *The Operation of the Initiative, Referendum, and Recall* (New York, 1915). On the direct primary see Charles E. Merriam and Louise Overacker, *Primary Elections* (Chicago, 1928). V.O. Key, Jr's *American State Politics* (New York: Knopf, 1956) is of prime importance for an understanding of the consequences of the direct primary. See especially, Chs 4–7.
2. Walter Dean Burnham, *Critical Elections and the Mainsprings of American Politics* (New York: W.W. Norton, 1970) pinpoints the changes in American politics which he terms 'electoral disaggregation' in the structural reforms of the progressive period.
3. George E. Mowry, *The California Progressives* (Chicago: Quadrangle Books, 1963), pp. 299–300.
4. David P. Thelen, *The New Citizenship: Origins of Progressivism in Wisconsin, 1885–1900* (Columbia: University of Missouri Press, 1972), p. 50.
5. See, for example, Samuel P. Hays 'The Politics of Reform in Municipal Government in the Progressive Era', *Pacific Northwest Quarterly*, October 1964, pp. 157–69. Hays calls the Progressive advocacy of direct democracy 'paradoxical' and then seems to suggest that such devices were merely tactical in nature, to be used when convenient, then dropped. But the direct primary was not dropped and while there was a great deal of 'rigging' by setting the requirements for qualifying initiated legislation too high, this was done mostly by the opponents of the reforms. The reformers, Hays concludes, did not intend to institute a direct democracy or the rule of the people – which is true, of course, but it leaves unclear just what, in Hays' view, 'direct democracy' or real political democratization would have entailed. Thus while Hays' article is rightly regarded as a key contribution

to the 'revisionist' argument, it has the same basic failing in so far as it accepts, or seems to, the Progressive identification of democracy with the devices of direct democracy. Moreover, he fails to see that the institutions of direct democracy were compatible with the reformers' goal of a rationalized, efficient government modelled on the modern corporation headed by a powerful executive.

6. Henry Jones Ford 'The Direct Primary', *North American Review*, July, 1909, p. 3.
7. Russell B. Nye, *Midwestern Progressive Politics* (East Lansing, Michigan: Michigan State University Press, 1951), p. 110.
8. Henry Jones Ford, *Representative Government* (New York, 1924), pp. 271–2.
9. Victor L. Berger, *Berger's Broadsides* (Milwaukee: Social-Democratic Publishing Co., 1912), p. 35.
10. Emanuel L. Philipp, *Political Reform in Wisconsin*, abridged and edited by Stanley P. Caine and Roger E. Wyman, (Madison: Wisconsin State Historical Society Press, 1973).
11. Ibid., p. 78.
12. *New York Socialist Call*, 12 April 1914, quoted in Isaac A. Hourwich, 'Direct Primaries', *The New Review*, Vol. 2, No. 8 (August, 1914), pp. 453–4.
13. Jonathan Bourne, Jr, 'Functions of the Initiative, Referendum and Recall', *The Annals*, Vol. 43 (September, 1912), p. 9.
14. Quoted in Thelen, *The New Citizenship*, p. 298.
15. Quoted in P.A. Culbertson, 'History of the Initiative and Referendum in Oregon' (Ph.D. dissertation, University of Oregon, 1942), pp. 81–2.
16. Herbert Croly, *Progressive Democracy* (New York: Macmillan, 1914), p. 306.
17. Ibid. pp. 291–302. Oregon today has a 'citizen legislature' which meets only for short periods and is unpaid, apart from expenses and a small stipend. As a result, the executive dominates the state and, as one prominent Oregon business lobbyist explained to me, laughingly, the legislators were a 'pushover' to deal with. Term limits, pushed by right-wing newspapers like the *Wall Street Journal* and supported by a powerful, wealthy and shadowy lobby is another case of Progressive-style reform and evidence of the way in which the Progressive ideology instilled in students over many decades of American high school civics courses and reinforced by the newspapers and media, permeates American political culture. Ross Perot's advocacy of term limits and 'teledemocracy' fits in well with his role as a man on horseback – a somewhat ludicrous image, to be sure, in Perot's case, but a familiar one to anyone knows the Progressive movement's love of great men – Colonel House's progressive dictator, 'Philip Dru', is only one such example. Tom Watson wrote an admiring biography of Napoleon while Upton Sinclair promoted William Randolph Hearst as a potential dictator in his novel, *The Industrial Republic* (1907). Perot's latest version of this and the mania for General Colin Powell, who fits the image a lot better, are both symptomatic of the deep sickness of American politics. As in the case of the direct democracy changes before World War I, term limits weakens representa-

tive government, strengthens the executive, and enhances the power of large corporate interests. And, as in the previous era, it has a great deal of popular support, from middling people who lack effective organizations of their own and enraged at 'the system' feel helpless to affect it through organized politics.

18. On the other hand, one ought not to discount the cynicism of politicians and professional lobbyists who are employed by business opponents of legislation. The lead lobbyist hired to lead the charge on the administrative implementation of the California Political Reform Act of 1974, 'Proposition 9', told me in an interview, with a mischievous twinkle in his eye: 'You just watch what I do. I make a helluva lot of noise, say that the operation of this law will drive business out of California, ruin the economy, and so forth. I just carry on something fierce. I'm at every meeting of the Commission, I raise objections to every point. Pretty soon these guys begin to get worried and then, well, by next year they'll be eating of my hand.' True to his prediction, the reformers' Fair Political Practices Commission was indeed eating out of his and the other lobbyists' hands within a year. I must say, Lincoln Steffens-like, I soon came to appreciate the cynical intelligence of the lobbyists, especially when viewed against the dense (to put it politely) minds of the Common Cause reformers who actually believed their own rhetoric.

    So too, after the passage of the initiative and referendum and the direct primary in state after state it didn't take very long for the professional politicians and the 'machine' to take hold of the new mechanisms and turn them to their advantage. The major difference was that their unchanged behaviour could now be presented as the triumph of the new democratic spirit in American politics.

19. Richard Hofstadter's discussion of the direct democracy movement in *The Age of Reform* (New York: Knopf, 1955, pp. 254–69) distinguishes between the two schools of reformers without seeing that the conservative wing which 'looked to the new forms of political organization under responsible leadership' regarded the direct democracy devices as a necessary prerequisite to that end. The real question, which Hofstadter's otherwise insightful discussion does not raise, is *not* whether the reformers could 'create organizations of their own, with discipline enough to survive, that would be cleaner and more efficient then those they were trying to break up' but whether such organizations could or should be designed to be *democratic* to serve the needs of Progressivism. The answer was clearly 'no' – as the experience of the Lincoln-Roosevelt League in California amply confirms (see Mowry, *California Progressives*, p. 11). Democracy – the fact, not the term – was never the objective of the dominant wing of Progressivism: its hostility to organized parties and espousal of a sham system of democracy was the means to create a new dominant elite made up of the upper middle-class 'Mugwump' types who formed the core leadership of the Progressive movement and

who had access to or owned newspapers (as La Follette did) which could reach 'the people' directly.

20. See Beard and Shultz, *Documents*, pp. 349–83 for U'Ren's draft plan of the Oregon system.
21. Horace E. Flack, 'The Initiative and Referendum in California', *American Political Science Review*, Vol. 5, No. 3 (August, 1911), p. 436.
22. See Charles A. Beard, 'Reconstructing State Government' *The New Republic*, IV (August 21, 1915), Part Two. Beard wrote about the Oregon system that 'many leading advocates of the initiative, referendum and recall are coming to hold that a reorganized and responsible representative machinery is full of promise for democracy'. Democracy here meant 'concentrated executive power in the hands of the governor'. Croly's editorials in the *New Republic* analyzing the New York Constitutional Convention of 1915 are very important for understanding the development of administrative progressivism.
23. *Report of the Committee on Efficiency and Economy of California* (State of California, March, 1919), p. 20.
24. Culbertson, 'History of the Initiative and Referendum in Oregon'; see also Richard L. Neuberger's article, 'Liberalism Backfires in Oregon', *Current History* (March, 1939), pp. 35–6, 39.
25. Chester Rowell, leading California Progressive, quoted in Mowry, *California Progressives*, p. 102.
26. See H.G. Nicholas, 'Political Parties and the Law in the United States', *Political Studies*, Vol. II, No. 3 (1954), pp. 258–70; James Fay, 'The Legal Regulation of Political Parties', *Journal of Legislation*, Vol. 9 (1982); Austin Ranney and Willmore Kendall, *Democracy and the American Party System* (New York: Harcourt, Brace, 1956); Austin Ranney, *Curing the Mischiefs of Faction: Party Reform in America* (Berkeley: University of California, 1975); Leon D. Epstein, *Political Parties in Western Democracies* (New York: Praeger, 1967).
27. See Maurice Duverger, *Political Parties* (New York: John Wiley, 1965), Ch. 2, and Ranney, *Curing the Mischiefs of Faction*. See especially Austin Ranney's dissection of the APSA report on 'responsible party government' in which he points out the contradiction between the call for responsible parties and the unwillingness of the committee to take a clear stand on the issue of the direct primary and the creation of membership parties. Austin Ranney, 'Toward a More Responsible Two-Party System: A Commentary' *American Political Science Review*, 45 (1951), pp. 488–99.
28. Thus the Socialist Party in 1914: 'We have the precious Primary Law. Under that law the control of our party is taken out of the hands of the men and women who worked so hard to build it up, and put into the hands of the enrolled voters, many thousands of whom are not party members, and cannot understand the needs of the party' (Hourwich, 'Direct Primaries', p. 453). The SP's foreboding was amply borne out when politicians from the old

parties encouraged non-members to invade their primaries. The result was to deny the socialists the right to run their own candidates. Of course, this could be turned around – thereby reinforcing the illusion that the old parties could be 'taken over' via the direct primary – as when Upton Sinclair won the Democratic party nomination for Governor in 1934, both enraging the old-line politicians and at the same time destroying the Socialist Party in California. His campaign book, *I, Governor of California* is an example of Emanuel Philipp's warning about individuals taking the place of parties with 'organized personal followings'.

29. Epstein, *Political Parties*, pp. 111–29.
30. Duverger, *Political Parties*, pp. 23–7. Duverger, it should be said, considered the British Labour Party an 'indirect caucus' party which has been altered in a more mass democratic direction by the creation of the constituency parties.
31. Robert F. Hoxie, 'The Socialist Party and the American Convention Methods', *Journal of Political Economy*, Vol. 20 (July, 1912), pp. 738–49.
32. Alvin Gouldner, 'Metaphysic Pathos and the Theory of Bureaucracy' in S.M. Lipset and Neil Smelser (eds), *Sociology: The Progress of a Decade* (Englewood Cliffs, New Jersey: Prentice-Hall, 1961), pp. 80–9.
33. See Mowry's account of the Progressive's hostility to organized labour in California, *California Progressives*, pp. 143ff.
34. Harold F. Gosnell, *Democracy – The Threshold of Freedom* (New York, 1948), p. 266; for Gallup's views see George Gallup and Saul F. Rae, *The Pulse of Democracy* (New York, 1940).
35. See Werner Sombart's remarks on how the AFL supported the 'Winnetka system' of examining candidates of the existing parties because 'they think in this way they have permanently removed the threat and danger of an independent Socialist workers' party'. The same point applies to Gompers' support for the direct primary and the initiative and referendum which he clearly saw as a 'democratic' alternative to the formation of an independent labour or socialist party. *Why Is There No Socialism in the United States?* (White Plains, New York: M.E. Sharpe, 1976), pp. 53–4.

Chapter 2: Populism and Direct Democracy

1. The main works which attempt to support this thesis are: Daniel Bell (ed.), *The New American Right* (New York: Criterion, 1955) which contains pieces by Bell, David Reisman, S.M. Lipset, Nathan Galzer and Peter Vierick; Edward Shils, *The Torment of Secrecy* (Glencoe: The Free Press, 1956); Richard Hofstadter, *The Age of Reform: From Bryan to the New Deal* (New York: Knopf, 1955). For a devastating reply see C. Vann Woodward, 'The Populist Heritage and the Intellectual', *The American Scholar*, Winter, 1959–1960, pp. 55–72. In a wonderful tongue-in-cheek manner, Woodward

pointed out that several proponents of the populism-leads-to-McCarthyism thesis, had not the slightest historical knowledge of the Populist movement and the geographical areas of its strength. As their arguments were largely based on the claim that the Midwest was the greatest hotbed of McCarthyism and populism, Woodward's reminder that it was in the West and South that populism had its major sources of support, is thoroughly deflating. Of all of these works, Shils' is by far the most conservative in its conclusions. See also, William Kornhauser, *The Politics of Mass Society* (Glencoe: The Free Press, 1959) as an example of how 'mass society theory' utilizes the idea of a 'populistic mentality'.

2. Seymour Martin Lipset, 'Fascism – Left, Right and Center', Chapter IV, in *Political Man* (Baltimore: Johns Hopkins University Press, expanded ed., 1981), p. 167.
3. Michael Rogin, *The Intellectuals and McCarthy: The Radical Specter* (Cambridge: MIT Press, 1967).
4. Hofstadter, *Age of Reform*, pp. 11–12.
5. Ibid., pp. 15–17.
6. Ibid., p. 17.
7. Ibid., p. 19.
8. Woodward, 'The Populist Heritage', p. 57.
9. Edward Shils, *Torment of Secrecy*, p. 98.
10. Ibid., p. 101.
11. Ibid., pp. 101–2.
12. Ibid., p. 104.
13. Ibid., pp. 48–9.
14. Kornhauser, *Politics of Mass Society*, p. 230.
15. A personal footnote to history may help to illustrate the seismic shift that the new Cold War-born liberalism brought about. In 1951, I was fortunate to hear several lectures in my introductory political science class at Berkeley by Peter Odegard, a representative of old-fashioned democratic liberalism which still believed that democracy requires popular participation. He fulminated against the 'new' elitist ideas, derived from Schumpeter, which were sweeping away the foundations of his kind of liberalism – a liberalism that was to all but vanish in the repressive McCarthyite atmosphere during the rest of the decade – until the 1960s when it was revived by the New Left advocates of 'participatory democracy', a revival which left, in theoretical and political terms, much to be desired. Looking back, I think that Odegard must have felt a bit like King Canute. I must admit I didn't fully understand the source of his anger until seven or eight years later when I heard a series of lectures by Professor Eugene Victor Burdick in a course to which I was a teaching assistant. How Odegard would have raged at Burdick whose views at least had the virtue of being explicit in their outright antipathy to democracy. How Eugene Victor Debs, for whom Burdick's undoubtedly disappointed parents named him, would have spun

in his grave. Burdick's now forgotten novel, *The Ninth Wave* (1959), ought to be read by anyone who wishes to get the flavour of the decay of democratic liberalism in the era of McCarthyism and the Cold War. Turn Burdick inside out and you have a demonstration of how a number of the students who formed the New Left learned their scorn for democracy from their professors such as Burdick or Kornhauser. The latter, much to his credit, following the Free Speech Movement in 1964, repudiated the conservative views of *The Politics of Mass Society*.

16. Robert Michels, *Political Parties: A Sociological Study of the Oligarchical Tendencies of Modern Democracy* (Glencoe: The Free Press, 1949); Beatrice and Sidney Webb, *Industrial Democracy* (London: Longmans Green and Co., 1902).
17. Carl Landauer, *European Socialism* (Berkeley: University of California, 1961), p. 1094.
18. Michels, *Political Parties*, p. 347.
19. Ibid., p. 350.
20. Karl Kautsky, *Der Parlamentarismus die Volksgasetzgebung und die Sozialdemokratie*, (Stuttgart: Dietz, 1893) and the revised, 2nd edition, *Parlamentarismus und Demokratie* (1911).
21. This is precisely what the major study of French revolutionary syndicalism by Louis Levine attempts to do: *Revolutionary Syndicalism in France* (New York: 1913). Cf. John Spargo, *Syndicalism, Industrial Unionism, and Socialism* (New York: Huebsch, 1913). The social conditions which bred the anarchist and anarcho-syndicalist movements in Spain are brilliantly analyzed by Gerald Brennan in *The Spanish Labyrinth* (Cambridge University Press, 1960), Chs. VII and VIII. The hostility to politics and political parties and to democracy as necessarily 'authoritarian', was, of course, a standard belief among the French syndicalists, especially those associated with Sorel and Lagardelle.
22. Webb, *Industrial Democracy*, Chs I and II.
23. Ibid., pp. 3–8.
24. Ibid., pp. 19–21.
25. Ibid., p. 21.
26. Ibid., p. 26.
27. Ibid., p. 36.
28. Ibid., p. 37.
29. Ibid., p. 59.
30. V.I. Lenin, *What is to be Done?*, in 'Collected Works', (New York: International Publishers, 1929), Vol. IV, p. 214.
31. Ibid.
32. Ibid., pp. 61–2.
33. Seymour Martin Lipset, James Coleman and Martin Trow, *Union Democracy* (Glencoe: The Free Press, 1955), p. 54.
34. Ibid.

35. 'Social Stratification and Political Power', in Reinhard Bendix and Seymour Martin Lipset (eds), *Class, Status and Power* (Glencoe: The Free Press, 1953), pp. 596–609.
36. Michels' account of the attitude of the German workers toward Lassalle is typical of his approach. Lassalle treated the movement as 'his' movement and demanded unconditional loyalty to his personal dictatorship. Even if one argues, as one could with some truth, that the German workers remained relatively docile before the authority of their leaders, there can be little question that both officially as well as in fact, such 'Bonapartist' tendencies declined considerably in the course of the maturation of the German socialist and working-class movements. Compare Michels' treatment with Eduard Bernstein's far superior discussion of this question in his biography of Lassalle, *Ferdinand Lassalle* (London: Swan Sonnenschein, 1893). Bernstein wrote under the direct influence of Engels and at the same time came into contact with Fabians like the Webbs, an encounter which was give rise to his revisionist views. His discussion of the way in which the German workers threw off Lassalle's dictatorial rule complements the Webbs' approach in *Industrial Democracy*.
37. 'Ought the Referenda to be introduced into England?', *Contemporary Review*, April 1902, pp. 492–3.
38. One of the best accounts of Napoleon III as a 'harbinger' of fascism, is to be found in J. Salwyn Schapiro, *Liberalism and the Challenge of Fascism*, (New York: McGraw Hill, 1949) Ch. 13.
39. Karl Marx, *The Eighteenth Brumaire of Louis Bonaparte*, in Lewis Feuer, (ed.) *Marx and Engels: Basic Writings on Politics and Philosophy* (New York: Doubleday Anchor, 1959) pp. 338–9.
40. Albert Guerard, *Napoleon III* (Cambridge: Harvard University Press, 1943).
41. Ibid., pp. 245–6.
42. Ibid., pp. 253–4.
43. Ibid., pp. 118–19, 284–90.
44. Ibid., pp. 284–90.
45. Ibid., pp. 118–19.
46. Interview with Saul Landau, 'Cuba: The Present Reality', *New Left Review*, Issue No. 9 (1961), p. 15.
47. George Gallup and Saul Rae Forbes, *The Pulse of Democracy: The Public Opinion Poll and How it Works* (New York: Simon & Schuster, 1940), Ch. 9; Lindsay Rogers, *The Pollsters: Public Opinion, Politics and Democratic Leadership* (New York: Knopf, 1949).
48. The exception would seem to be tiny, rural communities, isolated from their neighbours, with a highly homogeneous population. Even here, one is entitled to wonder whether 'direct democracy' in the form, for example, of the New England town meeting, is actually democratic. The existence of class differentiation plus other factors such as religious intolerance may well mean that public voting leaves dissenting individuals open to social

pressure or economic reprisal. The Quaker system of reaching all decisions by consensus is another variant of the spurious democratic form. Critics have not inaccurately termed this practice 'Quaker totalitarianism' because in practice it is used by leaders (who may or may not have a formal position) to impose ideas upon the participants. A variation on this is, of course, the refusal to take a vote in nominally democratic organizations on the ground that it will lead to 'division'. More often than not, such a refusal (usually by evasion rather than by direct refusal) to allow a vote allows the dominant elements to make the decisions and interpret the sense of the meeting as they will. This happens in a wide variety of organizations, from trade unions to academic institutions.

49. C. Wright Mills, *The Power Elite* (New York: Oxford University Press, 1956). See especially Ch. 13.
50. Ibid., p. 310.
51. At the end of the twentieth century, this characterization accurately describes proposals for 'teledemocracy' (Ross Perot) or the many varieties of cyber-democracy concocted by, among others, Newt Gingrich's 'Freedom and Progress Foundation' and his intellectual gurus, Alvin and Heidi Toffler, as well as the proposals by the British 'independent' think-tank, Demos, for a 'party-free politics' in a 'lean democracy'. See Alvin and Heidi Toffler, *Creating a New Civilization: The Politics of the Third Wave*, Foreword by Newt Gingrich (Atlanta, Georgia: Turner Publishing Co., 1994); Geoff Mulgan, 'Party Free Politics', *New Statesman*, 15 April 1994, and *Politics in An Antipolitical Age*, (Oxford: Polity Press, 1994); *Demos*, 'Lean Democracy', no. 3 (1994). See also: Lawrence K. Grossman, *The Electronic Republic: Reshaping Democracy in the Information Age* (New York: Viking Press, 1995); James S. Fishkin, *Democracy and Deliberation* (New Haven: Yale University Press, 1991).
52. As the books by Fishkin, Grossman and the Tofflers demonstrate, these conceptions remain deeply embedded in the culture of American politics.
53. Chester McArthur Destler, *American Radicalism, 1865–1901* (Chicago, Quadrangle Books, 1966), pp. 254–69. Hofstadter, in *The Age of Reform*, for the most part limits his discussion of the direct democracy movement to the Progressives. It is clear however, from the evidence, that its origins, while among the same elements who were the forerunners of progressivism, were also closely tied to the agrarian middle classes who joined the People's Party.
54. Howard Quint, *The Forging of American Socialism* (Indianapolis: Bobbs-Merrill Co., 1953), pp. 249–50.
55. Samuel Gompers, *Seventy Years of Life and Labor* (New York: E.P. Dutton and Co., 1943) Vol. II, p. 83. I have not dealt here with the reasons for Gompers' eager advocacy of direct democracy. The explanation, however, is simple enough: it was as counterweight to his socialist opposition in the 1890s and, in the period before World War I, to the strong sentiment

favouring electoral support for the Socialist Party or the formation of a labour party on the model of the British Labour Party. See 'Initiative, Referendum and Recall', Report of the Executive Council of the American Federation of Labor to the Seattle, Washington Convention of the AFL (AFL: Washington, DC, 1913).

56. J.W. Sullivan, *Direct Legislation by the Citizenship through the Initiative and Referendum* (New York: True Nationalist Publishing Co., 1893).
57. John D. Hicks, *The Populist Revolt* (Minneapolis: University of Minnesota, 1955), pp. 146–7.
58. Michael R. Hyman, *The Anti-Redeemers: Hill Country Political Dissenters in the Lower South from Redemption to Populism* (Baton Rouge: Louisiana State University Press, 1990), especially Chapter 2 and Conclusion.
59. Ibid., pp. 200–3.
60. Hicks, *The Populist Revolt*, p. 147.
61. Ibid., p. 70.
62. S.M. Lipset, *Agrarian Socialism* (Berkeley: University of California Press, 1949), pp. 47–8, 67.
63. Ibid., p. 70.
64. Hicks, *The Populist Revolt*, pp. 406–7.
65. Donald Edgar Walters, 'Populism in California' (Berkeley: Ph.D. dissertation, 1952), pp. 396–7.
66. Cf. Hicks, *The Populist Revolt*, p. 406 and Hofstadter, *Age of Reform*, pp. 64–5.
67. Hicks, *Populist Revolt*, p. 408.
68. *The Coming Nation*, 137 (4 January 1896).
69. M. Ostrogorski, *Democracy and the Organization of Political Parties* (New York: Macmillan, 1902), Vol. II, Ch. 8.
70. Ibid., p. 659 *et passim*.

Chapter 3: Attacking Democracy: State Funding of Political Parties

1. Interview in *The Commonwealth* (The Commonwealth Club, San Francisco), Part II, 16 December 1974, pp. 30–l.
2. Commissioner Tony Quinn, Meeting of FPPC, 7 July 1976. Quinn was responding to Commissioner (later Judge) Carol Brosnahan, a sincere and intelligent proponent of Proposition 9, who had objected to changing the regulations 'every time the political or ideological or intellectual complexion changes ...'. I was fortunate to observe the formative years of the FPPC in which the new commissioners were set the task of formulating the regulations to interpret the law. Terms such as 'substantial time' to define who was a 'professional lobbyist' baffled them and they decided when confronted with one commissioner who thought it must mean 20 hours, and another (obviously a true believer) who thought it must mean ten, to (a direct quote)

'cut the difference' at 15 hours. Thus were the naive reformers introduced to the arbitrary world of the Regulatory Commission. I think the high point of my association with the founding members of the Commission was after the first year when the Chairman, Daniel Lowenstein, who had been the legal architect of Proposition 9, told me in an interview that the mass of regulations and the enforcement powers of the Commission (similar to those of the FEC) were no more burdensome to citizens and professional politicians or threatening to them than the regulations and enforcement policies of the Internal Revenue Service. For anyone who wants to consider the otherworldliness of this statement, it would be worthwhile to read David Burnham, *A Law Unto Itself: Power, Politics, and the I.R.S.* (New York: Random House, 1990.) Someone may someday write a similar book about the FEC and its sister state bodies, but not until the prevailing orthodoxy has passed.

3. US Republican Congressman Bill Thomas, quoted in 'Politics: Are US Visions and Values Drying Up?', *International Herald Tribune*, 18 March 1990.
4. For the concept of 'civil society' see John Keane, *Democracy and Civil Society* (London: Verso Books, 1988) and the very useful collection, edited by Keane, *Civil Society and the State* (London: Verso Books, 1988).
5. Herbert E. Alexander, 'Money and politics: rethinking a conceptual framework', in Alexander (ed.), *Comparative Political Finance in the 1980s* (Cambridge: Cambridge University Press, 1989).
6. See the essays in Alexander, *Comparative Political Finance*, none of which, I think, whatever the conclusions of their respective authors, gives much support to the advocates of these devices. Far from being a liberal demand, the need of business-oriented parties to divorce themselves from direct or even indirect pressures from particular business interests in order to better represent the interests of capital as a whole and to avoid the appearance of being their paid (as opposed to unpaid) servants in order to secure majority electoral support, has often been the motive behind the institution of controls on contributions and public financing. See Arnold Heidenheimer and Frank Langdon, *Business Associations and the Financing of Political Parties* (The Hague: Martinus Nijoff, 1968); Arnold Heidenheimer, *Adenauer and the CDU* (The Hague: Martinus Nijoff, 1960) for an analysis of Adenauer's reasons for introducing state financing of the parties. In Japan, the scandals which engulfed the Liberal Democratic Party in 1989 led, if the British newspaper reports are to be trusted, to Japanese business leaders concluding that 'corporate donations are out of control, damaging Japan's political leadership and the country's image abroad' (*The Times*, 4 August 1989). Their solution was to approach the Socialist party, to show that they could be even-handed in their generosity, and hopeful that the Socialists would be favourable to business (Ibid., 26 July 1989). But, more significant, there was talk of a new business party, for a few days, which would not be as visibly or directly dependent on business contributions or as corrupt as the

LDP and therefore all the better able to serve the larger interests of business, not as a lackey tied by chains of gold, but by ideological conviction that what is good for Japanese big business is good for Japan. The idea faded away and the LDP went on to win the election, but in the long run it is possible that such a party, given the democratic upheaval borne of public disgust with the LDP's deep-rooted corruption, may emerge with business support, particularly if the JSP wins more popular support.

7. 'Kick-back amnesty for French politicians' by Ian Davidson, *Financial Times*, 22 June 1989. See also *Le Monde*, 22 June 1988.
8. See the account of this case by Khayyam Zev Paltiel, 'Canadian election expense legislation, 1963–1985: a critical appraisal or was the effort worth it?' in Alexander, *Comparative Political Finance*, pp. 59–64.
9. 'Sudden Sanctimony: U.S.Congress Seeks to Shun any Hint It Is In Debt to Big Givers', *Wall Street Journal*, 11 August 1989. For a statement of the case for reform from a journalist sympathetic to Common Cause, see Elizabeth Drew, *Politics and Money: The New Road to Corruption* (New York: Macmillan, 1983). A devastating critique of Drew's book and of the entire record of campaign reform in the US may be found in Robert Walters, 'The Failure of Campaign Reform', reprinted in *Current Issues in American Politics, 1987–1988* (Guilford, Ct: Dushkin Publishing Co., 1987). An excellent but ignored critical view of this issue may be found in David Nichols, *Financing Elections: The Politics of an American Ruling Class* (New York: Franklin Watts, 1974). Nichols' book is ignored precisely because it doesn't fit in with the Progressive/Common Cause assumptions which permeate American politics.
10. Quoted in 'Politics: Are the US Visions and Values Drying Up', *International Herald Tribune*, 19 March 1990.
11. This is an area of great controversy. Frances Fox Piven and Richard Cloward argue that the key is the undemocratic registration laws, while Curtis Gans of the Committee for the Study of the American Electorate, argues that the real problem is one of political culture and the Tweedledum-Tweedledee nature of the two parties. See Cloward and Piven, *Why Americans Don't Vote* (New York: Pantheon Books, 1988). For an interesting exchange of views between Howard Reiter and Thomas Ferguson see *The Nation*, 23 May 1987.
12. Quoted in Hobart Rowen, 'The Democrats Get a Wake-Up Call', *International Herald Tribune*, 22 March 1990.
13. It is an important insight into the political sociology of American political reformers to note that Common Cause's own organization is undemocratic and does not allow for membership control. A plebiscitarian structure was created in place of genuine control by the members, thus mirroring the American political party system which Common Cause has never dreamed of questioning. Common Cause was at least consistent in being opposed to democratic rights for third or minority parties, as evidenced by

its views on 'equal time' and laws restricting third party access to the ballot. The campaign reforms were quite explicitly advocated to shore up the 'two party system' and to 'restore confidence in it'. On the undemocratic nature of Common Cause see Chapter 7 below.

14. James MacGregor Burns, 'Democracy: Lessons on Both Sides', *International Herald Tribune*, 9 February 1990.
15. See Austin Ranney, *Curing the Mischiefs of Faction: Party Reform in America* (Berkeley: University of California, 1975); James Fay, 'The Legal Regulation of Political Parties', *Journal of Legislation*, Vol. 9 (1982); Leon Epstein, 'Will American Political Parties be Privatized?', *Journal of Law and Politics,* Vol. 5, No. 2 (Winter 1989).
16. Leon Epstein, *Political Parties in the American Mold* (Madison: University of Wisconsin Press, 1986) and 'Will American Parties be Privatized?'.
17. See Epstein, 'Will American Parties be Privatized?, for a review of the legal arguments. The most important recent case, *San Francisco Democrats v. March Fong Eu, California Secretary of State* (22 February 1989) was a major advance for democratic control over the parties. On the need for 'responsible parties' see *Party Line*, newsletter of the Committee for Party Renewal, which is an APSA-recognized group of scholars who advocate 'strong' political parties and have been active participants in the various efforts seeking to deregulate the American parties through lawsuits. David Nichols' *Financing Elections* also advocates strong political parties as an alternative to public financing, but unlike the Committee, believes, as I do, in the desirability of *membership* parties. In the 1990s, these views, which fell on such barren soil in the 1970s, will, I think, find renewed life following the debacle of campaign finance reform legislation.
18. For background on British political finance, see Michael Pinto-Duschinsky, *British Political Finance, 1830–1980* (Washington: American Enterprise Institute, 1981); and, by the same author, 'Trends in British Political Funding, 1979–84' in Alexander, *Comparative Political Finance*. See also Keith Ewing, *The Funding of Political Parties in Britain* (Cambridge: Cambridge University Press, 1987). Expenditure controls in individual parliamentary campaigns exist but such controls, as their many foreign admirers often fail to note, do not include national party expenditures or the kinds of coordinated expenditures made 'independently' by big business, the Government itself, and the Tory-controlled press – or, the non-Tory controlled press, for that matter. (See the discussion of this above.) Serious questions have been raised by third-party expenditures during campaigns: as for example, the desire of ecology or other single-issue causes, to defeat a particular candidate. With the breakdown of party rigidities and possibly because of the collapse of the center parties, and with the growth of American-style issue organizations, I think this will be a more serious issue in the 1990s, raising important democratic questions about this long-standing legislative control.

The Tory wish to destroy the Labour party by requiring the trade unions to conduct political fund ballots backfired. Legislation to control union participation in politics through funding restrictions is an old story in Britain. Simple prohibition was beyond even an authoritarian Thatcher government; Tories undoubtedly swallowed some of their own propaganda in this case, and in the legislation requiring trade unions to hold democratic elections for their officers and strike ballots. Their belief was that the rank and file were less radical than their union leaders, who were seen as manipulating them into strikes, and that the members resented the use of trade union funds for the party. The consequence, paradoxically enough, was to give greater legitimacy to the trade union funds and to the trade union organization of industrial action and hence to make the unions more democratic. But to say that this legislation, any part of it, was genuinely intended to democratize the trade unions, as Michael Pinto-Duschinsky does, can hardly stand up to scrutiny. In any case, the acceptance of state money for ballots, although now generally acquiesced in by the unions, has opened up a major hole in the ability of the state to control the internal life of the unions (Michael Pinto-Duschinsky, 'Trends in British Political Funding, 1979–1984' in Alexander, *Comparative Political Finance*). The Tories' tender concern for democracy did not, it should be noted, extend to the contributions made by companies: they resisted a Labour Party bill to require balloting of shareholders.

19. See Gian Franco Ciaurro, 'Public Financing of parties in Italy' in Alexander, *Comparative Political Finance*; and Donald Sassoon, 'The Funding of Political Parties in Italy' in *Political Quarterly*, Vol. 46, No. 1 (January–March 1975), pp. 94–8. Sassoon points to the centralizing function of the Italian system. The interpenetration of all of the political parties and the state is, it may be added, thus directly reinforced by this system which is not, I would suggest, unconnected to the support given to the system by the Communist Party whose cadre is drawn from the state sector and municipal bureaucrats. See Armando Cossutta, *Il Finanziammento Publico dei Partiti* (Rome: Ruiniti, 1978).
20. See Pilar Del Castillo, 'Financing of Spanish Political Parties' in Alexander, *Comparative Political Finance*. For a view of the Socialist Party freed from the financial constraints of trade union funding, written from a trade union standpoint, see Dan Gallin's article, 'What Spain Tells Us About Socialism' in the *News Bulletin* of the International Union of Food Workers (Geneva: Nos. 1–2/1989). The Spanish Socialist Party 'has been hijacked by middle class technocrats with a conservative agenda'. See also Paul Heywood, 'Mirror Images: The PCE and PSOE in the Transition to Democracy in Spain', *West European Politics* (1987). On Germany, see Uwe Schleth, *Parteifinanzen: Eine Studie urber Kosten und Finanieriung der Parteientatigkeit, zu deren politischer Problematik und zu den Moglichkeiten einer Reform* (Meisenham an Glan: Verlag Anton Hain, 1973). On Japan, see Professor Rei Shiratori, 'Public

Financing of Elections in Japan: Two Contrasting Aspects of the Scheme' (unpublished paper).

21. On Holland, see Ruud Koole, 'The "modesty" of Dutch party finance' in Alexander, *Comparative Political Finance*, and Chapter 7 in Ewing, *Funding of Political Parties in Britain*.
22. John Keane, *Democracy and Civil Society*. For the views of the democratic oppositional thinkers on the relationship between the state and civil society, I have drawn on the writings which have appeared over the last decade in the *East European Reporter* (London) and *Across Frontiers* (Berkeley, California). Timothy Garton Ash's writings are invaluable for understanding the developments in Eastern Europe, especially the intellectual dimension: see *The Uses of Adversity* (London: Granta, 1989) and *We the People* (London: Granta, 1990). See Keane (ed.), *Civil Society and the State*, Section 3, 'Eastern States and the Possibility of Democracy' which has essays by Jacques Rupnik, Jeno Szucs, Mihaly Vajda, Z.A. Pelczynski, and Vaclav Havel. On the role of social movements see, in the same collection, the article by Alberto Melucci, 'Social Movements and the Democratization of Everyday Life'.
23. See Chapters 4–7, below.
24. Quoted in *Militant*, 28 November 1975, p. 17. On Japan, see Rei Shiratori, 'Public Financing of Elections'.
25. The question of financing the emergent political parties has arisen most clearly in Hungary and East Germany, although, of course, money and resources from the West played a crucial role in Solidarity's election victory in 1989. In Hungary, because of the lack of a mass movement akin to Solidarity, the opposition has been, to put it mildly, ambivalent about such a movement, with a few exceptions. The utter apathy and distrust which has greeted their efforts under the liberalized (but not democratic) regime has forced them to confront the issue of 'building a grassroots network to combat disillusionment and widespread pessimism brought on by one-party rule' which Ferenc Koszeg, leader of the Alliance of Free Democrats, says has 'numbed' the population. *The Times* report goes on to note that 'this may prove difficult with the opposition's meagre finances and limited access to the state-run television network, whose director is a member of the Central Committee. Funding of opposition political parties from abroad may be a solution.' The British Foreign Office has offered support, 'however, proposed regulations now under consideration in talks between the Hungarian Communist Party and opposition groups would forbid direct funding from foreign governments, forcing a channelling of money through independent sources or private foundations' (*The Times*, 7 August 1989).

    In the Soviet Union, the 'Foundation of Deputies Initiatives' which is playing an important part in the nascent independent party system, is, we are told, 'researching legal ways for voters to make financial contributions. (the *Observer*, 'Radical Deputies break Soviet single-party mould', 30 July 1989). Here, is the licensing situation in which the state's permission is required to receive contributions: the doctrine of freedom of association and the spirit of free speech which underlies the American First Amendment, which is so alien to many of the advocates of controls, dictates that all such regulation be abolished – a point I have had occasion to make with some effect to East European democrats grappling with this issue in their own countries.

26. The money given to both the Spanish socialist and conservative parties by the Ebert Foundation and the Adenauer Foundation, although coming from the German state, was at least mediated by the political parties; a similar process is now underway in Eastern Europe where parties have been set up with money from their sister parties in Western Europe, especially, once again, Germany. There is, I think, a difference between this and the American government's direct intervention of the kind which occurred in Nicaragua, if only because the political parties are at least one remove from the state. This is a matter which deserves much more attention than it has been given by scholars.
27. FDP Parliamentary Secretary in *Die Welt*, 5 September 1964, quoted in Henry Jacoby, *The Bureaucratization of the World* (Berkeley: University of California Press, 1973).
28. Interview with Samuel P. Huntington, *US News and World Report*, 8 March 1976, p. 52. Cf. Huntington, *American Politics: The Promise of Disharmony* (Cambridge: Harvard University Press, 1981). For the Trilateral Commission's 'report on the governability of democracies', see Michel J. Crozier, Samuel P. Huntington, and Joji Watanuki, *The Crisis of Democracy* (New York: New York University Press, 1975), pp. 178–83. From the absorption of parties by the state to proposals for a system of plebiscitarian non-party democracy is only a short step. See Thomas E. Cronin's *Direct Democracy: The Politics of Initiative, Referendum and Recall* (Cambridge: Harvard University Press, 1989). In this programmatic book for American politics, parties simply don't exist, not even to be dismissed.
29. See Timothy Garton Ash, *We the People*, pp. 131–56.
30. For an interesting recent attempt to discuss some of these issues, see Alan Ware, *Citizens, Parties and the State* (Oxford: Polity Press, 1987).

Chapter 4: Political Reform as a Danger to Democracy

1. This essay first appeared in *The California Journal* (Sacramento, California: April 1975).

Chapter 5: Regulating Politics

1. This essay first appeared in *Series in Ethics and Politics* Number 1. (Center for Ethics and Social Policy, Berkeley: Graduate Theological Union, June 1977).

2. The terms of this provision tells us a great deal about the reformers' naive, civics-book understanding of the legislative process and the ways in which powerful interests can exercise their power. When its rationale was explained by the law's chief Common Cause drafter – an eminent professor of law – to the meeting of lobbyists referred to earlier in this article, it was greeted by general hilarity mixed with incredulity that anyone could be so foolish. In my opinion, even if the provision had not been successfully challenged in court, it would have been easily circumvented by most lobbyists and lobbyist employers – with one exception, the organized labour movement. In the first round of filing, not surprisingly, fines for late filing were assessed (later withdrawn) against a large number of lobbyists, including a large number of the 'public interest' lobbyists and – most ironically of all – Common Cause itself.
3. Common Cause's repeated attempts to pass 'lobby reform' legislation at the federal level have come apart when the liberal activist lobbyists realized that they would be their chief victim. Distinguishing a 'lobbyist' from anyone who attempts to influence legislation is of course impossible unless it is defined as someone who receives payment for his or her services. But, as Common Cause recognized, that is easy to evade in the case of 'organized, special interests' hence the requirement that anyone, paid or unpaid, file reports on contacts with or other efforts to influence Congress.

Chapter 6: Democratic Rights and the Regulation of Politics

1. This essay first appeared in *Political Reform in California*, Tom Leatherwood and Arthur Lipow, eds (Berkeley: University of California Institute of Governmental Studies, 1978).
2. For recent analyses of the Federal Election Commission, see Brooks Jackson, *Broken Promises: Why the Federal Election Commission Failed* (New York: Priority Press, 1990); Anthony Corrado, *Paying for Presidents: Public Financing in Federal Elections* (New York: The Twentieth Century Fund Press, 1993); Common Cause, *The Failure-to-Enforce Commission* (Washington, D.C.: Common Cause, 1989). It requires a great deal of forbearance in light of the chapters in this section, written nearly 20 years ago, not to comment – or crow – about the last item.

Chapter 7: 'Common Cause': The Dangerous Lobby

1. This essay was co-authored with James Fay and first appeared in *The California Journal* (Sacramento, California: November 1977).
2. For non-American readers, and probably a great many Americans as well, Common Cause was founded in the early 1970s by John Gardner, former

Secretary of Health, Education and Welfare in the Kennedy administration. A liberal Republican – as many good government reformers have been from the Progressive era onward – Gardner saw the need to restore 'confidence' in government and the existing two-party system in the aftermath of the Watergate affair. Common Cause's national membership grew rapidly and it soon became a force in Washington, playing a key role in the passage of legislation establishing state funding of presidential elections. Its state chapters and individual members were mobilized to support reform legislation by the use of the WATS (wide area telephone service) line. Largely upper middle-class, and disproportionately composed of women volunteers (the necessity of the two-income family and the subsequent entry of large numbers of women into the labour force had just begun), the organization inveighed against the corrupting effects of money in American politics. Its top-down structure was briefly challenged as the organization's influence grew, but the leadership, committed to 'democracy' opted instead for a plebiscitarian system of membership polls to advise them on policy. California provided an ideal laboratory for the study of Common Cause because of the organization's strength in the state and because of the long history of Progressive reform. Common Cause remains active today, although only a shadow of its former self. In its social composition and anti-party ideology, Common Cause was an almost perfect example of the Progressive-type electoral reform movement which has done such damage to American politics. By dealing only with the symptoms and framing the issues in the simple-minded language of Progressive reform, it contributed to the even greater cynicism of the American people about politics and politicians. The conservative-inspired 'term limits' movement which has even further eroded the American political system owes a large debt to Common Cause's incessant and utterly thoughtless campaign against the 'incumbency factor'. As this article and the others in this volume which deal with the political reforms of the 1970s makes clear, Common Cause, in common with the historical Progressive movement, has always been tacitly hostile to the idea of democratically organized membership political parties. Its own organization and the plebiscitarian form of a 'polling democracy' which it used to govern its membership are a reflection of this. In this they are, of course, very American and very much part of the Progressive tradition of top-down electoral reform. This article, as the others in this book dealing with post-Watergate political reform, was based on close observation of Common Cause in the 1970s, not only in California but nationally as well. Having kept up with the organization in the 1980s and 1990s as it has tirelessly pursued the issue of campaign finance reform along with the twin issue of lobby reform, I can see no reason to alter my view of Common Cause and the deleterious effect it has had upon American politics.

Chapter 8: Karl Mannheim: Turning Marx Upside Down

1. See Roger Kojecky, *T.S. Eliot's Social Criticism* (New York: Farrar, Straus and Giroux, 1971) esp. pp. 169–97.
2. In a paper given to the Moot in 1940, Mannheim urged his listeners to 'look to elite groups in our society, e.g., the Moot, or enlightened Civil Servants, to use these techniques for different ends. The new techniques [of managing modern society] constitute a new opportunity and a new obligation. We want to mobilize the intelligent people of goodwill in this country who are waiting for a lead. At the same time there must be a popular movement to back what the elites are doing. You cannot build up a great movement without the dynamism of social leadership ... We are too lazy to move. Hitler started with six people ...'. (Quoted in Kojecky, *T.S. Eliot*, p. 175.) See F.A. Hayek's sharp comment on Mannheim in *The Road to Serfdom* (Chicago: University of Chicago Press, 1972), p. 158.
3. For a discussion of 'bureacratic collectivism', see Michael Harrington, *Socialism, Past and Future* (London: Pluto Press, 1993) and my introduction to the same volume, 'A Guide for the Perplexed'. See also: Ernest Haberkern and Arthur Lipow (eds), *Neither Capitalism nor Socialism: Theories of Bureaucratic Collectivism* (Atlantic Highlands: Humanities Press International, 1996); Arthur Lipow, *Authoritarian Socialism in America: Edward Bellamy and the Nationalist Movement* (Berkeley: University of California Press, paperback edition, 1991).
4. Robert Merton, 'Karl Mannheim and the Sociology of Knowledge', in *Social Theory and Social Structure* (Glencoe: The Free Press, 1957, revised edition).
5. Karl Mannheim, *Ideology and Utopia* (New York: Harcourt, Brace & Co., 1936, Harvest Books Edition), p. 98.
6. Mannheim, Introduction to *Ideology and Utopia*, p. xxiv.
7. For a discussion of their contributions, and of the problem as a whole, see Reinhard Bendix, *Social Science and the Distrust of Reason*, University of California Publications in Sociology and Social Institutions, Vol. I, No. 1 (Berkeley: University of California Press, 1950).
8. Mannheim, *Man and Society in an Age of Reconstruction* (New York: Harcourt, Brace, 1949), p. 377. Cf. Hayek, *Road to Serfdom*, p. 158.
9. For Mannheim's earliest views on epistemology, see 'The Structural Analysis of Epistemology' in *Essays on Sociology and Social Psychology* (New York: Oxford University Press, 1953).
10. Paul Kecskemeti, ed., Introduction to Mannheim, *Essays on the Sociology of Knowledge* (New York: Oxford University Press, 1952), pp. 8–9.
11. 'On the Interpretation of *Weltanschauung*' in Mannheim, *Essays on the Sociology of Knowledge*, p. 46.
12. Mannheim, *Essays on the Sociology of Knowledge*, pp. 61–2.
13. Mannheim, *Ideology and Utopia*, p. 163.

14. 'The Problem of a Sociology of knowledge', in Mannheim, *Essays on the Sociology of Knowledge*, p. 137.
15. Merton, *Social Theory and Social Structure*, p. 492.
16. Mannheim, *Essays on the Sociology of Knowledge*, p. 144.
17. Merton, *Social Theory and Social Structure*, p. 492.
18. Mannheim, *Ideology and Utopia*, pp. 265–6.
19. Ibid., p. 77.
20. Merton, *Social Theory and Social Structure*, p. 503.
21. Mannheim, *Ideology and Utopia*, p. 283.
22. Ibid., p. 284.
23. Raymond Aron remarks that 'It was left to a "bourgeois Marxism", as Mannheim's doctrine has been called, to go beyond Marxism itself and to fall into a thorough-going historical relativism, of which the sociology of knowledge is only the self-styled scientific expression' *German Sociology* (Glencoe: The Free Press, 1957), p. 55.
24. I have drawn upon Robert Merton's paradigm for the analysis of the sociology of knowledge. See 'The Sociology of Knowledge', in Merton, *Social Theory and Social Structure*, pp. 460–1.
25. Mannheim, *Ideology and Utopia*, p. 276.
26. See especially Mannheim's essay, 'On the Interpretation of *Weltanschauung*', and also 'The Problem of a Sociology of Knowledge', *Essays on the Sociology of Knowledge*, p. 143.
27. Mannheim, 'Conservative Thought', in *Essays in Sociology and Social Psychology*.
28. Mannheim, *Essays on the Sociology of Knowledge*, p. 186.
29. Ibid., pp. 123, 125.
30. Ibid., p. 184.
31. Ibid.
32. Merton, *Social Theory and Social Structure*, p. 498.
33. Mannheim, *Ideology and Utopia*, fn. p. 97.
34. Ibid., p. 194.
35. Ibid., p. 98.
36. Ibid., pp. 195–6.
37. Ibid., p. 194.
38. Ibid., p. 266.
39. Ibid., p. 133.
40. Ibid., pp. 279–80.
41. Ibid., p. 281.
42. Kecskemeti, Introduction to Mannheim, *Essays on the Sociology of Knowledge*, p. i.
43. Mannheim, *Ideology and Utopia*, pp. 11–12.
44. Ibid., p. 149.
45. Ibid., p. 154.
46. Ibid., p. 155.

47. Ibid., p. 157.
48. Mannheim, 'The Problem of the Intelligentsia. An enquiry into its past and present role' in *Essays on the Sociology of Culture* (New York: Oxford University Press, 1956).
49. Ibid., p. 101.
50. Ibid., p. 121.
51. Ibid., p. 169.
52. Ibid., p. 167.
53. Mannheim, *Man and Society*, p. 99, 167.
54. Ibid., Part I, Chapter 1.
55. Ibid., p. 40.
56. Ibid. See Part I, Chapter III. One is more often than not overwhelmed by the way Mannheim successively discovers 'crucial events' and 'decisive facts' of the modern era.
57. Ibid., p. 44.
58. Ibid., pp. 49–50.
59. Ibid., pp. 53–4.
60. Ibid.
61. Ibid., p. 54.
62. Ibid., p. 58.
63. Ibid., Part II, Section VIII.

Chapter 9: Alienation and the New Slavery

1. *Work in America: Report of a Special Task Force to the Secretary of Health and Welfare* (Cambridge: MIT Press, 1972). Irving Kristol charged the Task Force with 'Neo-Marxism' (*Wall Street Journal*, 18 January 1973). In the ensuing exchange, the chairman of the task force, James O'Toole sputtered that 'as a Republican and a capitalist who has served loyally in the Nixon administration … I find it pathetically laughable to be accused of participating in a neo-Marxist endeavour'. How could Professor Kristol, O'Toole wondered, brand as 'Marxist a report that offers methods to business to increase productivity, that offers the government ways to cut its costs, and offers ways to improve the quality of life for all Americans – and working within the capitalist system to achieve each goal' (2 Feburary 1973). Such are the vicissitudes of the concept of alienation nowadays. See also 'Worker Alienation' (Hearings before the Subcommittee on Employment, Manpower and Poverty of the Committee on Labor and Public Welfare, US Senate, 25 and 26 July 1972).
2. Two examples of this kind of treatment of 'alienation' stand out: Ada J. Finifter (ed.), *Alienation and the Social System* (New York: John Wiley & Sons, 1972) and Gerald Sykes (ed.), *Alienation* (New York: Basic Books, 1966, 2 Volumes). Sykes in his introduction resolutely refuses to define

alienation and thus through two fat volumes we are greeted with every complaint against society anyone has ever made – or so it seems. Finifter's introduction and own contribution as well as the principle of selection make it clear that alienation is an infinitely expandable term which, in logical terms, makes it utterly meaningless.

3. Daniel Bell, 'Two Roads from Marx: The Themes of Alienation and Exploitation and Workers' Control in Socialist Thought', in *The End of Ideology* (New York: Collier Books, 1961), Ch. 15. See also, for a slightly different emphasis, Bell's essay, 'The Debate on Alienation' in Leopold Labedz (ed.), *Revisionism* (New York: Praeger, 1962), pp. 195–211, and Bell's excellent, if flawed, discussion of work, *Work and Its Discontents* (New York: League for Industrial Democracy, 1971). Bell's discussion of alienation was stimulated by Robert Tucker's *Philosophy and Myth in Karl Marx* (New York: Cambridge University Press, 1961). Of the many replies to Bell and Tucker on the 'two Marxes' question, the best are: David McLelland, *Marx before Marxism* (New York: Harper & Row, 1970); Shlomo Aveneri, *The Social and Political Thought of Karl Marx* (London: Cambridge University Press, 1968); Bertell Ollman, *Alienation: Marx's Conception of Man in Capitalist Society* (Cambridge: Cambridge University Press, 1971); Michael Harrington, 'Marx vs. Marx' (*New Politics*, Vol. I, No. 1, Series l, Fall 1961). On the persistent muddle between 'anomie' and 'alienation', see Steven Lukes' outstanding article, 'Alienation and Anomie' in Finifter, *Alienation*, pp. 24–32.
4. The publication in English of the *Grundrisse* (London, Allen Lane Books, 1973) should put this point of view to rest once and for all. The earliest, and one of the best, replies to Bell, Michael Harrington's 'Marx vs. Marx', also incisively discusses Hannah Arendt's contribution to this debate.
5. Bell, 'Two Roads from Marx', p. 358.
6. Ibid., pp. 360–1.
7. Ibid., fn. 130, pp. 334–5.
8. Ibid., pp. 366–7.
9. Ibid., p. 387.
10. Ibid., pp. 388–92.
11. Reinhard Bendix, 'Socialism and the Theory of Bureaucracy', *Canadian Journal of Political Science and Economics* (1949).
12. *From Hegel to Marx* (New York: Humanities Press, 1950). See especially chapters 1, 3, 6 and 9. Also Hook's still valuable study, *Toward the Understanding of Karl Marx* (New York: John Day, 1933).
13. Quoted in Hook, *Toward the Understanding of Karl Marx*, p. 286.
14. Karl Marx, *The German Ideology* (New York: International Publishers, n.d.), p. 69.
15. Ibid., fn., p. 193.
16. Karl Marx, from *The Civil War in France* in *Selected Works of Marx and Engels*, Vol. I (Moscow: Foreign Languages Publishing House, n.d.), p. 522.
17. Bendix, 'Socialism and the Theory of Bureaucracy', p. 503.

18. Karl Marx, *Economic and Philosophic Manuscripts of 1844* (Moscow: Foreign Languages Publishing House, 1959).
19. Ibid., pp. 69–70.
20. Ibid., p. 102.
21. Karl Marx, *Capital*, Vol. I (Modern Library Ed.), p. 83.
22. Ibid., pp. 92–3.
23. Bell, 'Two Roads from Marx'.
24. Marx, *Capital*, p. 264.
25. Marx, *Manuscripts*, pp. 129–34.
26. Karl Marx, *The Poverty of Philosophy* (New York: International Publishers, n.d.).
27. It is accurate, I think, to see *The German Ideology* (1845–46) as an important bridge between the young and the mature Marx.
28. Marx, *The German Ideology*, p. 20.
29. Ibid., p. 21.
30. Ibid., pp. 64–6.
31. Ibid., p. 66.
32. Ibid., p. 67.
33. Ibid., pp. 74–5.
34. Marx, *Capital*, p. 396.
35. Ibid., pp. 496–7.
36. Ibid., pp. 533–4.
37. Friedrich Engels, *Socialism Utopian and Scientific* (in *Selected Works*, Vol. II), p. 153.
38. Ibid.
39. Karl Mannheim, *Man and Society in an Age of Reconstruction*, (London: Routledge, Kegan Paul, 1949). See especially pp. 51–60, 74.
40. Clark Kerr, John T. Dunlop, Frederick Harbison and Charles A. Myers, *Industrialism and Industrial Man: Problems of Labor and Management in Economic Growth* (Cambridge: Harvard University Press, 1960). See especially Chapter 10.
41. See George Friedmann, *The Anatomy of Work* (New York: Free Press, 1961). Friedmann's criticisms of the tecnicians can serve, with appropriate alterations, as criticisms of Kerr and associates.
42. We do not here deal with the major part of *Industrialism and Industrial Man* which is an effort to create a framework to view the process of industrialization. The views of the authors summarized here are contained primarily in Chapter 10.
43. Kerr *et al.*, *Industrialism and Industrial Man*, p. 7.
44. Ibid., pp. 231–2.
45. Ibid., p. 232.
46. Ibid., pp. 282–4.
47. Ibid., p. 283.

48. Ibid., pp. 292–3.
49. Ibid., p. 283. The authors are, not surprisingly, all professional collective bargainers: negotiators. In the study of all utopias, one must always use as a rule of thumb, the analytic principle summed up in the phrase, '*cherchez le Dictateur*'. Thus we find a utopia by a B.F. Skinner, the behavioural psychologist, in which social control over man's unpleasant tendencies to antisocial activity is happily eradicated through a program of early conditioning by psychologists. *Walden Two* is not an anti-utopia, either. Both Cabet and Fourier made themselves the dictators of their utopias. Sociologists, or at least a sociologically trained elite, and intellectuals more broadly, are a critical element in Karl Mannheim's theory of a new ruling class in his version of 'elite democracy'.
50. Kerr *et al.*, *Industrialism and Industrial Man*, pp. 283–4.
51. Ibid., p. 287.
52. Ibid.
53. Ibid.
54. Ibid.
55. Ibid., p. 295.
56. Ibid., pp. 294–6.
57. Ibid., p. 294. Note the disciplinary function of the occupational association – trade unions, primarily, one assumes. What the meaning of the term 'pluralism' is here is a mystery, at least if Kerr's earlier work on 'liberal pluralism' is any guide. But the whiff of bureaucratic corporatism is certainly strong and that is, after all, one of the important strands in pluralist thought. Individuals belong to the association, or in this case, to their employer: it isn't exactly slavery, but a step toward a bureaucratic corporate society in which individual citizenship devolves into membership in occupational or functional groups. See Judith Kornbluth and Frederic Pohl's classic science fiction novel, *The Space Merchants* (London: Penguin Books, 1953) for a dystopian view that might be said to mirror Kerr's utopia for managers and mediators.
58. Kerr *et al.*, *Industrialism and Industrial Man*, p. 295.
59. Ibid., pp. 295–6.

Chapter 10: The Authoritarian Socialism of H.G. Wells

1. This chapter originally appeared in *Tribune*, 5 March 1993. For Michael Foot's critical response see the issue of 12 March; and my rejoinder to Foot, 19 March 1993.
2. Michael Coren, *The Invisible Man: The Life and Liberties of H.G. Wells* (London: Bloomsbury Press, 1992).

Chapter 11: Right Face: Sociology Under Attack

1. This essay is reprinted with the permission of *The Times Higher Education Supplement*, and first appeared 13 May 1994.

Chapter 12: *Culture of Complaint: The Fraying of America*: A Review

1. This review is reprinted with the permission of *The Times Higher Education Supplement*, and first appeared 9 July 1993. Robert Hughes, *Culture of Complaint: The Fraying of America* (New York: Oxford University Press, 1993).

Chapter 13: Civil Society, Democracy and the Cold War

1. John Lewis Gaddis, *The United States and the End of the Cold War* (New York, Oxford: Oxford University Press, 1992).
2. Irving Kristol, 'The Soviet Union's Albatross States', *The Wall Street Journal Europe*, 25 July 1988. See also his article, 'Changing Foreign Policy', ibid., 25 January 1988, as a fascinating statement about the crack-up of American Cold War policy from a neo-conservative viewpoint.
3. *Giving Real Life to the Helsinki Accords*, European Network for East–West Dialogue, November 1986. For a succinct account of the new democratic peace movement in Eastern Europe see Brian Morton and Joanne Landy, 'East European Activists Test Glasnost', *Bulletin of the Atomic Scientists*, May 1988, pp. 18–26. A complete overview may be found in Catherine Fitzpatrick and Janice Fleischman, *From Below: Independent Peace and Environmental Movements in Eastern Europe and the USSR* (New York: Helsinki Watch Report, October 1987).
4. The anti-democratic side of the socialist movement before the rise of Stalinism and its expression when the latter became full-blown, as well as the meaning of the 'other soul' of socialism, democratic socialism 'from below', is discussed in my book, *Authoritarian Socialism: Edward Bellamy and the Nationalist Movement* (Berkeley: University of California Press, 1982).
5. See John Keane, *Democracy and Civil Society* (London: Verso Books, 1988) and the very useful collection, edited by Keane, *Civil Society and the State* (London: Verso Books, 1988).
6. The far right's view is succinctly conveyed in Ralph Harris and Arthur Seldon's, *Welfare without the State: A Quarter Century of Suppressed Public Choice*: 'It is clear that the machinery of representative parliamentary democracy has so far proved unsuitable as the mechanism for translating personal preferences into day-to-day practice. Profoundly disturbing questions must be

raised about the imperfections or obstacles in the representative political process that frustrate the wishes of the sovereign populace it is ostensibly designed to 'represent' ... The weight of evidence is that a vote is much less effective than purchasing power ... the market is potentially more democratic than the state.' (Quoted in Susanne MacGregor, *The Poll Tax and the Enterprise Culture*, Manchester: Centre for Local Economic Strategies, 1988, p. 15.) Mrs Thatcher, if recent press reports are to be believed, has found her perfect capitalist utopia during her recent trip to Singapore where she met the dictator Lee Kuan Yew. According to an account in the *Independent* (1 August 1988) 'She shares with Mr. Lee the same views on everything, from the values of ruthless capitalism, encouraging competition and standing up for the free world, to not imposing sanctions on South Africa. "I have learned so much from your prime minister," Mrs Thatcher told a group of telecommunications officials ... "We believe in the same things" ... Nothing she saw disturbed her infatuation with the Singaporean dream. As she walked around the spotless shopping malls, she had a glint in her eye which seemed to say, "Yes, this is the way things should be. This is what we are working towards."' I suppose this is the equivalent of Lincoln Steffens's 'I have seen the future and it works,' when he visited the Soviet Union. Anyone who has watched the Iron Lady for the last decade knows that the reporter's portrait of her state of mind in the litterless utopia rings true. No difficulty in understanding either her sympathy for Gorbachev or imagining the kind of Europe which she envisages.

7. Rosa Luxemburg, *The Russian Revolution* and *Leninism or Marxism?* (Ann Arbor: University of Michigan, 196l), p. 70. For examples of an argument favouring Gorbachev's 'socialism' from above, see Anthony Barnett, *Soviet Freedom* (London: Picador Books, 1988) and Moise Lewin, *The Gorbachev Phenomenon* (London: Radius Books, 1988).
8. See C. Wright Mills, *The Causes of World War Three*, (New York: Simon and Shuster, 1958) for an early but still pertinent statement of the case against Cold War liberalism and the 'military metaphysic' of the arms race. Mills was a lone voice in academia who was dismissed as a radical by the guardians of public order in academic life. And then, just as surely, after his tragically early death, Mills was turned into an icon by people he would have scorned. Mills was close to the 'third camp' independent left, publishing several of his essays, including one of the most insightful of them, 'Liberalism in the Modern World', in *Anvil and Student Partisan* (New York, 1951–58), edited by Michael Harrington, and he also drew upon the pioneering discussion of the 'permanent war economy' by T.N. Vance which appeared in *The New International* between 1950 and 1953 for *The Power Elite*. Mills got outside the cage of Cold War politics and rattled its doors for a non-academic audience (for which he was denounced as a 'mere journalist'). He angered its Cold War liberal keepers, 'the best and the brightest' (who were heading to the crimes of the Bay of Pigs, the Cuban missile crisis and, the last stop, the

Vietnam war) but then was effectively ignored. The vacuum in American politics created by the absence of a political opposition swallowed up his views, and Mills himself.

9. One of these purest of pure Cold Warriors, whose 'anti-communism' remains undiluted, recently told the editor of a journal reporting on the East European opposition that he found sympathetic articles on the struggle for conscientious objection in Eastern Europe 'unacceptable' because of the bad example it would set in the West.
10. 'A Joint Statement of the Third Camp', reprinted in *Independent Socialism and War* (Berkeley: Independent Socialist Committee, 1966).
11. See, for example, Tair Tairov, 'Democracy must be guaranteed', *New Times* (Moscow, 1988, No. 22, pp. 23–4) who calls for the 'democratization of the Party' and restoration of the 'initial concept of the Soviets scrubbed clean of all alien coatings'. The most alien of coatings, which Tairov must know, is the idea of Soviets composed of a single party, even one which was as relatively democratic as the Bolsheviks were in 1917–18.

    Tairov calls for the creation of 'civil society' in which a multiplicity of organizations enrich public life in the Soviet Union. But not political parties or independent trade unions, although he carefully does not say he is against them. The Communist Party is to remain the sole party, but 'what is needed,' he says, is 'a clear-cut concept of the Party's place in the political system, one that will rule out the possibility of monopolizing and absolutizing power both at local level and in the centre'. He does not tell us how this is to be done. Suppose there are differences of opinion within the Party and that although such expressions of differences are allowed, those who have differences with the majority decide not to speak as individuals but to organize themselves into a group. Tairov speaks of guaranteeing by law the means for 'each individual not only to express his individual (or collective) view, but also to take part in decision-making on issues affecting the people and the state'. In plain language the idea of a 'collective' expression of opinion means the organization of a faction. But it is, as I am sure others will point out to him, only a hop-skip-and-a-jump from a faction to an independent party, which is why they were outlawed in the first place. The political logic of this is clear: the faction in a minority meets as a group, chooses leaders, decides strategy, issues statements, writes public letters, and then, without necessarily planning it, when it finds its way blocked, seeks support among the lower ranks of the party and then among the people outside the party. It is already half or three-quarters of the way to being an independent party. If it chooses voluntarily to abstain from going all the way, that may be fine for it but perhaps not for its followers who may decide to form their own party anyway. In any case, if the faction ('collectivity' of individuals) abstains from doing this because it is illegal or because they succumb to pressure from above, how can we speak of democracy? And what about those who obstinately believe, correctly, in my opinion, that the Party is the instrument of the Soviet ruling class and who despite all the sweet cajoling possible (we ignore for the sake of argument the KGB beatings and arrests and harrassments which still go on) wish to organize their own independent party? It is a travesty to speak of democracy in such a situation. One must suspect that Tairov knows it. [Note (1995): Tairov has emerged as a principled opponent of the Yeltsin regime, denouncing both the war in Chechnya and Yeltsin's assumption of executive power.]

12. Moise Lewin provides an almost simon-pure example of this kind of sham, plebiscitarian, system in the name of 'democracy' (*The Gorbachev Phenomenon*, pp. 134–5, *et passim*). Behind his support for Gorbachev is a theory of socialism from above (the backward Russian masses aren't ready for real democracy) combined with a neo-Trotskyist cum Platonist view of the Soviet Communist Party as somehow the eternal continuation of the Bolshevik Party of 1917, despite his admission that it was 'literally buried alive by Stalin and Stalinism' (p. 134). Usually people and parties which are buried alive are pretty dead after 50 or 60 years. But for Lewin there is the public ideology of 'socialism' (which it is, literally) and the fact that the Party presides over state property. Hence it must be 'socialist' (state property = socialism). The idea that it might be a new form of class society based on state property is unthinkable for Lewin, hence his belief in the reformability of the society from the top. Fortunately, it is not unthinkable for the opposition nor, from what I can gather, even from within the establishment. (Boris Kagarlitsky, in *The Thinking Reed* [London: Verso Books, 1988] uses the term 'statocracy' to grapple with this idea of new class society.) Lewin's sentences are, it is true, couched in the conditional tense, as if the outcome he desires is dependent on the Party listening to the good advice of its liberal well-wishers, but the underlying disbelief in real democracy is utterly clear. Thus Lewin writes: 'On crucial points the party could turn to the population by calling for a referendum or by allowing [*sic!*] serious debate within the soviets and having them become a more potent [?] political forum.' Lewin does not tell us who will decide what is a 'crucial point' or at what point it could or could not choose to call a referendum or when it will 'allow' serious debate. As for the democracy of referendums from above, one would think that a Professor of History would know something about Napoleonic plebiscites and the manipulation of democratic forms. If the Soviet Communist Party took the old Bolshevik party as its model, Lewin tells us, 'the new leadership could aim for a system of comparable political maturity. Of course it will be a complicated process: there is considerable backwardness in the urban society; public opinion is not always enlightened or forward looking; and the broad layers of the population are particularly inexperienced, for obvious reasons, in politics' (p. 134). We have here echoes of John Stuart Mill's views of the 'child-like' Indians and other natives of the Empire who were to be denied democracy until raised up by their British rulers combined with Beatrice and Sidney Webb pontificating on the

civilizing mission of Stalin's Communist Party to the backward Russian masses.

Gorbachev is no Stalin, for which the Russian people must be very grateful. But he is no democrat either. The Soviet people did not elect him nor do they have the right, much less the power, to throw him or the Communist Party out of office. Even if they do get the chance to vote for him as the new President, as seems promised, there is no more democracy in it without the right of effective opposition than in the 'demonstration elections' which dictators everywhere love to put on to show that they have the support of the people. Such elections are derided by the left as frauds when arranged by right-wing dictators. On present form, they will not be similarly derided when arranged by Gorbachev, not at least by the new true believers in Gorbachev. Intellectuals, as Orwell long ago pointed out, at least some of them, love dictators – witness the silence about Castro. Such is the state of the 'left' and of 'socialism' after the poisonous years of Stalinism.

These are not matters which are relevant to Professor Lewin who sneers at a 'Westminster-style multiparty republican system' but claims that the goal is 'to increase citizens' participation in political life, [and] to enhance political and other freedoms'. The sham view of democracy which he proposes may just be a lot closer to the 'Westminster' model than Lewin knows, but in any case without the right to organize independent political associations or parties 'citizen's participation' must be a fraud. As for the unfitness of the masses of people for democracy, the reasons for which (as he acknowledges) are the domination of the very Communist Party which Lewin now calls upon to play a liberating role, there is no simple answer: only in the school of democracy can people learn to exercise self-government which means they must be permitted to learn through their own experience. That's Karl Marx and it's also Rosa Luxemburg, but if that's old hat nowadays, then John Dewey will do as against the authoritarian, anti-democratic views exemplified by Lewin, who is only one example in many of the way in which the 'left' still remains incarcerated in the Cold War cage. Fortunately, in the Soviet Union itself, sections of the democratic opposition have already called for the right to form independent political parties. Perhaps Professor Lewin will give them a lecture from his book if the authorities fail to convince them to give up their ideas about the need for a real opposition party to push the reforms forward, to secure them from the Stalinist right, and at the same time to go beyond reforms to establish the basis of genuine democracy in the Soviet Union.

13. Cf. Rosa Luxemburg in *The Russian Revolution* and *Marxism or Leninism?* and the discussion in Lipow, *Authoritarian Socialism*.
14. Just such an extraordinary and moving exchange took place in 1987 in the Tufts–Moscow University satellite television program organized by Martin Sherwin. The very fact that it could be organized is evidence how far things have gone toward openness in the Soviet Union. The willingness of the

Soviet students to pose really damaging questions to their own leaders is an important sign of the new critical spirit which Gorbachev has permitted out of the bottle. It cannot, in my opinion, be put back in even when Gorbachev veers again to the right. Sadly enough, according to Sherwin, the American students did not ask questions as critical of American policies as their Soviet counterparts. It seems likely that the Americans, given the political vacuum in the US, may have to run to keep up with the Russians.

15. Arthur Schlesinger, Jr, *The Vital Center: The Politics of Freedom* (Boston: Houghton Miflin Co., Sentry paperback edition, 1962), pp. 235–6.
16. Just how threatening such a unilateralism based on the kind of independent thinking advocated by Mills could have been to both establishments was revealed in the panicky American reaction, in July 1988, to the report that the Russians would unilaterally withdraw their troops from Hungary. They hastily 'leaked' the rumour in order not to be seen to be caught unawares and then breathed a sign of relief when it turned out, unfortunately, not to be true. For now. But the Soviets are wily and may (probably will, in my opinion) announce just such a withdrawal. And the American military Cold War mind (and their NATO friends) will just not know what to do, except perhaps to denounce it as a dirty trick. What the Western peace movement ought to do, and what a party of political opposition worth its salt ought to do, is welcome such a move and up the ante by unilaterally withdrawing a significant number of American troops (who have only a political not a military role) from Europe. The pressure within the bloc from the top would be enormous – the Hungarian leadership wants desperately to reduce its arms expenditures and obviously hopes for some sort of Rapacki plan to stabilize its rule – and the opposition would have a field day. In the Hungarian parliament, in which there exist a few independent voices, a deputy recently stood up and demanded a reduction in the Soviet-enforced arms expenditures. Unilateralism would increase the space in which this type of demand, put forward for whatever reason, could grow.

A Guide For Historians (1995)

With the end of the Cold War, a re-examination of its history has begun. For historians or others concerned to understand the present situation, in which serious writers can soberly speak of a 'new Cold War', it will be useful to study the ideas and activities of the independent peace and environmental groups in Eastern Europe as well as their Western counterparts in order to understand what might have been. Of course, one should start with the many books, pamphlets and articles by Edward Thompson, who devoted ten years of his life to END, providing both intellectual and practical leadership. The following are among the most useful sources:

Catherine Fitzpatrick and Janet Fleischman, *From Below: Independent Peace and Environmental Movements in Eastern Eurpoe and the USSR.* A Helsinki Watch Report, October 1987.

Across Frontiers. Quarterly journal, edited in Berkeley, California, by Peter Rossman. Reported on the democratic opposition in Eastern Europe and the Soviet Union. Circulated clandestinely behind the Iron Curtain acting as a means of information and communication between various democratic opposition groups.

East European Reporter. Quarterly journal, edited in London by Jan Kavan. Offered broad coverage of human rights activity in Hungary, Poland, Czechoslovakia and East Germany. Also circulated clandestinely.

East–West Dialogue. Quarterly Bulletin of the European Network for East–West Dialogue. Edited by Dieter Esche in West Berlin. Published documents, reports, and discussion of the independent movements, East and West.

END Journal. Bi-monthly journal of the European Nuclear Disarmament Movement. Reports and documents, discussion of 'détente from below' and 'breaking down the blocs'. Co-founders of END were Mary Kaldor and Edward Thompson.

New Politics. (Series I and II.) Bi-annual journal of independent, third-camp socialist thought. Carried articles and interviews with leading East European intellectuals, discussions of trends in Soviet Union, and American and European politics.

Peace Magazine. Bi-monthly magazine of the Canadian Disarmament Information Service (CANDIS). Published news and articles about the Canadian peace movement and the independent peace movement in Europe.

Peace and Democracy News. Bi-annual (now quarterly) newsletter of the Campaign for Peace and Democracy/East and West. Director, Joanne Landy. Sponsor of support campaigns for peace and democratic rights, East and West, North and South. It carried, and still does, news and analyses of cooperation and dialogue among social movements, East, West, and Third World.

Hal Draper (ed.), *Independent Socialism and War* (Berkeley, California: Independent Socialist Clubs, 1966). An invaluable collection of articles on the third-camp socialist critique of the Cold War. Available from The Center for Socialist History, Berkeley.

Chapter 14: The End of 'The American Dream': The Crisis in American Politics

1. *Parade*, 27 July 1995.
2. J.D. Kleinke, 'Medicine's Industrial Revolution', *Wall Street Journal*, 12 August 1995.

3. Wallace Peterson, *Silent Depression: The Fate of the American Dream* (New York and London: W.W. Norton, 1994).
4. David R. Howell, 'The Skills Myth', *American Prospect* (Summer, 1994).

Chapter 14: Transnationalism From Below: International Labour into the Twenty-first Century

1. See the account of Margaret Thatcher's visit to Singapore in the *Independent* (London), 1 August 1988.
2. The far right's view is succinctly conveyed in Ralph Harris and Arthur Seldon, *Welfare without the State: A Quarter Century of Suppressed Public Choice*: 'It is clear that the machinery of representative parliamentary democracy has so far proved unsuitable as the mechanism for translating personal preferences into day-to-day practice. Profoundly disturbing questions must be raised about the imperfections or obstacles in the representative political process that frustrate the wishes of the sovereign populace it is ostensibly designed to "represent" ... The weight of evidence is that a vote is much less effective than purchasing power ... the market is potentially more democratic than the state.' Quoted in Susanne MacGregor, *The Poll Tax and the Enterprise Culture* (Manchester: Centre for Local Economic Strategies, 1988), p. 15.
3. See the several recent annual reports on Human Development published by the UNDP (United Nations Development Programme), especially 1992 and 1993, in which the link between poverty and development and human rights and political freedom is systematically documented. There is no difference in principle nor in practice between developing countries and the developed countries of Western or Central/Eastern Europe in this matter – a point which was not lost upon the UNDP's critics. There can be little doubt that the concessions to the idea of democracy by the World Bank and the IMF in recent statements which concede that the question of poverty is one of distribution which is in turn determined by the ability of the poor and working classes to exercise political power through democratic institutions, is a direct response to the UNDP reports. The most recent (1995) *World Bank Report* takes up, for the first time, to my knowledge, the role of workers and even sounds a cautious but still positive note about the importance of trade unions. Hitherto, as a survey of World Bank publications, including those on the role of Non-Governmental Organizations in development, demonstrates, the organized labour movement simply did not exist for the Bank and one can only conclude that this was an expression of their most earnest wish, along with the IMF and the transnational corporations, for a union-free global order. An issue which is not taken up in the preceding essay, primarily because the international labour movement has not yet addressed it, is the need to raise the issue of reforming the World

Bank: a World Bank for Democratic Development on whose board representatives of the labour movement sit would seem to be a reasonable demand, the resistance to which would reveal, I am sure, the fact that the Bank is the servant of global capitalism. For the ILO see the annual reports of the Director General and its annual *World Labour Report*.

4. 12 April 1994 (Official Text, US Department of the Treasury).
5. *Far Eastern Economic Review*, 21 April 1994. Note that it is published by Dow Jones, publishers of the *Wall Street Journal*.
6. A glimpse of how the global nature of the labour market and transnationalization of production must inevitably affect C/EE was provided to me recently when I went into a store in California to purchase light bulbs and confronted the following choice: on one shelf, four light bulbs for $3.00 under the label of an American manufacturer but made in its factory in Hungary; on another a 'special' – eight bulbs made in China for $1.50. Even this price ratio only partially reflects the real ratio of Chinese to Hungarian wages. Twenty-to-one would be closer to the mark. The recent decision of Continental A.G. to close its plants (one among many such decisions) in Germany and move to the Czech Republic in search of lower wage and other costs, gives some indication of how far Western European wages and welfare provisions have yet to fall before being able to be able to compete with Chinese workers. Capital mobility is not decided on purely on consideration of wage rates: there are other factors determining the location of production, but the downward pressure on wages is present even without actual movement.
7. *Social Aspects of the Assistance Programme to Central and Eastern Europe and the Commonwealth of Independent States* (Brussels: European Trade Union Institute, 1993).
8. For a discussion of these issues see my Introduction, 'A Guide for the Perplexed' to the UK edition of Michael Harrington's *Socialism: Past and Future* (London: Pluto Press, 1993) and the introduction to the new, paperback edition of my book, *Authoritarian Socialism in America: Edward Bellamy and the Nationalist Movement* (Berkeley: University of California Press, 1992).
9. I have drawn upon interviews and material gathered in a research visit to Romania in November 1993, for this discussion.
10 *Privatisation in Romania* (Brussels: North Atlantic Assembly, 1994).
11. Charles Oman, *Globalisation and Regionalisation: The Challenge for Developing Countries* (Paris: OECD, January 1994).
12. *International Herald Tribune*, 30 April 1994.
13. See *European Social Policy, Options for the Union*, European Green Paper (Brussels: European Commission, 1994).
14. *In Europe* (London: Manufacturing, Science and Finance, 1988).
15. See Bogdan Denitch, *After the Flood: World Politics and Democracy in the Wake of Communism* (Hanover, CT: Wesleyan University Press, 1992) and, by

the same author, *Ethnic Nationalism: The Tragic Death of Yugoslavia* (Minneapolis: University of Minnesota Press, 1994). The capacity of an independent, democratic labour movement to provide an alternative to ethnic nationalism in Central/Eastern Europe is demonstrated by the existence in Belgrade of Nezavisnost whose 200,000 members provide a signficant basis of opposition to the Milosevic regime. The international labour movement has supported the union, assuring its survival under the most difficult of circumstances. I have not discussed this aspect of the labour movement's role but it ought to hardly need repeating, were it not for the Orwellian memory-hole into which the post-Communist governments have dropped the history of pre-World War II democratic and socialist labour movements which were the first victims of both the fascists and Communists. On the erasure of the past and the equation of democratic socialism with Stalinism or communism, see 'Socialism, the Memory Hole and the Tasks of Workers Education' by Peter Rossman (editor of the *IUF Newsletter*) in *Workers' Education*, Bulletin of the International Federation of Workers Education Associations (Jerusalem: Number 4, May 1994).

Index

Index by Judith Lavender